I ONLY LAUGH WHEN IT HURTS

By Adrian Street

Copyright © 2012 Adrian Street. All rights reserved. No part of this publication may be used or reproduced in any manner whatsoever without written permission of the publisher, except in the case of brief quotations embodied in articles and reviews.

Contact Information:

U.S. Mailing Address:

Adrian Street
1496 Oak Drive
Gulf Breeze, FL 32563

Email: daffodil777@bellsouth.net

Website: http://www.bizarebazzar.com

ISBN-13: 978-1477540657
ISBN-10: 1477540652

Cover:
The larger photo is one of several physique photos of me as Kid Tarzan Jonathan. The smaller two are me wrestling 'Tiger' Tony Woods (left), and 'Big Butch' Digby (right). More photos at the end of the book.

DEDICATIONS:

To my Father & Arch Nemesis - Your constant opposition guaranteed my success.

To my Mother - Without you I may never have been born.

To My Sister Pamela's LOVE.

To My Brother Terence's LEFT FIST.

To Uncle Fred - Who taught me to never give up.

To Peter Inge - My Best Friend - Who introduced me to Professional Wrestling.

To Raymond Plunkett. Who remembers more of my contests than I do.

To 'Wresting Heritage' & 'Wresting Furness' whose Great websites have immortalized 'THE GOLDEN AGE OF BRITISH WRESTLING'.

To Victor Rook whose advice and book 'Musings of a Dysfunctional Life' inspired me to complete my own stories.

I will be eternally grateful to those who told me I could do it. - And even more grateful to those who told me I couldn't.

I want to pay a SPECIAL tribute to every wrestler I shared the ring with. Friend or Enemy. You all taught me the lessons I needed to reach the top. I couldn't have done it without you.

INTRODUCTION

My book has been self written and self edited - there maybe mistakes - the only time I spent in Oxford or Cambridge was when I wrestled there. Throughout my life I have always done things one way - My way. - So for better or worse, This is my story.

I ONLY LAUGH WHEN IT HURTS

I'm The Merchant of Menace, purveyor of pain,
There's no quality of mercy in the name of my game.
I get my pound of flesh with every strangle hold.
To me all that glitters, is definitely gold.

Continuing from book number one, 'MY PINK GAS MASK.' My journey takes me out of the wild Welsh 'Hills of Fire and Iron'. Away from The Coal Mines and slag heaps to the Bright lights of London. Everyone I was leaving behind predicted I would never make it. My dream of becoming a professional wrestler, to them was ludicrous. But I was determined to make my wild dreams a reality and then live them to the full. Or die trying.

LONDON

The day I left Brynmawr for London, I left alone. My 'friend' Chewy, the gutless wonder, had chickened out and decided he didn't want to leave Brynmawr after all. But I got a promise for a replacement from an unexpected source. 'The Black Rat' Brian Heath asked if he could take Chewy's place and come with me instead. In fairness to Brian, I suggested that he should wait until I found out if the management of Acton Bolt Factory would be willing to employ him, instead of Chewy. I would write immediately after inquiring and let him know. It would be hard on me in the meantime. Chewy and I had agreed to share the rent of our bed-sit, and now I would have to pay for it on my own until The Black Rat came to join me. The day I arrived in London I had less than 8 pounds in cash to my name. I would have to make it last, as I would have to work in the factory for two weeks before I received my first week's wages. My job consisted of pouring steel trays full of round headed bolts into machines that cut the round heads into 6 sided bolts. I was in charge of three machines, and when I wasn't pouring, I was constantly checking the heads of the cut bolts as they popped back out of the machine to make sure they were perfect. Eventually the dye that cut the 6 sided shape would chip and a scratch, or sometimes a deep gouge would appear on one of the edges and I would immediately have to switch off the machine. I would replace and adjust the dye before turning it back on and continuing with the pouring and checking. Machines and I have a mutual dislike and distrust of each other, and I don't understand them anymore than they understand me. At least half of the workers were female, and I seemed to interest the younger ones from the first day I started work. They were always asking me if I would take them out. But I was already worried about the money situation, so I refused to get involved with any of them. Most of the men were Irish and were very quarrelsome. The Londoners I made friends with were very pleasant to me and often asked me if I would like to spend time with them after work. I did intend to until I found out the reason for their invitation.

"With all those muscles you're just the bloke we need with us for beating up wogs." They told me.

"Doing what?!" I asked, thinking I was getting ribbed again. They had already got on to me about the 'Welsh Mountain Goats,' I told them that I'd never seen a Mountain Goat in Wales. Although there were a lot of Welsh mountain Ponies and Sheep.

"They are talking about you, you silly bugger!" Explained Trevor Davis, an older Welshman who used to live in Abertillery. "That's what Londoners call the Welsh - Mountain Goats!" But they weren't ribbing this time, they were deadly serious. 'Wogs' was what they called Black people and the London. 'Race Riots' was just beginning to simmer. Only a few months later the whole of the Notting-Hill Gate area would erupt into a bloody battlefield. I was disgusted when I realized what they meant. Although I must admit that I had often gone out looking for trouble when I lived in Brynmawr. But that was different, it was a part of growing up in that environment and was almost regarded as a sport. I had almost no experience of Black people before living in London. In Wales we were not brought up to hate anyone based on whatever their race or color may be. Having said that, some of the Irish guys I was working with were getting on my nerves. There was Sean who was a weightlifter and was okay when he was talking about weightlifting. But when the subject got around to religion, a sore point with me anyway, they could really piss me off. They were all Catholics, and that was something that I knew nothing about at that time. Other than the conflict between Catholicism and Protestantism had caused about as much trouble in Europe as the Black Death. I wasn't looking for trouble as far as religion was concerned, I'd had more of that than I could handle from the first time I met Dad until I had left Wales. Their constant preaching about how ignorant and uninformed all Protestants, especially Welsh Baptists, were finally prompted me to take extreme action. I actually wrote to Dad and explained the situation. Basically that I had no argument to defend my own beliefs. I had no knowledge of what the difference between it and Catholicism was. I got a 10 page letter back from Dad so quickly that I almost began to believe in miracles. It began - "What a deluded people Catholics are ---," and got steadily stronger as it continued. I was only looking for a little defense against some of my more preachy workmates and not really attempting to start yet another Holy War. I decided to talk to Uncle Fred's wife, Aunty Pat. In spite of the fact that she was the owner of the filthiest mouth on a woman I had ever met, she had been brought up in the Catholic faith. I thought she might give me some advice to soften Dad's onslaught. The fact that she swore so much led me to believe that she wasn't particularly interested in religion. What I should have done was try to explain the situation to her first. But I made the awful mistake of giving her Dad's letter to read before I told her anything about the aggravation I had been getting at work. She was furious! She called Dad just about everything under the sun, and although she had always been one of my favorite Aunts, that ended our friendship for all time. She absolutely would not listen to any explanation for the reason behind the letter, and things were never the same between us again. Personally I couldn't care less what anyone believes or doesn't believe. They can shake a Monkey's skull at the moon or shake their pricks at the sun for all I care. As long as they don't do it outside a girl's school. If people's beliefs don't harm anyone else, let them get on with it. I'm too busy trying to live my own life to worry about it, and very often other people's eccentricities can make the world a more interesting place.

****

Almost the moment I arrived in London, I took a trip To Brixton, as I had learned that that was where 'Dale Martin's Wrestling Promotions' offices were located. I got off the bus in Brixton Road, and was surprised after asking a half dozen pedestrians where Dale Martin's offices were that no one seemed to know. I soon learned that if you need directions in London, don't ask a Londoner they really don't know.

"Can I help you?" Came a friendly voice with a London accent. I turned to look at the face of the ugliest Negro I had ever seen. He made King Kong look like Cinderella.

"I'm looking for Dale Martin's Wrestling Promotions." I told him, as I puffed up my chest and squared my shoulders hopping that he'd take me for a Wrestler.

"I'm going down there right now," he replied, "I'll show you exactly where it is."

"Thank you very much." I said and then proceeded in relating to him my life's history and my future ambitions, in the half a mile walk it took to reach our destination. There was a small crowd of Wrestlers, but none I recognized hanging about a low wall that separated the sidewalk from a car-park. That in turn separated the wall from an old 4 story brick building. It proved to be Dale Martin's Promotions offices, which were on the two top floors. A gym with weights and a wrestling ring on the ground floor, which could be reached from the level of the car-park by ascending a flight of stone steps. And a printers shop that produced all of Dale Martin's Wrestling posters and all their programs in the semi basement. All of the wrestlers seemed to know my guide, and I thought I heard them call him John. I was wearing my black Weider T-shirt that showed off my chest, arms and twenty-seven inch waist pulled in to the max - or should I say the min? With a wide studded black leather belt that held up a pair of jeans that was so tight they looked as though they had been spray painted on. They all scrutinized me balefully, and didn't speak to me until I asked them,

"Where will I find Dale Martin?" One of them asked me if I was looking for Jack or Les. Interpreting my puzzled expression he explained that Dale Martin's promotions belonged to Jack Dale and Les Martin. Jack had two brothers who were also part of their business. An older brother named Johnny and a younger brother named Billy. Jack Dale was the only one of them who had ever been a Professional Wrestler and had retired just a few years before. He had been 'The British Middle-weight Champion' for 15 years.

"You'll probably want to see Jack," I was told, "I don't think Les is in today." I had always thought that Dale Martin was the name of one person. I entered the front door and walked down the hallway after ascending the steps from the car park. I turned left and up a flight of rickety stairs to the floor above. I knocked on the first door I came to which I opened and entered Jack Dale's office. Jack was just replacing the phone into its receiver as I walked in. On the wall behind him was a huge photograph of the very same Blackman who had brought me down from Brixton. He was dressed in wrestling trunks and boots, very muscular and solid looking.

"Can I help you?" Inquired Jack Dale, his eyebrows rising.

"Who is that?!" I asked, pointing at the photo.

"The Black Kwango." He answered. 'WOW! I thought. I hadn't recognized him - I had heard of him but I had never seen him wrestle.

"Can I help you?!" repeated Jack Dale.

"Yes, Mr. Dale," I replied, "I want to become a Professional Wrestler."

"What Club do you belong to, how many years have you wrestled amateur, have you won any amateur championships?!" He demanded.

"Er - a - no, I've only just arrived in London from South Wales. I left the coal mines and came to London because I want to be a Professional Wrestler." I answered.

"Yeah well it doesn't work like that," he told me, "you need at least a few years amateur experience and even then you may not be good enough to turn pro."

"I'm already a good Wrestler," I blurted indignantly, "I've beaten everybody I ever wrestled with. I'll wrestle with any of those wrestlers standing outside right now if you want me to then you can see how good I am!"

"You need to become a good amateur first!" He insisted.

"Mr. Dale," I replied, "I can't earn a living as an amateur wrestler."

"Well," he insisted as he got up from behind his desk, walked across his office and opened the door, "you can't earn a living as a pro either you're too inexperienced, too small and too young."

"I'm nearly 17!" I protested, "And how do you know I can't wrestle if you don't give me a chance to prove it?!"

"Come back in a few years when you're older, bigger and a bloody good amateur." He told me, as he placed his hand on my upper arm and guided me out of his office door. I flexed my biceps and triceps furiously hoping he'd reconsider.

"Nice arm." He said and closed the door on my open mouth.

"I'll be back!" I said to the door – and that was when Arnold was still in diapers.

I wondered around London after work each evening and on the weekends looking for a gym that had wrestling and bodybuilding facilities. Asking in every one if Spencer Churchill or Milton Reid ever trained there. Milton Reid was a huge grotesque movie character actor, but also wrestled as "The Mighty Chang." There seemed to be plenty of bodybuilding gyms around my area but not combined with Wrestling. In despair I began going to the YMCA again, even though it was in the middle of the west end of London, and I lived far out in the north-west suburbs. There were quite a few Pro Wrestlers who trained at the YMCA. Amongst the first of many I encountered there was Londoner Reg Trood and Pasquale Salvo an Italian from Bermondsey. I had seen them both wrestle in Cardiff, so I went straight up to them and introduced myself. I congratulated them both on their fine wrestling skills. Then informed them that they could both expect to see me wrestling on the same cards as them in the very near future. They laughed so much I think I could have beaten them both before they recovered.

"If I was you I'd forget it and go back home to Wales before you get hurt," chuckled Pasquale through his tears, "you're too small little guys like you are 10 a penny, you'll never make any money as a wrestler."

"You'd never make a wrestler - period, ha-ha-ha!" Agreed Reg.

"I'll give either of you a pull right now if you want to get on the mat!" I challenged, pointing to the vacant mats where the wrestling took place.

"Fuck off!" Said Pasquale politely, as he and Reg walked away still chuckling.

I was furious. I was still smarting from the rebuke I'd suffered after my first meeting with Jack Dale. As there was no one on any of the wrestling mats I walked across the gym and up the stairs to the balcony, where the weights were. I'd take my frustration out on a heavy barbell until some unlucky wrestler got on the mat downstairs. Then I'd show anyone present that Adrian Street was in town, and he meant business. I heaved my barbell up to my chest and began pressing it with a vengeance. In between each set I'd march to the edge of the balcony, and glare down at the mats below. It wasn't long before a few guys came in and congregated around the mat, they paired off and began grappling. By this time I had simmered down enough to think about my plan of action. It wasn't enough for me just to go downstairs and wrestle with whoever would oblige me, I wanted an audience! I wanted my performance to explode with such a bang that even Jack Dale would hear of it and appreciate what a mistake he had made in not employing me on the spot. A strange feeling came over me and I realized that I'd been waiting for this moment for years. Well it seemed like years, in fact I knew I was going to experience this moment from the first time I saw the movie 'Somebody up there likes me'. I would be like Rocky Graziano when he got in the ring as a sparring partner to a future champ, and instead of sparring with him laid him out cold. He greatly impressed all the trainers, managers and promoters present. The only thing wrong here was there were not enough people in the gym to witness my triumph. Apart from a few wrestlers there were only a couple of gymnasts. And a tall blond, good looking man playing handball on his own against the far wall of the gym. I learned later that he was Roger Moore and had just started filming for his upcoming TV series 'Ivanhoe'. A few more men came down the stairs from the dressing rooms. Two of them had very impressive physiques and were obviously wrestlers. As I looked down on them they walked over to the mats, found themselves a space and began wrestling with each other. They were just what I needed to make my first impression. There was still not enough people in the gym for my liking, but the excitement had built up in me to such a pitch that I couldn't contain it any longer. I flew down the stairs as fast as I could go. I swaggered over to the mat and sized everyone up. Yes either one of the newcomers would do very nicely, as they were far more heavily built than any of the others. They both sported broken noses and huge thick cauliflower ears, their huge powerful muscles were thickly covered with hair knotted and writhed as I watched them wrestling. I felt as though I had been transported back in time and was watching as two brute Neanderthals were battling each other for dominance of their tribal cave. Wrestling had really left its mark on both of them and I promised myself that I would prove to be too good a wrestler to ever end up looking as gnarled and battered as either of these two. My impatience and excitement got the better of my manners. When a couple of the gymnasts began to make their way back to the dressing rooms, I was horrified to see my already very scant audience diminishing.

"Which one of you is going to give me a pull around?!" I demanded impatiently. I still can't remember who was the first one of them to oblige me. But as the other wrestler began to walk away, I added in a voice which I hoped would make the exiting gymnasts reconsider leaving, "Don't go away, - you're next!!!"

"Oh, okay." He answered meekly and stood on the edge of the mat and watched as his friend and I began to circle each other. This was it, now I would show the wrestling world what I was made of - Yeah, - right! They beat the crap out of me! whatever induced me to think that I had the slightest idea of what wrestling was about I'll never know. But I did learn a lesson AND that lesson taught me that I didn't have a clue! Mind you, that didn't mar Alf's or Frank's enjoyment. And they took delight in swapping places every time one of them pinned me. A competition seemed to develop between the two of them, to see which one of them could twist me into the most intricate and painful position. My opponents that day were Frank Nottingham and Alf Jacobs. They were both Amateur wrestlers. Although Alf had turned pro for a while, but didn't like it and had eventually managed to get himself reinstated as an Amateur.

"Have you had enough, son?" Asked Alf kindly.

"I haven't even warmed up yet!" I lied and got battered some more. When I finally crawled off the mat – and I do mean crawled. The only way I could get to my feet was to drag myself up the exercise bars that lined the gymnasium walls. I held onto them shakily not daring to let go in case I fell back onto the mat. "I'll be back." I said once more. But without much conviction, and staggered towards the stairway that led to the dressing room. I glanced at Roger Moore as I approached him. He was wearing an immaculate, whiter than white sweat-suit. Although he must have already been playing handball for over an hour, he didn't have a single hair out of place on his well groomed head. He looked quite magnificent, and I could just imagine what a splendid figure he would cut when dressed in Ivanhoe's shining armor.

"Are you alright?" He asked me, looking a little concerned. I didn't know whether he meant physically, or in the head, but I answered bravely,

"Yes, thank you." And staggered on to the dressing room. I had never been so utterly exhausted in my entire life. I collapsed into the first chair I came to, dropped my head onto my knees and didn't move for almost an hour. I just watched as the sweat that was pouring out of every pore in my body drip, drip, drip and formed a huge puddle all around the legs of the chair I was sitting on. Then make its way in little rivulets in a dozen different directions across the floor of the dressing room. I had never ever seen so much sweat and every drop used to be mine. When I finally made my mind up to move, at first I couldn't. My neck was so mangled that it wouldn't bear the weight of my head. I had to hold my head in both hands, and slide my arse forward off the chair. I then assumed a squatting stance before I could stand up, supporting my head with my hands all the time. When I undressed and took a shower I was so dehydrated that I must have drank half of my shower water. As soon as I dried myself and dressed I went to the café and ordered a pint of milk. Only to find it was almost impossible to drink. Thank goodness I was wearing a white T-shirt instead of my usual black one. I had to try to hold my head in position, and support it with one hand while I used the other to lift the milk bottle, and pour its precious contents into one side of my mouth. My neck was so weak that I couldn't control what I was doing, and most of the milk poured out of the other side of my mouth, and soaked my White T-shirt. I left the YMCA, a shattered brain in a shattered body; I wished I was dreaming - what went wrong? I'd really thought I could wrestle. What a bloody fool I would have made of myself in front of Jack Dale if he had taken me up on my offer, and allowed me to wrestle one of the Professionals who had been standing in the car park. Instinctively I looked for a mental diversion, and walked into Soho. I didn't see Jack 'Spot' so I carried on merrily. I found out later that Jack 'Spot' Comer was no longer operating as a gangster. He had hung up his razors and violent temperament for good. He was now a legitimate furniture salesman in Camden Town. Just over a year before in May 1956 Jack Spot had been ambushed outside his Bayswater Road flat by two of his arch rival, Billy Hill's thugs, Frankie Frazer and Alfie Warren. They had razor slashed the razor slasher badly enough, for him to finally call it quits. Possibly afraid of retaliation Billy Hill also retired and went to live in Spain. Of course their shoes were soon filled by many others. Most notably the notorious Kray Twins Reggie and Ronnie. I didn't see any gangsters that Mam had warned me to avoid but I did bump into the Women she had alluded to. 'Ladies of the night' were everywhere. I stood and watched them, amazed that they strutted and posed so brazenly for every male passerby. I was soon spotted by a half a dozen of them from the other side of the narrow Soho Street, and they all waved and shrieked at me to come over and join them. One turned her backside towards me bent down and called to me from between her own legs, "See anything you like love?!" She hollered. She was wearing a very short skirt, so I could almost see what she'd had for breakfast. I had always loved Women and Girls so I was surprised that I was finding this encounter so embarrassing. But not as surprised and shocked as I was, when a Lady who had crept up behind me suddenly slipped her arm through mine and asked,

"Would yer like a good time, luv?!" I leapt as though I'd been scalded.

"Err a n-no thank you!" I spluttered, "I've got to go somewhere - Er-um I'm late!" I tried to disengage myself, but as I hurried up the street she clung to my arm like a leach.

"C'mon luv, won't take long," She purred, "I got a place in the next street."

"No thank you!" I repeated as I lengthened my stride and almost broke into a run while the Lady still clung to my arm and tottered determinedly beside me her 5 inch heels clattering in time with my heartbeat. I careered around the corner into Old Compton Street with such force that the poor Harlot spun away, almost colliding with a lamppost.

"Come back when you have more time!" She chuckled at my retreating back, "Yer know where t' find me!" I had told Mam that I wasn't afraid of any Women. I found I was mistaken. That was the second lesson I had learned that day. I walked the length of Old Compton Street looking for what I thought was called 'The Two Eyes' coffee bar. I'd heard they had live Rock 'n' Roll bands playing there. It was the place where early British Rock Star Tommy Steele had been discovered a couple of years earlier. Now it seemed to be the Mecca for every would-be Rock 'n' Roll wannabe hoping to duplicate Tommy Steele's success. Not being able to find it, I asked a boy and his girlfriend who had just stepped out of a tiny shabby coffee house. I was surprised when told that that was it. I had imagined something about 20 times bigger. I also learned that it wasn't called 'The Two Eyes' but 'The 2 I's'. Apparently it used to belong to 3 Iranians, one of them left London and went back home to Iran which left 2 Iranians, who then called it 'The 2 I's'. I didn't see anyone playing as I entered, but the whole place was pulsating with loud Rock music. After ordering myself a cup of strong frothy espresso coffee I found my way to the stairs that led down into a small dungeon of a basement where it was all happening. The place was more crowded than 'The Black Hole of Calcutta' must have been. It took me almost an hour of maneuvering between the sardine packed denizens, to get from the bottom of the stairs the few yards it took to get right up to the low stage where a band was performing. I had never heard such loud music. It was absolutely fantastic and every atom in my body was leaping to every beat that pounded my eardrums in that tiny confined space. I could have murdered another cup of coffee but there was no way I would relinquish my space, once I had got right up to the stage. A half a dozen or more Rock bands got to strut their stuff, and I thoroughly enjoyed every one of them. When I finally left The 2 I's I was still staggering. Not from exhaustion as I had been when I left the YMCA earlier. I felt that the colossal volume of noise in so confined a space had intoxicated me as well as rejuvenated me. Although I hadn't drank any alcohol since before I had left Wales, I felt really dizzy. But instead of dragging my arse like I had earlier, I seemed to float across Old Compton Street on a cloud and even braved the Girlie gauntlet without fear or incident.

During my bus ride home I tried to focus my mind on my enjoyment of the 2 I's rather than on my devastating disappointment of my first real wrestling experience. And the ignominious embarrassment of being chased up the street by a professional Lady. But my mind wouldn't leave it alone. By the time I was just a couple of miles from home I had began to settle down and relax a bit. But when the bus stopped outside Harlesden Ballroom I felt my bottom jaw drop. I looked at, and recognized the two bouncers standing outside the front entrance. The tall one was Ken Richmond the winner of the Bronze Medal in the Wrestling heavyweight division in the 1952 Olympic Games. The short, yard wide one was none other than Bert Assirati. Although I was excited to see two of my Heroes standing there, I felt as though I had just received a kick in the guts. Uncle Fred's words of wisdom jumped up and slapped me in the face,

"There's no such thing as a full time professional Wrestler," he had told me, "they all have regular jobs like everyone else and they only wrestle in their spare time. They make a few quid, but it's more of a hobby - it's not a job."

There was Bert Assirati, not only was he one of the biggest names in professional wrestling but his wife Marge Assirati was a wrestling promoter. If Bert Assirati wasn't a full time professional wrestler, and needed to subsidize his income by working part time as a bouncer, what chance did I stand of becoming one? I felt sick, but I forced it to the back of my mind, and I absolutely refused to accept the evidence of my own eyes.

'I will be a full time professional wrestler.' I told myself stubbornly.

When I finally got back to my room I was delighted to see that Mrs. Lewis had left a plate of goodies for me on my table. Mrs. Lewis lived with her husband on the same floor as me and she worked for a high class caterers. She was allowed to take home any spare left over canapés and hors d'oeuvres and such. And it wasn't unusual to find a big plate full of them when I returned home at night. I would devour them with relish, and a nice hot cup of coffee before turning in. Although I was not used to eating that kind of fare. It was quite delicious, and quite delightful trying to identify some of the tastes of the delicacies that were not recognizable to my unsophisticated eyes or palette. On this occasion there was a taste that was tantalizingly familiar amongst the tasty tidbits, that I didn't recognize until I'd already devoured most of it. Crab! I had only ever eaten Crab once before in my life. One Saturday night a couple of years before I came home ravenous after a night of drinking most of the Scrumpy in Wales, and then spent the rest of the night throwing it all up. I thought I might have gotten over it. No such luck, I spent the rest of the night on the floor of my room wrapped around a plastic bucket being violently sick. What a bloody awful end to the most memorable and enlightening day I had yet spent since I'd arrived in London.

****

After inquiring if it would be possible for 'The Black Rat' Brian Heath to take my friend Chewy's job, working in Acton Bolt Factory I had received an affirmative answer. Straight away I wrote to Brian, and told him the good news. Although he had never been a particularly great friend of mine he had been one of the lesser members of our old gang. I found that on the day I went to meet him off the train at Paddington railway station, I was really looking forward to seeing him. When he alighted from the carriage he was carrying all his worldly belongings in an average sized suitcase. Greetings over we caught a bus to where I lived in Harlesden. The financial situation would be easier on me now that Brian had arrived to share the cost of our rent - or so I thought. After paying his train fare to London the Black Rat informed me that he had almost no money left to last him till he got his first wages from the factory. That would be 2 weeks after he commenced working there. So until he got paid I would be worse off than ever as I had to pay for his food and any tube or bus fares as well as his half of the rent. 'Oh well,' I thought, 'at least it will only be for 2 weeks.' I couldn't wait to show London off to the Black Rat who had never been there before. Brian had no interest in some of the things I loved, like wrestling or lifting weights. But I knew what would appeal to him. So I wasted very little time before I introduced him to Soho. Much to my delight on this occasion the Ladies of the night were out in force, and much to my surprise with the Black Rat's immoral support I enjoyed their bawdy banter no end.

"Where are you from?" Inquired a buxom red-head detecting our Welsh accents.

"From South Wales." I answered.

"Oh yes, I thought so," she said, "all you bleed'n Welsh are the bleed'n same ain't cha? Men's pricks and boy's bleed'n pocket money!" We were flattered as well as amused and laughed all the way to the 2 I's, and for the rest of the night. We exploded with laughter when ever one of us reminded the other of what the big red-head had said to us. We both planned to spend our Christmas vacation back in Brynmawr. Even though Christmas was still a few months away, I decided now that I had Brian to share expenses I would use the few pounds I had saved to put down as a deposit on a new suit. I knew that I couldn't really afford it, but I was determined that my appearance when I returned to Brynmawr would suggest success. And, therefore shoot all my friends and enemies alike up the nose for doubting my ability to make something of myself in London. In order to make a more unexpected statement I decided to abandon my Edwardian style of dress, and take a walk on the tame side. I would dress not only smartly, but as soberly as I could.

Although Brian worked in a different part of the factory from me we would always walk to work together each morning, and then meet in the canteen for lunch. It was in the canteen that the Black Rat noticed a girl named Carol whom he fancied, and from then on the three of us would always share a table while we ate. Unbeknown to us at that time, making friends with Carol raised the ire of a git named Joseph Mackey one of the hostile Irish gang. He also fancied Carol, but at first he just fumed in silence.

At last the Friday that the Black Rat would get his first weeks pay crept around. Not too soon for me as Friday was also rent day, and this would be the first time I wouldn't have to pay it all myself. I had been working at my machine for just an hour or so after lunch that day, when the factory manager walked up to me and said,

"Well your friend didn't last long did he? It was a waste of time giving him a job here." I had no idea what he was talking about.

"What's happened," I asked, bewildered, "did you fire him for something?"

"No," replied the manager, "he came to my office this morning, and asked for his cards and his 2 weeks wages. He told me he was going back to Wales today. I told him that I would have his cards and wages ready for him by this afternoon and I'm just now going to my office to see if they are ready for him."

"Can I go and see him?" I asked, "This is the first I've heard of it and the twat owes me money!"

"Okay, but turn your machines off and don't be long." He said. I had to ask him for directions to where Brian was working, and found it was in an adjoining building. When I saw him he was standing with his back towards me and he didn't see me approaching him. I was amazed to see that not only was he dressed in his suit instead of overalls. But he also had his suitcase all packed and ready to go sitting on the factory floor beside him. I gave him a slap on the back that could be described as VERY hearty.

"What's happening?!" I asked him in a loud voice. I thought he was going to shit in his pants.

"Er-ugh-um-err-um-ugh!" He said.

"Come on Brian," I told him, "you know I don't speak Welsh, WHAT'S HAPPENING!!!" It's strange, I had never heard him stutter before and now he couldn't stop. "Take a breath," I told him quietly, "and tell me in English, what's happening?"

"I've got to go home," he replied, eventually, "but I'm coming back!" He added.

"How come you're waiting for your cards and your wages then?" I inquired, he began to stutter again.

"What about all the money you owe me?" I asked him.

"I was going to leave it on the table in your room for you - with a note honestly!" He answered.

"If you were going to leave it on the table, why have you got your case with you already packed? It looks as though you were going straight to the railway station from here." I suggested.

"Oh no, I was going to go back to the flat to leave you your money!" He insisted.

"How much were you going to leave?" I inquired.

"I don't know," he answered, "I was going to leave you some and send you the rest when I get another job."

"That won't do," I replied, "I want it now, and I'll wait with you till you get paid."

"I can't give it you all now," he whined, "I've got to pay my train fare, and what's left has got to last me till I can get another job."

"You will give it all to me now," I corrected him, "unless you want to take your trip home in a fucking ambulance." He glowered and shuffled about but didn't answer me; he still hadn't looked me in the eye. "Why didn't you tell me you were going?" I asked him, "It's obvious that you were going to try and cheat me out of the money you owe me." I still didn't get a reply so I added, "Do you think I wouldn't come looking for you when I came home for Christmas?" Still no response. So I brought out the heavy guns, "After I'd found you missing today and realized what you'd done, the first thing I would have done is drop my Brother Terence a line. He would enjoy collecting my money for me." At the very mention of Ter's name the Black Rat shuddered and turned a lighter shade of pale. When the manager arrived with the Rat's cards and wages, I held my hand out for them which he gave me with a little smile on his face. I handed Black Rat his cards, I opened his pay-packet, extracted what I figured he owed me, and dropped the remainder on the floor of the factory. If the manager hadn't been present I would probably have kicked Brian in the face as he bent down to pick it up. But he was, so I didn't. The Black Rat retrieved what was left of his money, picked up his case and shuffled out of the factory, without a glance at me or uttering another word.

"See you Christmas!" I called after him, hoping he would detect the hint of menace in my fond farewell. Well, I was on my own again with the only person I had ever met that I could rely on - me!

"Bert Assirati is wrestling at the Seymour Hall Wednesday," Uncle Fred informed me, "I'll take you to watch, my treat if you come to White City with me this week."

"Okay, you've got yourself a deal!" I told him enthusiastically. White City was where Uncle Fred liked to spend his time gambling on the Greyhounds and occasionally racing his own Dog Jerry. Usually in some minor track somewhere outside the London area. Not that Jerry was a minor class Dog, far from it. But Uncle Fred along with some of his Greyhound racing buddies, would often change Jerry's name and disguise him in some way to improve the odds when racing him out in the sticks. I've seen the naturally brindle hued Jerry dyed almost every color a Greyhound can be. I was taken along as a bit of extra muscle in case things got a bit hairy as a result of their attempted subterfuge. I used to enjoy my little excursions to the track with Uncle Fred. The only drawback was it would take me away from the gym for an evening. And I was always loathe to miss a session with the weights. I wasn't very interested in gambling, but I would risk a shilling or two on each race to make the evening a little bit more interesting and even exciting - if I won that is. If I was lucky enough to win a bet on one of the early races I'd put the rest of my money back in my pocket, and just play with what I'd won. Uncle Fred on the other hand, would lay pretty hefty bets on the forecast and would rarely win as a result. I never studied form like Uncle Fred, but would make a bet on a Dog if its name appealed to me. Having made my choice, Uncle Fred would often roar with laughter and tell me this one or that one that I fancied didn't stand a chance. The week before we were due to go and watch Bert Assirati in action I had been winning steadily all night. I decided to bet a couple of pounds on an outsider in the last race which was over the hurdles. I made my choice for no other reason, than the fact that the Greyhound weighed 84 pounds and was the heaviest Dog running that night. It won - so I told Uncle Fred that the treat would now be mine instead of his, when we went to the Seymour Hall to watch the wrestling. I was suddenly the richest I had ever been. I had fretted over my extravagance when ordering that new suit, which I could barely afford when the Black Rat had come to London, and was supposed to share expenses. When he suddenly left I didn't know how I would manage to pay the balance. Especially if I was to pay for it before Christmas. With the money I'd won in White City that night, not only did I have sufficient funds to pay off the balance on my suit, but I bought an overcoat, shirt, tie and new shoes to go with it. And plenty over to buy a nice Christmas present for Mam, Dad, Ter and Pam. Things were looking up.

    The following Wednesday, both Uncle Fred and I were sitting in the front row of the balcony in The Seymour Hall looking right down onto the ring. I was of the opinion that we would have a much better view of the action sitting there, than the more expensive ringside seats. The wrestling was excellent. But we were informed that Bert Assirati's scheduled opponent hadn't turned up, and he would be wrestling a substitute wrestler from Tonga. In years to come when I learned a lot more about the Legendary Bert, I realized that it was a very common occurrence for Bert Assirati's scheduled opponent not to turn up. That night Bert's performance gave me a very obvious clue as to why. The Friendly Islander got anything but a friendly reception from Bert, who brutalized him unmercifully from the sound of the first bell. He finally caught him with one of his specialties. A double elbows drop. It was applied by purposely making a slow clumsy grab for both the Tongan's legs. This gave the Tongan an easy opportunity to counter it by grabbing Bert around his huge chest as he was bent in front of him. Bert would then lock his arms around the elbows of his opponent trapping them firmly and securing the huge Tongan face down on his own broad back. Then he would launch himself into the air and drop backwards with the hapless, helpless opponent upside-down behind him. The back of his opponent's head would break Bert's fall. On this occasion the 260 pound Bert threw himself back with such a tremendous force that he, and his even heavier adversary crashed right through the wooden boards of the ring. It collapsed completely as all 4 corner posts imploded into a tangled melee of wood, canvas, metal and rope that used to be a ring. Uncle Fred and I must have been two amongst no more than a few dozen fans who were in a position to see what happened next. Both Bert and the Friendly Islander were now struggling at the bottom of a canvas canyon in the middle of the wreckage. Bert was on top of the Tongan, and was hacking blow after blow down onto his defenseless opponent's unprotected face with the edge of his fist like a butcher chopping meat. Blood was splashing and splattering everywhere. The best part of it all was, that almost no one in the hall was aware of what was happening. They couldn't see either of the wrestlers from the angle where they were sitting. So the only reason Bert was punishing the poor Tongan so brutally must have been solely, for his own enjoyment. Uncle Fred scowled with revulsion, then looked at me and said, "Are you still sure you want to be a professional wrestler?!"

"Yes, I do." I replied, in a tone that I hoped sounded convincing. Uncle Fred gave me that pitying look and just shook his head. Over the next few years I learned that Bert's bestial behavior that night was anything but an isolated incident. If you remember earlier in my story I mentioned the time I spoke to Mike Marino in Cardiff. And my description of his badly scared face, badly broken nose and two cauliflower ears. That damage wasn't the result of many years wear and tear in a very rough business. It all happened to him in one night whilst wrestling with Bert. Bert was double tough, the harder he was kicked, slammed and smashed the better he liked it. His ring strategy was very simple. He would allow an opponent to kick, slam and smash him all night long. As long as you could give it Bert would take it. But never mind how fit, strong and energetic his opponent was. Pummeling the rock solid Bert for an indefinite period while he just kept coming back for more, would eventually exhaust and demoralize him. When he couldn't give any more, then it would be Bert's turn and what would happen next was not for the squeamish. Marge Assirati, Bert's wife and wrestling promoter had a reputation as an instigator of Bert's ultra violent temper. Especially if the night's receipts didn't come up to par. While her wrestling venues were full she would be fine. Too many empty seats - then look out. When the doors were opened to admit the fans at Marge's wrestling shows she would always be in the box office selling the tickets. More often than not Bert would be in there too standing behind her. As the Wrestlers she had booked on that night's card would arrive, they'd give Marge a wave and say hello as they walked past on their way to the dressing rooms. If business was good that would be fine. If Marge thought business could use a boost she would make a special fuss of Bert's opponent that night and after they were out of sight she'd say to Bert,

"What a nice young man he is, all the ladies love him, I'm not surprised either he's really so good looking."

"Hurum!" Bert would grunt and sentence would be past. Bert's opponent might be good looking going into the ring, but coming out he'd look like he'd had an argument with a combined harvester. That would satisfy the most hardened fan's bloodlust and by the time the word went around next week's turnout would soar. Marge didn't do it to be spiteful or vindictive it wasn't personal - just business. She knew when to feed the Lions and Bert was just the right tool to get the job done. That's how Mike

Marino got to look the way he did, and he certainly wasn't alone. Before Les Thornton went to wrestle in the States he wrestled in Europe as Henri Pierlot. He was an extremely handsome young man, and a very tough one. When he wasn't wrestling he was playing Rugby. Much to his wife's chagrin. She was terrified that Henri's looks could easily get damaged. Especially his perfectly even whiter than white teeth. And, if you've ever seen a photo of a smiling Rugby team you can easily see why her fear was justified. Marge was promoting in Cardiff and Henri was wrestling Bert, and receipts were down.

"Oh, isn't young Henri a really handsome boy, Bert?" Sighed Marge as Henri made his way to the dressing room after stopping to wave and flash a dazzling white smile. "He's got the most perfect white teeth I've ever seen." "Hurum!" Grunted Bert. When the Main Event was over Henri staggered back to the dressing room. His face looked like a squashed Strawberry. As he examined his teeth in the small wall mirror he found that all that was left of his front teeth, were a few bloody jagged stumps. After assessing the damage, as tough as he was the now ex-handsome Henri broke down and cried like a baby. Not just for himself, but for the horror, anguish and distress his Wife would suffer as result of his injuries. Henri's perfect teeth were his wife's pride and joy and now - well fangs ain't what they used to be. By the time Bert entered the dressing room Henri was bent forward sitting in a wooden chair, with his battered face in his hands weeping unashamedly. Bert looked down at him for a few moments. Then in an uncharacteristic and extremely rare show of compassion he gave poor Henri a gentle slap on his shoulder with a ham like hand and said,

"Never mind son - have a nice hot cup of tea, you'll be alright." Hey, but the next week Marge's show was packed. I'm sure Henri and his Wife would have been deliriously happy and completely pacified to know that.

Bert Assirati may have been the biggest name and the biggest draw in Britain if not Europe in those days. But for reasons, some of which I've just described also made him the most feared and unpopular opponent there too. Black Butcher Johnson was booked to appear in 'Bellevue' Stadium in Manchester one Saturday night, and was making the trip by train. A few stops before the train reached its destination, another wrestler who was scheduled to wrestle on the same card got into Butcher's compartment. The Butcher was taken aback to see the astonished expression on the other wrestlers face as he realized Butcher was on the train.

"My God, I didn't expect to see you tonight Butch!'. The wrestler told him.

"Why not?" Butcher retorted indignantly, "I thought that everyone would know."

"Oh, I knew you were billed, but I didn't think you'd turn up." The other replied.

"Why not?!" Repeated Butcher.

"Well you know who you're wrestling don't you?!" The other inquired.

"Yes of course," said Butcher, "the promoter told me I'm wrestling Jack Pye."

"He lied," the other informed him, "you're on with Bert!" Black Butcher Johnson's black face turned white.

"What - Are you sure - you're fuckin' with me - right?! Croaked Butcher.

"No I'm not," he was assured, "look here's the card." The wrestler told him as he fished a program out of his pocket, and passed it into the Butchers trembling hand. Sure enough there it was in black and white, 'Main Event – Bert Assirati versus The Famous Negro Mule-Kick Expert Black Butcher Johnson. Butcher got off the train at the next station. Before he caught the next train back to London, he went into the telegraph office and sent a telegram to the promoter in Bellevue Stadium - it read,

'I've gone home in agony! Love, Butcher.'

There was also the time when four Heavy-weight Wrestlers were traveling together from London, by car to a show in Saint James's Hall in Newcastle. Newcastle is 300 miles north of London. And in those days, on those roads in Britain a 300 mile trip was an all day affair just getting to an arena. And an all night affair getting back home to London, after the matches had finished. I can't remember the names of the four wrestlers involved, so I shall refer to them as Tom, Dick, Harry and Jim. From the time they began their drive from London, Tom, Dick and Harry seemed to be sharing a secret joke at Jim's expense.

Every now and then Tom, who was driving would adjust the mirror so that he could catch Jim's eye as he sat in one of the back seats with Harry. He'd shake his head in mock sympathy, then he'd glance at Harry and Dick and all three of them would chuckle gleefully.

"What's so funny?!" Jim would demand.

"Oh nothing, nothing at all, he-he-he!" Tom would snigger. Then he would shoot a look at Harry and Dick and they'd all roar with mirth. This childish behavior was carried on all day for the rest of the trip. Punctuated by one of the other three asking Jim periodically, if he felt okay. Needless to say long before they reached their destination Jim was royally pissed off with each of the other three wrestlers. A little way into the City of Newcastle Tom slowed the car to a halt beside a wall that was plastered with posters advertising that night's Wrestling promotion. There billed as main event was Jim versus none other than - yes you've guessed, Bert Assirati!

"Oh shit!" Exclaimed Jim, as he gazed with horror at the posters. Most wrestlers have a very cruel sense of humor and Tom, Dick and Harry all chortled with pleasure at poor Jim's distress. All three of them had been aware of the fact that Jim would be wrestling with Bert that night. And, they had been enjoying the fact all day that Jim didn't know. They were cruelly looking forward with anticipation to poor Jim's reaction when he did find out.

"Better get going," said Tom smiling at Jim, as he started the car, "we don't want to be late and upset Bert do we?"

"Stop this fuckin' car right now," roared Jim, "I'm getting out!" With the volume and fury of Jim's voice screaming at the back of his head Tom slammed on the brakes, which brought the car to a screeching halt.

"Where are you going?! Asked Tom, as Jim leapt out of the car.

"Give me the car keys," he demanded, "I want to get my bag out of the back!" After retrieving his bag Jim flung the keys back to Tom through the car window. He walked a few yards back down the road and stuck his thumb up with the intention of thumbing a lift back to London. Tom, Dick and Harry looked at each other with eyebrows raised before Tom started the car to resume their journey. A whelp from Harry who was now sitting alone in the back seat caused him to brake once more.

"Stop the car, I'm getting out too!" Yelled Harry.

"Why?! Demanded Tom.

"If Jim doesn't turn up who do you think will have to wrestle Bert?! He replied.

"YOU!" Answered Tom and Dick in unison. Harry leaned forward snatched the keys from the ignition and was out of Tom's car in a flash, after recovering his bag and returning Tom's keys he called down the road to Jim,

"Hey Jim, hang on, I'm coming with you!" As Tom began to start his car again he suddenly stopped and looked at Dick,

"Shit!" He exclaimed, "If Jim and Harry don't turn up one of us two will have to wrestle with Bert!" Tom and Dick stared at each other in horror for one whole minute. Tom started his car swung it around and drove back south down the road where Harry and Jim were still trying to thumb a lift.

"Get back in the two of you," ordered Tom, "were going home!" The four wrestlers traveled south on their long 300 hundred mile journey back to London in complete silence, until Jim said,

"Well at least we'll get home a bit earlier than we would have."

"Yes – and in one piece." Added Tom.

In December 1957 the great American World Heavyweight Wrestling Champion Lou Thez defended his title against Dara Singh - Champion of India in London's Royal Albert Hall. Their match ended in a 15 round draw. As the result was being announced who should emerge from the audience to challenge Lou Thez to a match for his World Title, was none other than Bert Assirati. In spite of the fact that Lou was reputed to be one of the world's greatest shoot [real] wrestlers, he refused to accept Bert Assirati's challenge. Many years later I asked Lou about that night, and he claimed that he didn't refuse Bert's challenge at all. But, the fact that the match never took place does tend to cast a little doubt on the credence of that claim.

****

What a small World I thought. I was having a conversation one lunchtime with Carol and Trevor Davis. The older fellow Welshman who worked near me in Acton Bolt Factory and hailed from Abertillery, which was only a few miles from Brynmawr. I had been relating the epic massacre I'd just witnessed between Bert Assirati and the Friendly Islander - or should I say the Flattened Islander from Tonga. Trevor was both appropriately impressed and horrified with my story and when I completed it he said,

"We used to have a chap back in Abertillery who would have taught Bert Assirati a lesson or two; he was a Mountain Fighter and a good Wrestler too."

Although I was amazed by what he had just said I managed to keep a straight face as I knew exactly what he was going to say next - so I jumped in and said,

"Oh yes, I think you're right, that's the chap who used to drive around Abertillery on a horse and cart delivering fruit and vegetables from his greengrocers shop." Trevor's jaw dropped as I added, "peculiar fellow he used to fasten a smoked Kipper to the lapel of his jacket with a safety pin. Raced Horses and Pigeons too I believe." Trevor by now was pop eyed with amazement. I placed my hand on my chin as though in deep thought as I continued my musings. "A very tough man indeed - would have definitely given Bert Assirati something to think about. Ah, what was his name now, don't tell me it's right on the tip of my tongue - Yes, I remember now - Big Jim Arnold! I remember him well."

Trevor was almost speechless by now. But being Welsh that didn't last long.

"How could you possibly know that?! He gasped, "You're far too young to be able to remember Jim Arnold. He was probably dead before you were even born!"

"Oh no," I replied, "as a matter of fact he was very much alive last time I saw him. In fact we came close to exchanging blows. We had a very hot dispute over some of his prize Pigeon eggs that I took from his Pigeon loft to make myself an omelet." Now Trevor really was speechless. His astonishment wasn't much appeased even after I explained to him that Big Jim Arnold was my Great-Grandfather. So Big Jim Arnold was our main topic of conversation whenever Trevor and I had time for a chat. But even he couldn't tell me for certain who had won that famous marathon fight between Great-Grand-Dad Arnold and the Cowboy.

Talking about fighting, I hadn't had a fight since before I left Wales. Apart from the ones I was having on a regular basis on the wrestling mats in the YMCA. I didn't miss having a street fight either surprisingly enough. Away from the small town environment I found it was no longer necessary to assert myself that way. In a small town it seemed important to keep the tough guy persona well primed, and very much in the forefront of any would be rivals mind. In a small town everyone knew everyone, in the big City no one knew anyone and didn't give a damn either. So there was no need to pick fights all the time as there was no one to impress. Unfortunately that didn't last. Even though the Black Rat, Brian Heath had long gone Carol and I would still sit together and chat over lunch. There was no flavor of romance between us whatsoever, we were just friends. I believe she would have dated me if I'd asked her to but I was hardly making enough money to live on let alone spend any on Girls. I certainly hadn't lost interest in the fair sex I just couldn't afford them. But unbeknown to me trouble was brewing as a result of our friendship. The Irish git, Joseph Mackey was still smoldering with jealousy. He wouldn't have been a bad looking guy if it wasn't for the mean, ugly, scowling expressions he always adopted. His mouth was always compressed into a straight line and his eyebrows creased in a perpetual angry frown that surmounted his small shifty eyes. We had words on a number of occasions but on this particular day he walked right up to me and got right in my face. He told me to 'keep away from his girl if I knew what was good for me'. I didn't have a clue who his girl was and I told him so.

"Yeah, well you eat lunch with her every day!" He accused, "And that had better stop right now!"

"Oh, you mean Carol," I replied, "I've never seen her with you so how am I supposed to know she's your girlfriend?"

"Well you know now, 'cos I'm telling you so back off!" He snarled viciously.

"I'll tell you what I'll do," I told him pleasantly, "I'll run what you just told me by Carol and if she agrees that I should back off, I will be happy to oblige you both."

His face began to do some funny things, twitching, blinking and jerking. As startling as that was. I waited patiently for him for him to stop doing it for a few moments as I imagined that was what he did when he was trying to think.

"No!" He eventually shouted, "You are to never speak to her again - you've been warned!" Then he turned and stalked off. 'What an anticlimax,' I thought, after that great build up he performed with his face I was expecting so much more. I did run it by Carol next time I spoke to her and she said,

"Oh, that creepy bleeder, he's asked me out so many times he really gets on my bleed'n tit, I just tell Him to eff-off. I wouldn't bleed'n piss on him if he was on fire!" Well I suppose that more or less summed up her feelings on the subject.

But piss or not it hadn't quenched Joseph Mackey's feelings. I had long lost count of the threats and ultimatums that I endured from that lovesick Gaelic Git before he finally told me to meet him after work as he intended 'kickin' my teeth in!'

"No problem," I told him, "I'll be happy to oblige you and let you try." I was really quite surprised to find Mackey waiting for me near the main exit of the factory that day when work was over. I thought he was all piss and wind. He had threatened me with violence so many times by now, only to back pedal and flunk on his promise that I had long ago stopped taking him seriously. There was a wide alleyway between a couple of other businesses just across the road from the factory. That seemed a very appropriate venue for what we had in mind. So we just automatically made our way towards it without having to utter a single nicety. We walked about halfway down the alley before turning to face each other. When all at once a very large airplane fell out of the sky and landed on the back of my head. At least that was what it felt like. I hurtled forwards towards Mackey. I think I would have hit the ground face first at his feet if something hadn't grabbed me by the back of my jacket, which stopped me mid-flight. It dragged me backwards and spun me around in a single movement, and I caught sight of a big black bomb for just the tiniest fraction of a second before it exploded in my face. I was barely aware of the blood that gushed down and turned my vision into a blurred crimson, before I felt myself propelled through the air like a rag doll. My flight was rudely and abruptly arrested by the brick wall I bounced off. I landed heavily on a small flight of stone steps that I had completely cleared before hitting the wall; I immediately began flailing with my arms and legs. They all seemed to be working in spite of the fact that I couldn't feel my right side from my hip down, except a dull, numb ache. Before I had time to contemplate my plight, I vaguely felt a violent jarring of my deadened right foot. But I just kept flailing and kicking as I still couldn't see through the sticky mess that covered my face and filled my eyes. I don't know how long I lay there swinging my arms and legs like a Tortoise on its back. But I heard one of the London boys from the factory asking me if I could get up. About the same time it dawned on me, that if I were still being attacked something else should have happened by now. There was no sign of Mackey. But even in my dazed and confused state I knew that he wasn't the reason that I had just spent the last few minutes cart wheeling madly through a field of flying meteorites. The London boy who spoke to me, and pulled me back to my feet after I had ceased my flailing and kicking was Dave, who worked near me in the factory. He accompanied me back into the factory's wash room and told me while I washed the blood out of my eyes, and off my face what had happened,

"I didn't see it from the beginning," he explained, "I didn't even know what was going on in the alley until Big Sean the weightlifter, shot past me and right through the people who were standing around watching. I only saw you for the first time when Sean jumped on your back, spun you around, hit you and then threw you at the wall ----"

"What did he hit me with," I interrupted, "his head or his fist? It happened so fast I didn't see it coming."

"I'm not sure myself," Dave replied, "I was still standing behind him and there were a few people in front of me - But shit - you sure did a number on Sean, I don't think he'll be bothering you again."

"What are you talking about I asked him?" completely mystified.

"Yeah, go on act the bleed'n innocent!" He grinned.

"I'm telling you Dave, I don't know what happened. I had blood in my eyes and I was just trying to defend myself. I didn't even know who against!" Dave gave me that old fashioned look and I could see he wasn't convinced.

"Okay," he said, deciding to humor me, "You kicked Sean in the gob and nearly scored a field goal with his bleed'n head. When you kicked him, he fell flat on his arse, got right back up and ran off with blood squirting all over the bleed'n place!"

It was strange I thought, that it didn't strike me as odd when I walked back up the alley to cross the road back to the factory, that I had followed a trail of blood. It veered off up the nearside pavement as I neared the road. I was probably still dazed and too preoccupied to give it a second thought. I remembered then the jarring feeling I'd felt with my right heel as I instinctively kicked away, and that was when I must have made contact with Big Sean's chops. He didn't come into work for a couple of days but when he did, his face bore evidence of the damage I had inflicted on it. The gash, which was about an inch under his bottom lip was almost as wide as his ample mouth. It was still red and swollen and stitched all along it with a thick, ugly black thread. He had also lost two or three of his bottom front teeth. He caught my eye and saw me blatantly inspecting my handiwork but didn't say anything to me and acted as though nothing had happened between us. I decided to leave well alone and not seek further revenge and not because Sean stood 6 feet tall and weighed 235 pounds to my one 179. For one thing I was satisfied that even though he had Pearl Harbored me, he had fared a lot worse than I had. Also it was now obvious that if you had bother with one of the Irish mob you had bother with all of them. As for the original instigator Mackey, he seemed to have vanished off the scene completely and I didn't set eyes upon him again for over a year - but that's another story.

****

As a result of my association with some of Uncle Fred's Greyhound fancying friends I learned there was a job going in Wembley Stadium which paid a lot more money than I was making in the Bolt Factory. I applied for it and got it, things were looking up. I began work there just a few weeks before I went back to visit Brynmawr for Christmas, I lost count of the gleeful faces that said,

"Oh, so you're back from London then?!" Only to sour when I replied,

"Yes, but only for a few days over Christmas, I just can't wait to get back. I got a great job in Wembley Stadium." It wasn't a really great job but it was a lot better than the bolt factory and of course anything was better than the pit. The work consisted mostly of sweeping and painting and there was an awful lot of Wembley Stadium to sweep and paint. It was also compulsory to work on one of the two nights a week when they held Greyhound racing. Unfortunately for me I had started my new job right in the middle of a very cold winter and I was one of 6 workers who would have to re-rake the frost hardened dog track after every single race. Before the first of the racing punters had bought their entrance tickets, I would be filling giant wheelbarrows full of coke. Then running around the stadium with it filling and lighting the braziers. We put them under the stands all around the Stadium to help warm the customers. I was thus engaged one night and had just lit about 7 or 8 braziers that were set out in a fairly tight circle. It was a blustery night and the wind was blowing the thick smoke everywhere. I was in the process of stacking the coke into all of blazing braziers and I would take a huge breath of fresh air before running back into the circle to replenish each of them in turn with a large shovel full of coke. I would hold my breath until I ran back out of the circle, where I'd take some more deep breaths before running back in with another shovel full. Everything was going fine until the blustery wind suddenly changed in the wrong direction at the wrong time. I breathed in a huge full lung capacity breath of thick, toxic, coke dust and smoke and almost past out on the spot. I was really quite ill as a result and still seemed to be capable of coughing up lumps of coke for the next month. I was forced to take over a week off from work. That hurt my pocket and upset an unsympathetic management. They didn't appreciate me taking time off even though I was sick from a work related incident. They let me know in no uncertain terms that that was strike one.

****

I was no longer training at the YMCA. Frank Nottingham had told me about the famous 'Foresters' Wrestling, Boxing, Gymnastics, Bodybuilding and weightlifting Club. It was in North Kensington and was only a few miles away from where I lived. The Foresters was a great club, one of the best in London at that time. I started off there in my usual style by making a fool of myself, I told the Wrestling Coach Bill Smith, that I had been wrestling with amateur and pro wrestlers in the YMCA. Now I only wanted to wrestle in the professional style. Bill explained that they were an amateur club and only taught that style. I insisted that I was more of a submission wrestler and submissions were against the rules in the amateurs. Bill invited me to join him on the mat and suggested that I could use any style I wanted, while he would wrestle strictly amateur. I didn't really want to take advantage of him as he was looking a little long in the tooth, but in order to prove my point I accepted his offer. Once again I got the crap beaten out of me. Boy was I ever a slow learner?! I persevered and improved.

Whenever I had the time I still frequented the 2 I's Coffee Bar. Especially after I found out that it now belonged to two professional wrestlers, Paul Lincoln and The Giant Tasmanian, Ray Hunter who I had watched wrestling a number of times in Cardiff. I was in there one day sitting at the counter drinking a coffee. I would have preferred to have been down in the basement listening to the noise and enjoying the action. But I thought that I would stand more chance of spotting one of the wrestlers where I was. I was rehearsing in my mind for the 300th time what I would say to either of them, if I was lucky enough for one of them to walk in while I was sitting there. All of a sudden the door burst open and in swaggered about four guys who looked as though they were walking right towards me. The leader of them stopped beside a teenager who was sitting at the counter a few stools away from mine. The leader paused for effect, then his top lip curled up in his best Elvis impersonation and he drawled,

"You're sitting in my seat - get off!" The teenager hesitated for just two seconds before he picked up his coffee from the counter slid off the stool, and walked to a table a few yards away, without even replying.

'How bloody rude!" I thought, and wished with all my heart that it had been me sitting in his seat. I glared at the Elvis wannabe hoping to catch his eye. But his friends had gathered around, shielding him from the heat of my eyes. 'If you'd spoken to me like that,' I thought, 'I'd make your lip curl up permanently!' When they had finished their coffee one of them said,

"Time to go downstairs 'arry." And they all went downstairs to the basement; I followed wondering if 'arry would give me an excuse to belt him. They maneuvered themselves down to the stage. And as they were spotted by the denizens of the dungeon to my surprise they were cheered and slapped on their backs. A few minutes later they were on stage rocking for all they were worth. Young 'arry turned out to be Harry Webb, soon to be known as Cliff Richard. He brought out a record 'Move it' and when I heard it, instead of wanting to do him grievous bodily harm I became an avid fan. I thought he was great! He must have been great as I actually paid good money on two separate occasions to watch him perform on stage in Chiswick Empire. I also went there to watch another up and coming Rocker named Marty Wilde who was very good, but no Cliff Richards. There were many more bands that performed in the 2 I's that I admired. One was belonging singer Tony Sheridan. I had asked him on a number of occasions to sing a new Buddy Holly song, 'Think it over'. He told me that he had never heard of it but would get it, learn it and sing it for me. Every time I asked him he said he hadn't got it yet. I think he must have got fed up with my perpetual request. One night he told me,

"If you know it, you sing it." Much to his surprise I was on stage beside him in a flash. I began to sing and to my surprise the rest of his band seemed to know it and played the music along with me. After that if Tony saw me in the crowd he'd often call me up to sing what was by then my favorite song. What I liked most of all was that Tony, who never seemed to be able to remember my name would always introduce me to the audience as the 'Wrestler.'

When I had returned to work after Christmas, The Circus in

Wembley Empire Pool was still going. Some of us would be detailed to clean up there early each morning. Other times we worked as usual in the Stadium. One evening those of us on duty at the Greyhound track were all taking it easy in the Stadium staff room. When Freddy one of our co-workers rushed in and breathlessly ordered us all to follow him down to the Empire Pool.

"You're not going to believe this!" he promised. As we approached the building, Freddy put his finger up to his lips to signal us all to silence. And we began to tip-toe stealthily between the caravans and trailers belonging to the Circus people. He was correct, we were not going to believe this. We peered around a truck and there in full view of anyone who may have happened by was a beautiful long-legged Circus Show girl almost bent over double. Behind her standing on a box to bring him within range of his objective, was the ugliest and most completely naked Dwarf I had ever seen. Even though this was winter the sweat on his body glistened and reflected the lights from the caravans and trailers that surrounded him as he humped away viciously. One of the Kennel Girls in our company began to giggle with embarrassment, and another one named Dian told her to "shut up!" As she obviously didn't want the copulating couple to be disturbed by our presence. I had the feeling that they were both well aware of our presence and enjoyed having an audience. That feeling was confirmed when the Dwarf disengaged long enough to give us all a good view of his tackle before slamming it back with a vengeance.

"Jesus Christ, did you see the size of that?!" exclaimed Dian.

"It's not real!" Squawked Morris. Morris was acting foreman whenever our official foreman wasn't around. Normally he was okay but put the foreman's mantle on him and he turned into a real jerk. Dian the Kennel maid was his girlfriend. She had a real sense of mischief and seemed to enjoy winding Morris up as much as the rest of us did.

"What do you mean, it's not real?!" Demanded Dian, not appreciating anyone attempting to diminish the spectacle that had obviously impressed her so much.

"Come on, everyone back to work!" Ordered Morris ignoring Dian's question.

"What do you mean it's not real?!" insisted Dian, "Are you jealous or what?"

"Oh come on Dian," Morris whined, "or we'll all get fired." Most of the guys began to move away but Dian and the other girls wouldn't budge.

"I'm going to watch and check him out again," answered Dian, "he's got to take it out sometime." Almost as if the Dwarf heard her he uncoupled again and stood proudly on the box blatantly displaying himself. He looked like a cross between a grotesque little Satyr from ancient Grecian mythology and a tripod.

"Jesus Christ look at the size of that!" Ordered Dian. I was thoroughly enjoying Morris's discomfort.

"Do you still think it's real, Dian?" I asked, hoping to encourage her.

"It's as real as Morris's!" She laughed.

"Only bigger!" I added.

"Much bigger!" She agreed. Morris marched off furious. Which caused both Dian and I to collapse in a fit of giggles – 'OOPS! Strike two' I thought.

****

I hurried along Burrows Road from Uncle Fred's house filled with the anticipated excitement of another upcoming wrestling event to be held at the Seymour Hall. Not only was Joe Cornelius, one of the biggest names ever in British wrestling going to be main event that night. But Spencer Churchill a bodybuilding idol of mine even before I knew I wanted to be a professional wrestler myself was also on the card. Just the thought of it was the very reason for my haste. I was on my way to the Forrester's gym. The club wasn't due to open for at least another hour. But just contemplating the fact that I would soon be seeing two of my greatest idols for the first time in action made me long for the weights and the wrestling mats like a heroin addict longed for the needle. I spun around the corner at the end of Burrows Road in a dream and almost collided with a face I hadn't seen for a few years. But a face I had seen in my mind's eye on a very regular basis. The look of shock and surprise on his face must have mirrored my own. Although I realized immediately that I shouldn't have been surprised. After all, this is where Bobby Selsden lived. The wrestling fantasy that had enveloped me before I turned that corner evaporated and I could feel my features darken into a vicious scowl. I'd waited a long time for this moment. But coming as it did out of the blue I had to struggle to rearrange my mood. I scrutinized my enemy; he had grown into a very handsome young man. And to my disappointment bore not the slightest scar or facial disfigurement, as a result of his boxing activities. Either he had given up boxing or he was too good at it to have suffered any noticeable injuries. He had also outgrown me and was both taller and heavier than I was. Hey, but that had never stopped me before, and it certainly wouldn't stop me now. To add to my surprise Bobby's face cracked into a wide grin,

"Hi, Adrian," he said, "I heard you were living here now, is it true you're wrestling, you look in great shape; you're lifting weights too, right?"

"Yes!" I answered sullenly, bracing myself for what was to come next; Bobby's face sobered a little as though aware of my stony visage for the first time.

"Where are you training?" He asked, ignoring my obvious air of hostility.

"The Forrester's." I answered.

"I train in a club in Kensal Rise," he told me, "you should come there and have a workout with me one night."

"I don't box, I wrestle," I responded, "why don't you come down to the Forrester's one night and I'll show you around the wrestling mat!" Bobby threw his head back and laughed,

"Shit, no Adrian, I know better than to want to wrestle with you. Damn, I can still remember you throwing me all over the street last time we met – and the time before that. I haven't boxed for ages - I'm into bodybuilding now, like you!"

Bobby held his hand out, in a gesture of friendship and with little hesitation I shook it gladly. I knew he wasn't afraid of me and would have given a good account of himself if I'd forced him to. We chatted like old friends instead of old enemies. After I'd said goodbye and I continued on my way to the Forrester's I realized that Bobby Selsden had outgrown me in more than just size.

It was about that time that I began training with a new guy at the gym, he stood a little over 6 feet 4 inches tall and possessed the first pair of genuine 19 inch upper arms I had ever seen. Big Sony Colindos was from Trinidad in the West Indies, but now lived less than a couple of miles from me in London. He invited me to workout with him in his own little gym that he had set up in his garage. We worked out there on Saturdays and Sundays as well as our usual five nights a week in the Forrester's. I couldn't wait to write to my Brother Ter and tell him all about my new training partner. As I had never been to a gym in Wales that had had more equipment than a couple of old rusty barbells. I had never used the bench-press as an exercise before. I found it very strange and awkward to perform at first as I was only used to pressing weights above my head. Once I got the hang of it the poundage I used increased dramatically, until I got close to using 200 pounds. Then it was as though I had hit a brick wall. It was frustrating for me more so, since I had been able to lift that kind of weight above my head for at least a couple of years already. My amateur wrestling was improving but not fast enough to satisfy me. I had won more club and interclub matches than I had lost but the fact that I lost any was not the way I had visualized my invasion of the wrestling World. Plus they were amateur matches not professional. I have always been very strong which was a good thing considering the only thing that really worked well for me in competition, was a head chancery and arm bar that I was able to apply equally well, whether facing my opponent on our feet or from the strong position on our knees. If I got that hold on my opponent he was really in trouble. If I didn't then I was. I don't ever remember winning an amateur contest with any other move. I really was a one hold wonder. One of the last amateur interclub competition matches I had, was against a tall, skinny East Indian from a club in Finsbury Park. I must admit I felt as though I had been insulted after he had striped for action and I found that I could almost count his ribs from my side of the mat. There was little glory I thought in vanquishing such a puny adversary. I glared at Bill Smith who had chosen me to wrestle him. Bill smiled back innocently. I sighed a great sigh and looked back at my opponent who was scrutinizing me with such a look of undisguised contempt on his face that I just couldn't wait to get at him. I intended making very short work of him, and then have a word or two with Bill Smith about the quality of opponents he'd choose for me in future. Well we met in the centre of the mat and after pulling, grabbing and grappling around the mat for what seemed to me, an embarrassingly long time, I found I couldn't do anything with him - He was just too bloody tricky - He couldn't do anything with me - I was just too bloody strong. We had both become very frustrated with each other. The Indian was getting very angry and showing it, I got very angry because he did. He bulled into me and tried for the fifteenth time to take my legs and stuck his head just where I wanted it for my specialty. I had despaired of ever catching him with it but now he had thrown caution to the wind and given it me for free. He realized his mistake too late, and we crashed down to the mat with him underneath me. Only for him to wriggle and squirm his way to the edge of the mat where I was told to break my hold and let him up. I did, but I was not happy about it. We were ordered back to the centre of the mat to begin again. That had been the first, and I was afraid, possibly the last chance I would get to pin him. But somehow after what seemed like a month of Sundays I managed to trap him in a front chancery again. Down to the canvas we went and I tried in vain but failed to prevent him wriggling to the edge of the mat once again. I was once more ordered to release him. I was fuming and couldn't wait to get at him again. In disgust I kicked him, and ordered him myself to get back to the centre of the mat. He didn't have to, as I was disqualified on the spot. I glared at him with unfeigned hatred. He held my gaze only long enough to convey an ugly look of triumph before mingling with his team-mates where he may have felt safer from further confrontation with me. Bill Smith didn't say a lot, only that I would probably be better suited to wrestling professionally as the pros appreciated that sort of behavior more than the amateurs did.

Wrestling nights in the Foresters was on Monday, Wednesday and Friday in a large room apart from the rest of the gym's activities. On Tuesday and Thursday the wrestling mats were used for gymnastics. Weightlifting and bodybuilding in the main building was Monday till Friday. The gym instructor offered me the use of one of the mats that I could practice my wrestling on, with anyone who wanted to join me there on the gym nights, if I would sign up for his classes. I didn't have to practice gymnastics but as he didn't have many students, the more signatures he had, the better it looked for him. Often I would find that it was only me, along with a small group of would be pro wrestlers that I had recruited that would be using the facilities on gymnastics nights.

'Butch' was a little shy of 6 feet tall and weighed close to 230 pounds, plus with his huge neck and shoulders and close cropped hair he really looked the part. He was my favorite opponent, and it's a wonder either of us ever survived our marathon battles to become pros. As we hammered lumps off each other at every possible opportunity.

****

Back at work, Morris was becoming more of a foreman than an acting foreman. The more authority he was given the more of a pompous self-important twerp he became. Most of my workmates began to jump when Morris said 'jump,' but I just couldn't seem to make myself take him seriously. Until very recently he had just been one of us. Dian only made things worse, she didn't seem to take Morris seriously either. But being his girlfriend she obviously got away with things that I couldn't. That didn't stop me from trying especially when Dian was around to erg me on. Just a couple of days after the 'horny Dwarf' incident I was busy sweeping up mountains of discarded betting slips from the Greyhound meet the night before. I saw Morris and Dian walking towards me on their way to the main exit. Morris was laughing at something he had just said. Dian walked beside him hunched up against the chilly wind with her hands in her pockets. And not looking very amused at whatever witticism Morris had just imparted. Neither one of them had spotted me so far. On the spur of the moment I kicked off the boots I was wearing and kneeled down on them making me look quite dwarf like. I put my broom between my legs with about 2 feet of the handle sticking up in front at a most erotic angle.

"Hey, Morris," I shouted, as the two were just a few yards

away, "do you think this is real or not?!" Morris's giggling died in his throat to be replaced by Dian shrieking the Stadium down with laughter. In the second that they both saw me both of their expressions reversed. Morris from laughter to fury, Dian from misery to hysterics. 'Just the way it ought to be.' I thought. Morris's pace increased as he walked away from me. He turned back to urge Diana to hurry. Just in time to catch her looking at me, pointing at him with a finger on one hand. while demonstrating a pumping motion with the other. Whatever Morris was about to say again died in his throat and he almost ran from the scene. 'That went well.' I thought, a little apprehensively 'I can't see him letting that pass.' Sure enough later that day, Freddy came looking for me.

"Morris, told me to fetch you," he said, "he has another job for you."

'Here it comes I thought.' I walked slowly after Freddy who rushed ahead of me.

"I'd hurry if I were you," Freddy called over his shoulder, "you know what he's like if you keep him waiting!"

"Fuck off Freddy," I told him, "what's wrong with you, is your head cold and you can't wait to get it back up Morris's hot arse?!

"I don't like Morris any more than you do!" He protested.

"Yeah right," I agreed, "if your head was any further up his arse Morris would have two heads and still have no fucking brains!" Freddy was beginning to piss me off almost as much as Morris did. We used to be friends especially after I'd introduced him to my little scam. On the Greyhound nights if we weren't busy, I would pretend to be until I could melt into the crowds of punters. Then run around the stadium, sneak out past the kennels and spend the rest of the evening in the nearest cinema. Then when the movie was over I'd sneak back into the stadium just in time to clock out and go home. Freddy loved my idea of getting paid to watch a film. But now since Morris started getting almighty Freddy seemed to be hovering around him like a fly around shit,

"Do you want a coffee? Morris, shall I do this for you Morris? Would you like me to do that for you Morris?" Freddy was still Freddy when Morris wasn't around and could be great fun. But as soon as the acting foreman was on the scene Freddy Jekyll turned into Freddy Hyde.

"Took your time, didn't you Street?!" Accused Morris, as we approached him.

"What a bloody stink!" I complained. No, I wasn't talking about Morris. Not this time at least. Freddy had led me behind one of the toilets where Morris was impatiently waiting. He indicated the source of the smell. A drain was overflowing.

"What do you suggest, Street?" Asked Morris.

"Call a plumber." I suggested.

"Don't you know how to fix it Street?" He asked sarcastically, "I thought by the way you talk you knew everything!"

"Everything except plumbing," I told him, "especially if it stinks."

"Well now is your chance to learn, Street," he sneered, "get that drain cleared."

"Get yourself fucked." I told him and walked back towards where I'd been working before Freddy disturbed me. Morris ran a few paces behind me and screamed at the back of my head,

"I've given you a direct order Street; if you disobey me I'm going straight to the manager to report you!"

"Fuck off, Morris!" I told him, without turning or slackening my pace. I hadn't even reached where I'd left my broom when Freddy came running up behind me and breathlessly told me to go see the big boss. The look I gave Freddy shriveled him. And he gave me his best 'don't kill the messenger' look before scurrying back to tell his master that I'd been told. 'Jesus Christ,' I thought 15 minutes later as I walked out of the boss's office, 'it's just like being back in school. I'm surprised he didn't try to cane me.' Well, I'd been warned. If I wanted to keep my job I did whatever I was told to do by my superiors. And under no circumstances was I to tell my superiors to fuck off. I didn't know whether to feel proud or ashamed of myself. That I had managed to keep my mouth shut when he said 'to my superiors,' and I hadn't told him that as far as I was concerned I didn't have any superiors. Most especially if he was referring to Morris. Thank God for both of us that Morris wasn't hanging around to gloat as I made my way back once more to my broom. A few weeks later, just as I was leaving work through the main exit after clocking out, Freddy called to me and asked me to wait for him.

"I'll be with you in a minute," he told me, "I've just got to go and clock out!"

"Okay, but hurry up, Freddy," I called back, "I want to catch the first bus, I've got a match tonight in the Forester's!" Well I waited and waited and there was no sign of Freddy. A couple of the other guys were coming by and I asked them had they seen him.

"Yes," answered one of them, "I saw him going out past the kennels."

"The stupid twat," I responded, "he asked me to wait for him." Freddy must have been sneaking around the kennels looking for one of the girls he fancied'; I thought and then I promptly forgot clean about him. That night in the Forester's was the night I had my match against the skinny Indian and got disqualified after a very frustrating battle. It put me in a filthy mood which resulted in a bad night's sleep. Next morning I woke late and had to rush out without breakfast in order not to be late for work. I have always been a breakfast person, and I am not awake or human until I have eaten and drank my coffee. I reached the stadium in plenty of time to clock in before 8, but as I was passing some of my workmates, Freddy, who was amongst them began to holler and scream.

"Hey Adrian, did you wait long last night? HA-HA-HA! I heard you were still waiting for me half an hour after I'd gone out the back way, HO-HO! What a joke!"

I lashed out and Freddy bit the dust. It wasn't because Freddy had played such a stupid unfunny prank. It was his loud, screaming, raucous voice that jangled my nerves first thing in the morning, and I just wanted to shut it off. Unfortunately for Freddy I caught my knuckles on the corner of his misshapen head, and I thought I'd broken my fist. This sent me into a fit of rage and I began doing a shithouse shuffle all over Freddy's head and ribs. If only to take my mind off the pain in my hand. Someone grabbed my hair from behind and happy for the diversion I spun around and lashed out again. Morris hit the concrete deck, like a sack of shit. His eye-glasses, which I'd punched right off his face didn't stop their flight until they disintegrated against the stone steps that led up to the lower stands. "OOOPS!" I barely had time to clock in before I was summoned once more to the boss's office. I was told to clock back out again as I no longer worked in Wembley Stadium. Well now I had a new job - looking for a new job, and not only did it pay exactly nothing - But the money I spent every day on bus and train fares looking for work soon helped in completely depleting my already scanty savings.

****

Every time I had gone to visit my family in Wales after going to live in London, I had brought back to London with me as many of my collection of Swords and Daggers as I could comfortably carry. I had stored my entire collection, with the exception of my Japanese Samurai Swords, which were still in Wales, at Uncle Fred's home for safety. That turned out to be a terrible mistake. One of Uncle Fred's Greyhound racing friends saw my collection and in Uncle's presence asked me if he could have one of them. I didn't want to embarrass Uncle Fred by refusing his friend's request. Although to part with just one of my precious weapons, for me would be heartrending. He told me he wouldn't offer to pay for it as he claimed that paying for a knife, dagger or sword would sever a friendship, or some such crap. He was Uncle Fred's friend not mine and I was starving to death and unable to even pay my rent. So if I had to part with one of my swords, payment would have been not only accepted but most appreciated. Nevertheless I agreed to let him have one. He asked me which one he could take - That was like asking me which of my fingers would I like him to cut off. So I told him to 'take what you want'. That turned out to a bigger mistake. I left Uncle Fred's house and walked to The Forester's Club as I couldn't bear to watch him make his choice. Next time I checked on my collection I found that there was 9 swords missing, instead of the one asked for. According to Uncle Fred - his friend had taken my offer of 'take what you want' as, 'TAKE AS MANY AS YOU WANT.' I was shattered and all of a sudden my precious, but now depleted collection just didn't mean so much to me anymore. If I can't have it all, I don't want any of it. I gathered up what was left, tied them all into two large bundles and took them to 'German's Antique Armor and weapons Store' in Edgware Road. I asked the proprietor how much would he pay me for them. He looked at me suspiciously and then offered me a few pounds for the lot. I explained to him that I had paid much more than that for them over the years, and was certain that they would have appreciated considerably in value by now.

"I buy those things by the box full," he explained, 'that's all they're worth to me, take it, or leave it." So I took it. All the years of polishing floors for Mam, loading and unloading produce and running errands on the market. Working at a paper-round seven days a week, in the sun, rain and snow blizzards. To build up a collection of Antique weapons who's value amounted to less than 3 weeks off the arrears in rent of a one roomed bed sitter. In retrospect I imagine that German's Armor Shop's proprietor probably thought that I'd stolen the weapons I had sold him and that I didn't really appreciate the value of them.

There seemed to be no work to be found anywhere. And I suppose that with no jobs available for so many people and thousands of new emigrants swarming into Britain. From India, Pakistan and most especially the West Indies was the main cause of the Race Wars that were now at their climax. I soon fell into arrears with my rent payments and Mr. Murray my landlord soon lost patience with my promises to catch up as soon as I got a new job. But a new job seemed almost impossible to get. From early in the morning till late evening, I went everywhere looking for work. There was none to be found. In desperation I even tried to join the Merchant Navy. But they told me I was too old to train as a Midshipman and too young to be employed as an Able Bodied Seaman. That pissed me off, as I considered my body was as able as anyone's. I didn't really want to sail away from London and my wrestling anyway. I was desperate and I figured that a few months wages earned at sea, could set me up again whenever I returned. But I couldn't get a start with them. I had been paying regular visits to Dale Martin's Wrestling Promotions ever since the first time I went there. Now I told them it was vital that they give me a start as I was starving to death, but no joy from either Jack Dale or Les Martin.

"Come back when you're bigger, older and an amateur

champion." They told me.

"How can I get bigger or even much older if I can't afford to eat?!" I asked them in desperation. I got no sympathy from either of them. Talk about desperation I even inquired at both the Army and Royal Navy recruiting offices about joining up. I was told that they were no longer calling up recruits for either of the services. They were only accepting career soldiers or sailors. I was informed that I wouldn't have the option to serve only 2 years as when one is called up like my Brother Ter was. It would now have to be for a minimum of 9 years. I received an appointment from both services to go for a medical on the same day. One at 8 a.m. the other at 9 a.m. Normally I was a very early riser. But on that morning I remember laying in bed watching the clock and thinking about what both Jack Dale and Les Martin had said to me when I told them that I was thinking of joining up.

"Don't be so bloody stupid - you're not a bloody idiot are you? Only morons who can't think for themselves join the bloody army or navy!" 'Easy for them to say,' I thought, 'they can afford luxuries like food.' Still I lay there watching the big hand go past the first deadline. 'Too late for the army,' I thought, 'still I knew I wouldn't have looked good in camouflage; as I was made to be seen.' I continued to watch the big hand tick on and 'life on the ocean wave' was soon no longer an option either. So I jumped out of bed washed, shaved and dressed. Then before I had decided what my next move was going to be for that day there was a loud knock on the door. I answered it and there was Mr. Murray the eternal optimist hoping for some rent.

"Sorry, Mr. Murray," I told him, before he had time to inquire. "Still got no work." Mr. Murray invited himself in and said,

"I'm sorry Mr. Street, but I can't afford to let you stay here any longer. I have another tenant waiting to move in."

"Okay." I said and began to pack. I couldn't blame Mr. Murray, I hadn't been able to pay him a penny for weeks and I considered he had been very patient.

"I don't know when I'm ever going to be able to pay you what I owe." I told him. He looked surprised that I was going to leave his property without protest or argument.

"That's all right,' Mr. Street," He said, "We'll call it quits, have you got any money at all?"

"No I haven't." I told him honestly. He fished into his pocket and produced a 10 shilling note,

"Perhaps this will help you out." He said, and pushed it into my right hand as he shook it in a final goodbye, "Try the unemployment office," he called, as I walked down the stairs towards the front door with my suitcase in my hand, "Best of luck!"

So here I was nowhere to live, no work and just 10 shillings to my name. The unemployment office was in Harrow Road. I walked in then walked back out, it was packed with people like myself looking for work. I began immediately scouring through ads in shop windows for the cheapest of the cheap bed-sits I could rent for the night. I collected addresses then went to check them out one by one only to be refused a bed for the night from each of them. I spent the first night walking the streets until daylight, then started looking again. The case containing my worldly goods gradually seemed to gain weight. I decided to take it around to Uncle Fred's house and leave it where it would be safe until I had sorted something out. Uncle Fred was very distressed to see me out of work. He told me that if it was up to him he would give me a job working for him in his foundry, where he genuinely needed a strong back and arms. But he knew Aunty Pat wouldn't hear of it as she never ever got over Dad's anti-catholic letter. I began my second night wandering around London and finished it sleeping on a bench. I made my way back to the unemployment office and this time I was prepared to wait all day if I had to. At least I had somewhere warm to sit while I waited. When I was finally interviewed the Lady Unemployment officer, asked me what working experience I possessed. After I told her, she suggested that the best thing for me to do was to go back to Wales and get a job in the coal-mines. I lied and told her that the reason I had come to London in the first place was due to the fact that I had been laid off, and I had been unable to get any work in Wales. There was no way I would ever go back to the coal mines again. I was determined to live my dream, or die trying. After haggling on and on for what seemed hours, she finally gave me 4 pounds and told me to report back to the unemployment office next Thursday. I left and entered the first café I could find and with trembling hands fed on a crusty cheese roll washed down with a hot cup of coffee. I wanted work but realized that any employer would require my home address before giving me a job. I decided that now I had a little money getting a roof over my head was my first priority. No luck on the third night either so I slept on a bench in Roundwood Park. Early the next evening I lucked out and got a one room bed-sit in Scrubs Lane. It was no more than about a mile from the unemployment office, and no more than a 3 mile walk to the Foresters Club. The room cost me 1 pound-10 shillings a week and they had given me 4 pounds at the unemployment office. 'If they gave me that much every week,' I thought, 'I'd manage for a while whether I got a job or not.' Unfortunately that was not the case, all I was entitled to I was informed by the Lady in the office, was 2 pounds 10 shillings. So after paying my rent each week all I was left with for food and fares was 1 pound. My trim waist got trimmer by the day.

Paul Lincoln and Ray Hunter both used to wrestle for Dale Martins, but now I'd been told that they had started their own independent wrestling promotion. 'Well if Jack Dale won't hire me, maybe I could wrestle for 'Lincoln Promotions,' I thought. I made a B line for the 2 I's every time I was in the Soho area hoping to meet one of them. I then found out that Ray and Paul also owned another coffee bar, called 'Coffeeville' on the opposite side of Old Compton Street. I was told pro wrestlers often hung out there. I shot across the road and almost collided with something that looked like a Buffalo stepping out of the entrance of Coffeeville. It was 'Crusher' Verdu, I didn't recognize him at that time as he was fresh over from the States. But it was obvious from his size, shape, posture and general body language that he was a wrestler, I said to him,

"Excuse me, are you a wrestler?" He didn't answer me but glared at me as though I had just kicked him in the shins. Then still without a reply he carried on along Old Compton Street. "Okay!" I said, and watched as people leapt out of his path as his huge buckskin clad back and shoulders swayed from side to side as he strode away. As I entered Coffeeville I saw another wrestler and this one I recognized. - But only just - his face looked like it had been sewn together out of spare parts. Sitting alone at a table nursing a cup of froffy coffee was the Australian juggernaut, Big Bill Verna. Equal in size to the Bovine I had just passed outside.

"Hello, Mr. Verna." I said apprehensively, half expecting another rebuff. The jig-saw puzzle of a face looked up and with the semblance of a smile from the only side of his mouth that was still working, he said,

"'Ullo mate, call me Bill." Instantly relieved, I said,

"Thank you Bill, would you like another cup of coffee?"

"No fanks kid," he answered, "this is me firial cup already, if I drink anymore I ain't gonna stop pissin' fer a week." Again, I was instantly relieved as I couldn't even afford a cup of coffee for myself.

"Do you mind if I join you, Mr. Ver--, ah, - sorry, Bill?" I asked.

"Nah, come'n sit darn." He replied, through the corner of his mouth, "ain't cha gonna git yourself a cuppa coffee?"

"I've had 3 myself." I lied, "I've seen you wrestling in Cardiff," I told him.

"Is that where yer from?" He asked, "I fought cha talked funny."

'Listen who's talking.' I thought. "How did you injure your face?" I asked him, hoping he wouldn't take offence, but not wanting to miss out on a bloodcurdling wrestling tale. I wondered if he had recently wrestled Bert. "Did you do it wrestling?"

"Nah." He said and fished in his inside jacket pocket. He pulled out a wallet, which he opened and extracted from it a newspaper clipping. He handed it me before sitting back in his chair, the better to observe my reaction. He wasn't disappointed; I didn't have to get as far as reading the first paragraph before he must have got the facial expression he had expected. As I had unfolded the paper the first thing I saw was a large photo of Big Bill's face. It had a huge, jagged, ragged L shaped gash running from the left side of his left eye straight down the outside of his cheek. Then abruptly swerving at right angles down to just below the left side of his mouth. The flesh on either side of the bend in the cut almost looked as though it was hanging off the rest of his face. He was wearing a 'once upon a time' white shirt. That even in that grainy, black and white newspaper photo was clearly soaked and splattered with blood. I read the article from beginning to end and then sat for an hour or more as Big Bill retold me the whole horrid tale. According to Bill's story, he had been sitting in the very same seat in Coffeeville that he now occupied. When some guy walked in and in a loud voice, asked one of the waitresses if the big Australian was about. Apparently it turned out that he was looking for Ray Hunter. Ray, being the bigger of the two Australians who owned Coffeeville, he and Paul Lincoln. But Big Bill Verna, himself being a big Australian, thought that the guy was looking for him, and called over,

"Yeah mate, Whatcha want?!"

"Are you the big Australian?" The man asked Bill.

"Yup Mate, what can I do for you?" Replied Bill.

"I need to talk to you in private." The man said, "Come back here for a minute." Bill got up and followed him into the toilet at the back of the café. the man opened the door for Bill and once both inside the man turned his back to close the door behind them. When he turned back to face Bill it was with the speed of light, with an open razor in his left hand which he back slashed viciously across Bill's face. Before Bill had time to respond his attacker continued the impetus of his movement and brought an iron bar which he had been hiding up his right sleeve across the side of Big Bill's head. Bill dropped like a brick and couldn't say for sure whether the man hit him or kicked him again. All he knew is what he was told, by a couple of guys who heard a commotion coming from the toilet. They went to investigate and arrived just in time to interrupt the Thug before he hit poor Bill with a meat cleaver. The Thug instead put all his weapons back into hiding on his person. Looked in the mirror, straightened his tie and walked out as casually as though he had just taken a piss. Naturally, no one attempted to delay him.

I still frequented the 2 I's, but would always pay Coffeeville a visit every time I went to Soho; I became friendly with a waitress named Bridget who was also a dancer on the TV program 'Cool for Cats. Bridget was totally outrageous; I thought I had lost the art of blushing until I met her. We'd be walking together through the West-end and any time a pretty girl or woman caught her eye, Bridget would shout things like,

"Shit, Adrian, look at the fuckin' tits on her!" Or even worse, she'd stop one of them in the street and say, "Hey love, my boyfriend wants to fuck you and I want to watch!" As they hurried away almost as embarrassed as I was, she'd shout after them, "Oy, if you don't fancy him, I've got my dildo in my handbag!" She'd kiss and hug me whenever there was an audience, but we'd never do anything in private. She'd also introduce me to anyone she knew as her boyfriend but that's as far as it went. Even then it seemed obvious that she liked girls as much as I did. But I wouldn't have known what a Lesbian was in those days if one had fell on me. And wouldn't have believed what I heard even if it had been explained to me. Mind you, I didn't know as much about anything like that as I thought I did. Even though I had heard about things like oral sex. I didn't believe that anyone would really do it, or think of any reason why they would want to. I just thought it was some of the more disgusting boy's idea of a very sick joke.

About the same time I saw a couple of girls in Kensal Rise who smiled and said, "Hello." Then I met one of them again while I was on my way to the Forester's Club. She lived just around the corner from the gym in Kensal Road. Her name was Jean, her friend Maureen, lived a block away. I walked past both of their homes whenever I went to and from my workouts. I would stop and chat to Jean on the way to the club and often talk with her for an hour or more after I'd left the club. We began going out together although we couldn't go far on the money I had at that time. In fact I had worked out roughly what it cost me to live; I used to buy a box of porridge oats which I would cook in water, as I couldn't afford to buy milk. I'd sweeten the porridge with one spoonful of sugar and that was breakfast. One box of oats would last me about 10 days. Sometimes I'd eat lunch and sometimes I didn't. If I did it would always be two slices of bread with a few leaves of raw spinach. My third and last meal of the day would be a few spoonfuls of jelly. I could buy a little box of it for 4-pence and after mixing it with boiling water and letting it set I could eat half of it one night, before I went to bed and save the other half for the next night. That way I'd at least have something in my stomach when I went to sleep. All I ever drank was water as I could always drink as much as I wanted for free. I was hungry all the time. I wore a studded belt to keep my jeans up the same belt I had made for myself when I was 13. By now I was wearing it on the same notch that I had when I was 13. I'd lost so much weight. Even so I still practiced my wrestling and worked out with the weights as hard as I could for over 4 hours a session 5 nights a week, plus the weekend with Big Sonny Colindos in his garage.

I was continually looking for work and continually disappointed; in the unemployment office I saw a job advertised for an assistant manager of a store in Caracas, an island close to South America. I applied for it but thank goodness never got it. I didn't want to leave London but I was very hungry. I heard there was a fair in Roundwood Park and rushed up there to see if they would give me a job. That was something I had had experience with. But when I got there the fair was already going full swing. I could hear the loud Fairground music before I even entered the Park.

'Damn it,' I thought, 'oh well, maybe I can get a job on one of the rides.' I walked from ride to ride and stall to stall, but no one needed a hand and then, Manna from heaven. - A loud, raucous voice shouting,

"1 pound, a 1 pound note to anyone, who can last 3 rounds with 'Mad-dog' Davis!" The Boxing Booth Barker was a grey Rat of a man with a cigar stub stuck in one side of his mouth. It wobbled and dropped smoldering ash over his grubby shirt and jacket as he growled out his challenge into a megaphone with the other side. "And 3 pounds to anyone who can last 6 rounds wiv 'Big Bully' Kelly!" He added.

"I'll fight him!" I screamed, and fell over the bottom step of the wooden stairs leading to the platform that the Barker and his group of Boxers stood on. In order to claim a fight and a chance to win 3 pounds before anyone else could beat me to it. I scrambled the rest of the way on my hands and knees and as I straightened up in front of Big Bully, I found myself eye to eye with his nipples. I stood on tiptoe so that the top of my head grew level with the bottom of Bully's chin. I had to tilt my head right back to give him my most menacing glare. And almost lost my balance as I was determined not to take a step back from my intended opponent.

"Yew are too bleed'n small t' fight wiv Th' Bully kid!" The Barker barked at me, "I'll give yer a fight wiv 'Mad-Dog' if yer like!"

"How much will I get?" I asked.

"A quid - if yer last free rounds," He told me, "nuffink if yer don't!"

"I want to fight him for 3 quid!" I insisted, indicating The Big Bully, who was beginning to look amused and was in serious danger of losing his air of menace.

"I told yer, yer ain't big enough, you kin fight the Mad-Dog, take it or leave it!" Stated the Barker. Our little argument had caused more than a little interest with the would be paying customers, who were standing all around the stage at the front of the Booth listening to the Barker's spiel. Their interest wasn't lost on me and I noticed with gratification was obviously not lost on the Barker, who said to me,

"What's yer name kid?" Caught on the hop, I thought frantically for something that sounded dramatic. He already had a 'Mad-Dog' and a 'Bully'. I thought of some of my wrestling idols, Buddy Rogers - Don Leo Jonathan, -- I looked at the Barker hoping he would give me some inspiration.

"Come on kid, what's yer name?!" He coaxed.

"Er, - a – Jonathan, er, a, Kid Jonathan." I told him.

"Okay, the first match is a free round middle-weight bout, between 'Mad-Dog' Davis and Kid Jonathan," he called out to the punters, as he brushed me to one side of the stage - "Now who's gonna fight wiv 'Big Bully' Kelly? Free pounds, to anyone who can last 6 rounds wiv 'im!" Someone challenged him and the punters lined up to buy their tickets. I found that each boxing show consisted of 2 matches, a 3 round preliminary match and the main match which was a 6 rounder. Usually with one of the 2 Heavy-weights. As soon as the matches were over the booth would be cleared, and the Barker, who had doubled as a commentator would go back to the stage outside the front of the booth. His boxers would join him and he would shout to all the passing punters to drum up interest in the next show. It would commence as soon as he got a couple more challengers and had enough punters buying tickets. I was asked by my opponent if I had any boxing shorts I could wear. I told him "no." and I'd box wearing my jeans and shoes and just remove my t-shirt. Although I had lost a lot of weight I almost split the arse out of my jeans, just getting in and out of the ring. My waist was very small, but my thighs were proportionately very large from all the heavy squats I did. Well 3 rounds later I had lost a pint of blood from my nose but was 1 pound richer. When the Barker began his spiel again and asked,

"Who'll fight 'Lightning' Larry Smith, 1 pound if you kin last free rounds!"

"I'll fight the other one for 6 rounds and 3 pounds!" I shouted, at the top of my voice. I scrambled back up the steps of the front stage and indicated the heavy-weight waiting to be introduced. The tobacco stained Barker gave me that, 'Oh, no, not you again' look which evaporated as I got a big cheer from some of the punters who had just watched the show before.

"Yer kin fight wiv Larry," he told me, "are sure you're up to it, Kid?" He asked, past the 1 inch of cigar he still had, hanging from the side of his nicotine stained trap. So back in I went and 3 rounds later with 2 pounds now stuffed in my jeans pocket and 2 black eyes. I bounced back onto the front stage to issue my third challenge and found myself in my third preliminary of the day. Matched again in a 3 rounder and once again with 'Mad-Dog Davis' who re-blooded my nose with his first punch. I fought like a demented Demon for the rest of the match and caught the Mad-Dog with a few good shots of my own. I was afraid with all the blood I was splashing about that the referee might stop the match before the end of the third round and deprive me of my third consecutive pound. I was lightheaded, seeing treble and in spite of all the water I was guzzling totally dehydrated. But when the Barker began his spiel for the fourth time I was already staggering up the stairs to join him.

"I'll fight him!" I shouted, before I even knew who I was challenging.

"Not this time Kid," the Barker told me, "yer gotta give somebody else a chance." "Let him fight!" Shouted the punters who had already seen me fight. I was gratified and encouraged by their response and I could see a look of indecision glaze the Barkers greedy eyes. He managed to blink it away and said,

"Nah, you've 'ad enough fer now kid, come back later an' we'll see."

I'm okay." I told him feebly but he wouldn't budge. So I

wondered off around the Fairground looking for something to eat, now I could afford it. It was getting dark by the time I got back to the Boxing Booth and the Barker consented to let me fight my fourth and last match of the day and for the third time that day entered the ring to face 'Mad-Dog' Davis. Who much to my surprise asked me if I was okay, and actually looked as though he gave a damn. I met Jean later that night and if it hadn't been for my usual arrogant swagger and the same ancient black Weider t-shirt I wore. I don't think she would have recognized me. I looked as though I'd walked face first into an oncoming express train. From my first day of Boxing I had developed a headache from Hell, which stayed with me for weeks. Also, it wasn't unusual for my nose to suddenly pour with blood even when I wasn't fighting and for no apparent reason. For instance, one afternoon, I was sitting in a Café enjoying a crusty cheese roll and a hot cup of coffee. When without warning, I got a deluge of blood pouring from both barrels all over my crusty cheese roll. I got a startled look from the waitress which turned to horror, as I continued to munch away at my now red, soggy roll. I may have been earning some money now, but there was no way that I was going to waste one penny of it by throwing food away.

"Extra protein." I told the waitress, as I stuffed the last morsel of my bloody cheese roll into my battered mouth.

Next day I was back at Roundwood Park hours before the Fair opened for business and claimed a fight with 'Lightning' Larry, for the first match in the opening show. My bouts against Larry were matches made in heaven, well for Larry at least. With him playing the dashing Toreador to my charging Bull. A role I didn't overly relish, as we all know what eventually happens to the Bull. I missed the next show but on the third show I had another 3 round preliminary match with a black guy named Carl, who I hadn't seen the day before. My third match was with The 'Mad-Dog' once again. I was determined to give him at least as good as I got from him the day before. So as soon as the bell rang to start the contest instead of circling around and around the ring and getting out punched and snipped in the snout. I rushed across the ring and enveloped Mad-Dog in the corner like an avalanche. I remembered my days in the Amateur Boxing Club in Ebbw Vale, when these kinds of tactics were the only thing that had worked for me. As I have admitted before, I am not a great boxer. But I can punch very hard and I have tremendous energy and endurance. I managed to keep Mad-Dog trapped for about a minute with me wailing away like a windmill with both fists. I only stopped when the referee pushed me back to enable Mad-Dog to drag himself off the canvas, with the aid of the ropes before I was at him again. The crowd of punters in the booth were going nuts and I felt like a World Champion. Till Mad-Dog got his second wind and the battle was on, and then I found I had lost very little of my skill in blocking almost every punch he threw with my face. I had a few more surges myself and in spite of my lack of boxing skill before the match was over I had put Mad-Dog on his arse twice more. The crowd applauded at the end of the match till their hands must have stung as much as my face did. I thought I was great. There was an old bus behind the Booth where the Booth's boxers and the challengers got changed. I was there cleaning myself up and drinking water when the Mad-Dog climbed aboard and came up the isle between the seats.

'UH-OH!" I thought, 'Here comes trouble. He's probably pissed off because I knocked him on his arse a few times.' I also thought, 'Mad-Dog is in for a nasty surprise if he thinks he can get the better of me when I'm not wearing boxing gloves. And he finds, he's going to be fighting instead of boxing. Especially in the confined space afforded in the back of a beat up old bus.' But, to my surprise, he said,

"Hey Kid, are you okay?" Without waiting for my answer, he carried on, "You did great in there did you hear the punters? They loved you!" I tried not to look too shocked or smug as he continued, "Listen Kid, it doesn't have to be that hard, which do you prefer," he asked, "this or this?!" He punctuated 'this and this'- with a quick left and right to my face, with both his gloved fists.

"Twat!!!' I screamed and was out of my seat in a flash mad as hell, especially at myself, for letting him get the advantage.

"Hold it, hold it!" He shouted, "I was just showing you something!"

"Right, you twat," I told him, "Now I'm going to show you something!"

"Hold it," Mad-Dog insisted, "listen, we don't have to kill

each other every time we fight and I'm sure we'll be boxing each other again. I just asked you which punch you preferred, the heavy one or the light one?"

"What are you talking about?! I demanded, as suspicious as hell.

"Didn't you notice, the difference in the power behind each punch?" He asked.

"What are you talking about?" I repeated.

"Look at this," he said, "this is what I'm talking about." He threw two quick successive punches at the back of the padded seat next to me.

"Did both those punches look the same to you?" He asked.

"No," I answered, "you did one with your right and the other with your left."

"I'm not talking about that you pillock," he said, "I'm talking about the power behind them. Look at this now and don't get excited. I'm not trying to hurt you, I just want to show you something." He hit me on the chest with a stiff jab; I gritted my teeth and glared at him. "Feel that?" He asked, and jabbed me again but much lighter, "Feel the difference now?"

"Yes I do," I admitted, "What's the point?"

"The point is," he explained, "you're going to get 1 pound to go 3 rounds with me and I'm going to get the same whether we punch the shit out of each other or not. The punters don't know the difference. In fact we can give them a better show if we punch lighter, 'cause your gloves make a louder slap when they strike if you unclench your hands. You can punch just as fast. All you have to do is relax your fist instead of clenching it, and instead of us punching holes in each other we can have a bit of fun." I was totally unconvinced and I thought that because I had given him a hard time in our last match he was trying to devise some way of messing me up. But he persisted and got me to practice his method of lighter punching. "That's much better," he told me after a while, "You can throw haymakers all night without damaging anyone or knackering yourself into the bargain - What part of Wales are you from?" He asked, obviously recognizing my accent.

"Brynmawr in South Wales," I replied and then added, "What part of Wales are you from?" He too, I noticed had a Welsh accent.

"Cardiff," he answered, "I used to do a bit of sparring there with Joey Erskine."

"Joe Erskine's Manager, Benny is the Brother of a friend of mine, who's got a Greengrocers shop in Brynmawr," I told him, "Mickey Jacobs."

"Oh yeah, small World," he said, "look Taffy, I'll have a word with Pricey the Barker and get him to give us another 3 rounder. You just challenge me out front like you usually do." So I did, I got the fight and it was a classic. When he began to trust me after testing the force behind my huge slapping punches. He'd even purposely walk into the odd haymaker, Stagger back dramatically. Or even hit the canvas when he thought one of my punches warranted it. I took the lead from him and took a few very spectacular trips to the canvas myself when he charged in with a flourish. The punters were going ape-shit and they cheered and screamed as though they were witnessing the war of the Worlds. The blows Mad-Dog rained on me, were still ringing my bell but were not as damaging as they had been in our prior fights. Even Pricey the Barker was impressed,

"That wuz the best bleed'n match I've seen fer ages," he told us, "go'n git lost till to-night," he told me, "an' then come back just afore 8 o-clock an' I'll give yer another free rounder wiv Mad-Dog."

"Why can't it be a 6 rounder if it was that good?" I asked him.

"Not yet Kid," he replied, "we'll build it up over the next coupla days." Well it was another exciting match and the prime time punters gave us an even bigger ovation than we got on the earlier show. At the end of the match the referee couldn't pries us apart and 3 other boxers had to come in and help out before we could be separated.

"Give 'em another round - give 'em another round - give 'em another round!" all the punters chanted. Pricey jumped into the ring with his megaphone and told everyone that if I agreed. I would be fighting with 'Mad-Dog' Davis the same time tomorrow night in a 6 round grudge match – and don't forget to tell all your friends. Being greener than Ivy I wanted to settle it tonight, but Pricey wouldn't hear of it,

"Tomorra Kid," he told me, "They'll be back in droves." I kept on at him to such an extent that he agreed a compromise and gave me another 3 round match with Carl. Which turned out to be a chronic anticlimax, especially after the one I'd just had. Carl was a very conservative plodder mostly defensive. He never seemed interested in actually winning a match and he'd throw as few punches as he could get away with and stay allusive. He was hard to hit and impossible to generate any excitement with, he just wouldn't stay and fight. He had the most infuriating knack of just nonchalantly catching every punch that came close to scoring, in the palm of a glove and deflecting it with a casual flick of his wrist. It was a total let down for me after being the man of the moment in my previous match. I had already lost sight of the fact that I had originally only wanted to fight so I could get some money to afford something to eat. Now I wanted glory. I almost apologized to Pricey for my mediocre performance after the match as he paid me my sixth and final pound note of the day.

"Don't worry about it Kid," he said, "It's the fight yer had wiv 'Mad-Dog they're gonna remember an' tha's why they'll all be back tomorra - an' talkin' about tomorra, git yourself some better boxin' gear, it don't look good wearin' jeans an' shoes, 'specially fer main event." When I got back to the bus Mad-Dog was ecstatic,

"That was bloody marvelous," he told me, "we'll do another angle tomorrow and get another 6-rounder out of it!" The other boxers in the bus all congratulated me on a job well done. But I sensed an air of resentment, especially from 'Lightning' Larry. Which puzzled me at the time but became more evident as time passed. Flashy 'Lightning' Larry, had been 'Mr. Excitement' up until now. And had just been upstaged by an unschooled, unskilled newcomer who didn't know his elbow from his arse when it came to boxing. I didn't think so at the time. But looking back on it, I think my appeal and apparent drawing power was due more to the fact that as a boxer I was bloody terrible. I was so unorthodox that I was sometimes getting away with things that shocked everyone. Plus I was wild, very tough and resilient had boundless energy and endurance, and if I could land a punch, which I did rarely, I was capable of knocking someone's head off. No one knew what I was going to do next - including me most of the time. My punches were so wide and wild that the punters ringside were often in more danger of being hit than my opponent. But when I fought somebody got a good hiding, if the guy was like me and couldn't box the chances are it would be him. If he was a good boxer then the chances were it would be me. Either way the punters got plenty of action and value for money.

"You're like a breath of fresh air," Mad-Dog told me, "I'm looking forward to our match tomorrow myself."

"I've never seen you so enthusiastic." Larry said to him. He said it in a way that could have been interpreted as more of a reproach than congratulation.

"Pricey told me to get some boxing gear to wear tomorrow," I told them, "I've got some boots that will do that I wear for wrestling. But I only have wrestling trunks, where is the best place to get boxing trunks?"

"I've got some old ones you can borrow - Shit, you can keep them, they won't fit me anymore anyway - too small." Offered Mad-Dog. He rummaged around in a bag he had with some of his belongings in and produced a pair of crumpled, black satin boxing shorts. "Good grief," he exclaimed in disbelief as he held up the shorts. "I used to fit into these, once upon a time." I had noticed that Mad-Dog, as in the case of both the heavyweights boxing on the booth, were quite podgy around the midriff. But as Mad-Dog later explained to me that on the booth they didn't have to make a certain weight and their theory was, that a comfortable layer of fat around the tummy would absorb a lot of the damage that punch after punch, day after day could cause. I knew that I was far to vain to adhere to that theory and felt that with my muscular abs and tough body no boxer could hurt me - from the neck down anyway.

"Great!" I said as he handed me the shorts, "They're the same color as my wrestling boots, thank you."

"You'll probably need to give them a wash," he advised me, they've been marinating in my bag for months." I was glad he told me as with the condition my nose was in I couldn't smell anything. When I left the fairground that evening it was already too late to go to the Forester's. But I wandered down that way to see Jean and to tell her that I had made 10 pounds in 2 days. A lot more money than I had ever made working down the pit for 6 days a week or in any other job I had ever had. I showed Jean my newly acquired, old boxing trunks as though they were a trophy, she said,

"Phew! They could do with a good wash." So she volunteered to give them a wash and iron them if I would take her to Roundwood Park the next day so she could watch me box. I explained that I would be hanging around the boxing booth while she was still at work. But if she'd come up to the Fairground when she finished, that was where she'd find me and I'd make sure she had a good place from where she could watch me perform. By the time Jean got to the Fairground booth the next day, it was already past 6 in the evening, I had already fought 2 three rounders. The first with a guy named Tommy Bates and the second with 'Lightning' Larry. Who I was just getting ready to challenge once more as Jean arrived. Carl was missing again; as he had been, on the first day I had boxed on the booth. I was very happy about that as after the lousy match I'd had with him the night before, I didn't want a repeat performance. Especially if Jean was there to watch. I had been purposely kept away from 'Mad-Dog' Davis as that was going to be the highlight of the evening at about 8 o clock that night. I had the best match yet that I'd had so far against flashy 'Lightning' Larry and succeeded in knocking him down twice in the third and final round. I was feeling very good about that and thought that I must have improved. Until back in the bus after the match was over. Larry burst my bubble by informing me that Pricey had told him to take a couple of bumps in the third, to make me look good for the upcoming match I was going to have against 'Mad-Dog'. I preferred not to believe him and chose instead to think he was trying to preserve his own ego. But as 'Mad-Dog' had jumped into the ring as I was leaving it. Brandishing Pricey's megaphone the better and louder to announce, to everyone present what was going to happen to 'their own local, Roundwood Park hero' when he got me in the ring later that evening. Gave me the uncomfortable feeling that Larry was possibly telling the truth. Well the match I had later that night with 'Mad-Dog' exceeded all expectations. It went terrific with all the booth's boxing fans cheering till they were hoarse. Back and forth we battled from the first bell. In the sixth and final round - that to me had arrived so quickly I had 'Mad-Dog' reeling around the ring. Tottering about and hardly able to stay upright after staggering back to his feet from the canvas, where I had put him about 4 or 5 times in that round alone. Only the final bell saved 'The Mad-Dog' from defeat and total humiliation. Pricey was in the ring in a flash as the bell sounded, and almost knocked me out with his megaphone in his haste to shove it into my mouth,

"Tell the punters you want one more round to finish 'im off." He whispered. 'Great,' I thought, 'at least another 3 minutes of glory.' But after issuing my challenge and Mad-Dog at first shaking his head in refusal. And then finally putting his fists up ready to continue our fight. Pricey grabbed the megaphone back and said,

"No, I'm sorry, but you both signed a contract to fight for 6 rounds and that's got to be it - But, I can get another contract drawn up to-night and you can have a return grudge match right here in this ring, the same time tomorrow night!"

'What bloody contract!' I thought, as I knew for a fact that I hadn't signed anything. It was beginning to dawn on me without being told. I had my fifth and final match that night, again with Larry, and once more in the last round he took a dive to the canvas after I had delivered a vicious flurry of punches. As if to prove the point he had made earlier, he put both of his huge gloves up to the sides of his face to block the view of the punters and lay there with his eyes crossed. Even though only the Ref and I could see his face from that angle I was furious with embarrassment. But Larry smiled, gave me a wink and pouted his lips into a kiss before staggering up a second after the referee counted 10, to give me my first clear win by knockout. Again the crowd cheered enthusiastically and Pricey reminded them that the winner of this match was due to box in the fight of the century tomorrow night. Back in the bus after the match Larry just smiled at me again - he didn't say anything - he knew he didn't have to. 'Never mind,' I thought, '5 matches and 7 pounds richer in one day, things were looking up.'

Walking Jean back home from the park I was full of jubilation, I had had the chance to make money and pose as the big, victorious hero in front of her, while doing it.

"Did you hear the crowd cheer when I entered the ring?" I asked her, "And what about the times I knocked Mad-Dog down? They went nuts!" I declared.

"Talking about nuts, they cheered a lot more when you got knocked down," she told me, "you were not wearing any undies under your baggy boxing shorts and everyone could see everything you've got, every time you went down!"

That was the second time that night, I'd had my bubble burst. But Pricey hadn't complained about anything showing. Maybe he hadn't seen what Jean had. But I suspect that even if he had, he probably wouldn't have complained. As the wily, greedy old sod probably knew, that even in those days, sex, as well as violence put arses on seats.

****

I had just finished my breakfast of Porridge oats, made with milk that morning and sweetened with honey. Thanks to my newly acquired wealth, which I had earned boxing on the Fairground Booth. 'One last cup of coffee,' I thought, 'and I'll get ready to leave my bed-sit for Roundwood Park.' Then as I walked over to the one ring electric heater to pour the last of my hot milk over the spoonful of instant coffee powder in my only cup. I glanced out of my window and saw a lady whose back window was right opposite my own. I had seen her a number of times before and we had often nodded and smiled a greeting. She had been ironing some clothes but now as I looked over at her she removed her blouse and began to iron it. Wearing nothing from the waist up but a yellow bra, needless to say she had my full attention. I was sure that she knew I was there as we had performed our usual nod and smile no more than 20 minutes earlier. I wondered if she was doing it for my benefit, when she removed her bra which she also began to iron. She looked straight at me and smiled, then carried on with her ironing, as though I wasn't there. Then off came her skirt to expose knickers and garter belt that matched her bra. Then she stepped back behind her ironing board pulled off her knickers and ironed those too. I couldn't see her from the waist down at first as the ironing board was in the way. But then she folded it up and took it somewhere in the room that was out of my view. I was almost relieved that the show was over as I wanted to get to the fair early. But she came back into view and I found that the show had only just began. She walked back and forth across her room folding and stacking the clothes she'd spent the morning ironing. All she was wearing was a pair of black high-heeled shoes and stockings held up with the yellow garter belt. When she had completed her chores she picked up a magazine and sat in an armchair that afforded me the best possible view. As she sat back and opened her magazine to read it she threw one leg over the arm of her chair in a most unladylike pose - and I knew I was going to leave late that morning for the fair.

"Well fank goodness you've turned up at last," said Pricey the Barker, when I eventually turned up at the Boxing Booth. "That effin', bleed'n Carl ain't turned up ag'in, that bleed'n Bird of 'is is gonna get 'im bleed'n fired." It had been hit or miss as to whether the only Black Boxer who worked for Pricey would show each day or not. Rumor had it that he was having trouble with his girlfriend. She didn't like Carl boxing and wanted him to get a regular job - and kept telling Carl to get lost when he refused to do either. Or that she was keeping other male company when he was away and Carl was trying to catch her at it. Either scenario made sense as Carl was an unfriendly, moody git, at the best of times. And he did seem to have other things on his mind beside his job on the Booth. Pricey had already threatened to replace him for being unreliable. And, although he had never mentioned it to me himself there was another rumor "Mad-Dog informed me, that he was going to ask me to do it. As if to confirm the rumor when I stepped up to make my first challenge of the day against Larry. Two other punters did the same, so instead Pricey matched me with one of the challengers, and told the other one that he could fight with Larry on the next show.

"One quid to the winner - loser gets nuffink!" Pricey stated, 'Crafty bastard,' I thought, 'if I'd fought against Larry we both would have got a pound, win, lose or draw.' I did get my first pound of the day as my opponent wasn't any better at boxing than I was. And didn't have the energy, strength, punch, viciousness or the want of that one pound note that I had. He made it through the first round but wouldn't come out for the second. I had to bide my time through the next show as the other challenger got his fight with Larry. I was rearing to go by the time that show had ended. But as I stepped up and made my next challenge to my utter dismay found that it was with Carl, who had finally turned up. The look he gave me suggested that he had also heard the rumor that I might be asked to take his place on the booth. Or, he may have been mirroring the look I gave him knowing I was in for another boring, uninspiring match. As it happened it turned out to be the most exciting match that I was ever to have with Carl. I had decided to show Pricey that I had the stuff to make a good replacement for Carl and Carl had obviously made up his mind to show Pricey that I hadn't. We beat the living crap out of each other but I must admit, that Carl gave me a thorough boxing lesson. It depressed me at the time, as I wanted to make a better showing to impress Pricey. But looking back on it later, I took more than a little pride in the fact that even though Carl tried his best to take me out before the end of the match he couldn't do it. I fought Larry twice on two shows before my 6 round main event match with 'Mad-Dog' that night. And another twice after. Then later in the bus I caught Carl glowering at me just one too many times and had to be restrained by Mad-Dog from attacking him.

"Keep it for the ring, Taffy Bach," Mad-Dog told me, "Carl won't try anything; he knows he couldn't beat you outside the ring." Carl didn't contradict him and Mad-Dog's vote of confidence did wonders for my ego and in calming me down. 'He's right,' I thought, 'if I hit Carl now it would be like working overtime for nothing.' When I got home that night the Lady in the window was at it again. Although I was very tired after a full days boxing I couldn't bring myself to go to bed until after she had put out her light and left the room.

I left my bed-sit the next morning without breakfast and without looking through my window. I just had a feeling about what the day held in store and I was impatient to find out what it was. Instead I popped into a café for rolls and coffee to keep up my strength and got to the Fairground long before it opened. The first person I saw was Pricey who was already looking out for me,

"I want you out front today Kid," he told me, "you've got a

better body than any of my other blokes and I think it will be good for business. Go get yer boxing gear on and when we get started I want you standing up there with the others. He indicated the stage; so my feelings were correct it seemed.

"How much will I get paid?" I asked him.

"Same as the uvers get," he replied, "a quid fer free rounds, an' free quid fer 6." 'Wow, looked like I have a job at last,' I thought, 'but who would have thought it would be as a professional boxer instead of a professional wrestler.'

Well I became quite a hit on the boxing booth, pun intended and I always drew a good crowd. I thought it was due to my powerful physique and all action boxing style. Jean maintained that it did have something to do with my physique - mainly the parts of it that only showed when I got knocked down, as I still didn't own a pair of undies. As I've indicated looking back on it, and knowing what I know now. My appeal was probably as much to do with comedy as it was to do with action or drama, and the fact that I took myself so seriously probably made it even funnier. I missed fighting with 'Mad-Dog', but it wouldn't have seemed right for Fairground Booth Boxers to fight each other. So from now on I just boxed with whoever challenged me from amongst the punters. I would fight as many as 7 times in one day when the fair opened early and no less than 4 times when it didn't. It had also become obvious that Pricey didn't really care if the punters managed to stay conscious till the end of the match or not. He was getting his booth filled almost every show and a few more pounds that he would have to pay the challengers if they stayed the course didn't really make that much difference to him. The only advantage he thought there was in knocking someone out early, was that it would take less time and that way he might be able to squeeze an extra show or two into a day.

Even though I was now one of Pricey's stable I still sensed resentment and jealousy from all the other boxers. With the exception of Mad-Dog who I was getting along famously with. Although he was Welsh himself, he always called me Taffy, which is a nickname most Welshmen ever born have been called sometime or other, especially by non Welsh acquaintances. Carl was no longer with us. I don't know whether he finally succumbed to his girlfriend's demands and quit boxing. Or if

Pricey had fired him as a result of his tardiness and unreliability. Being young and very arrogant I chose to believe that I had frightened him off and I purposely didn't ask any of the other boxers just in case the facts conflicted with what I wanted to believe.

"Are you staying with the booth after we pack up here Sunday?" Mad-Dog asked me a couple of weeks later "Make your mind up Taffy; it's our last day here Saturday."

"I don't know I suppose I will." I answered vaguely. I knew I was going to have to commit one way or the other and very soon. I had been offered, what was for me a very well paying job and told that I could sleep in the bus as most of the other boxers did and that would save me paying rent, if I gave up my bed-sit. But I was loathe to leave London or my bed-sit. I was told we were going somewhere north to Luton or St Albans, not very far from London, but not London. That rankled me from the point of view that everyone back home had told me that I wouldn't make it in London, and I would soon be back in Brynmawr with my tail between my legs. Well I wasn't going back to live in Brynmawr and I never will. But it was also important to me to prove myself in London, as I said I would. As for the bed-sit I could always get another one whenever I came back and would have plenty of money to get a nicer one. Even get a TV, mind you I already had something much better to watch than TV in my present bed-sit and all I had to do was to look out of my window.

Carl had often doubled as the boxing booth's referee when he didn't have a match himself. When he didn't do it, Larry or Tommy usually would. I told Pricey right away that any kind of rules were not my strong point and I would probably make a lousy ref. As it happened the fact that I was now the lightest boxer on Pricey's booth, made me the prime target for challengers and I was fighting more often than any of the others. Another reason I supposed for the continued jealousy and resentment from the other boxers. With Carl gone, my favorite opponent Mad-Dog Davis was now almost always the new full time referee. He'd whisper advice to me throughout my matches. But his advice usually made me laugh more than helped my boxing. He had a really funny way of putting things. Well it was Saturday night. I had been fighting all day and although both

Pricey and Mad-Dog seemed to have taken it for granted it was a done deal, that I was leaving with them tomorrow. I hadn't actually said I was going and hadn't given up my bed-sit. I hadn't told Jean I would be leaving either. But quite honestly I couldn't see how I had any other alternative as it was the only option I had to earn money.

"What's yer name kid?" Pricey asked my challenger, in what I thought would probably be my last fight before we left London.

"Rocky Ryan, professional boxer!" He answered smugly, while giving me that look. His accent at first suggested he was Irish but I also detected a strong Gypsy flavor.

"Rocky Ryan versus Kid Jonathan," Pricey shouted through his megaphone. There was such a tremendous cheer from the punters, and not just from the fans that I had developed a following amongst. But from the tribe that had come to support my challenger. Opportunity gleamed in Pricey's avaricious eyes,

"Rocky Ryan in a 6 round, Main Event contest against Roundwood Park's own, Kid Jonathan!" He roared. 'Wow!' I thought, 'That's the first 6 rounder I've had since I ceased being a challenger, great - 3 quid instead of one!" Rocky Ryan was quite a bit taller and heavier than I was and could have easily got away with fighting one of Pricey's heavyweights. But I must have been doing something right in Pricey's eyes for him to promote me from a 3 round contest to a 6 rounder. And I certainly wasn't grumbling with 3 quid in the offing. Jean was standing near my corner as I entered the ring as she had been for my last couple of contests. The booth was jam packed and there was a lot of noise coming from the other side of the ring. As my opponent entered he was almost carried and was even lifted onto the ring apron by his rowdy, Pikey entourage. They then gathered all around his corner and immediately began jeering and booing me. Some of them were shaking their fists and waving an invite for me to go down and fight with them. Little did they know that in those days I was dopey enough to have obliged them. BUT - I knew there was 3 pounds cash riding on me staying in the ring so I did.

Mad-Dog, who was refereeing our match called us both to the centre of the ring and recited the rules and regulations. We then walked back to our respective corners the bell rang and we both charged out to do battle. The only success I ever had especially against someone who could box was to crowd and bully them into the ropes. Or better still into the corner, and then whale away with both fists. But this time I was the one who got crowded and bullied backwards into my own corner. I was punched and pummeled so fast and from so many directions, I could have easily imagined that every one of Rocky's friends had entered the ring and were all punching me at the same time. He didn't stop punching until I was in a heap on the canvas in my own corner and Mad-Dog made him stand back. Rocky's entourage were going nuts. Mad-Dog started to count over me, but I was out of the corner like a cannonball out of a cannon and caught Rocky a few good clouts right in his chops. We began whaling away at each other with me getting the worst of the deal. I was trying to keep my hands up high to protect my face. I wasn't really concerned about the rest of my body as I knew that no one could hurt it, especially while they were wearing big padded boxing gloves. God! If I was ever wrong about anything in my life, I was wrong about that. Boxing gloves or not his punches were ripping my guts out. I couldn't believe the power, or the resulting pain I was receiving every time his fists exploded into my ribs and stomach. Every punch was like a kick from a mad stallion. A sledge-hammer like blow smashed me full in the face and I felt a sharp pain on the outside of one ankle, followed almost immediately, by another sharp pain on the inside of both ankles. I found that I was upside-down in one of the corners and the pain I felt had been caused by first, one of my ankles hitting the top metal turnbuckle and then the second ankle hitting the first one. I had never been knocked out, but I didn't remember being knocked upside down. I only remembered finding myself that way. I managed to gather my thoughts and turn right way up before the 10 count, and walk into another barrage of flying leather before the bell sounded to end round one. Round 2 was a repeat of the first with me taking a terrible beating, especially to my ribs which I was sure were broken on both sides. British sports fans being such great supporters of the underdog, I was getting an ovation second to none. Except from Rocky's Gypsy friends who were now in competition with the rest of the punters, as to who could cheer and jeer the loudest for, or against their fighter of choice. Mad-Dog followed me to my corner as I staggered into it, I was in agony,

"Don't you think you'd better call it a night Taffy?" He asked me, "He's fuckin' killing you." 'How astute of you to notice.' I thought. It was an effort to answer him as it entailed taking a breath, which sent red hot scythes of pain searing through my ribs,

"The match is 6 fucking rounds not 2!" I barked at him. I didn't mean to snap at him as I could see he was concerned. But I was in pain and desperately trying to think what the hell I was going to do next, and with him talking I couldn't. He sighed and said,

"Well it's your funeral Taffy!" - 'What a wonderful way you have with words.' I thought as the bell sounded and here comes Rocky in for the kill. I don't know if it was to prove to everyone that I was still game for a fight after what Mad-Dog had said to me about quitting that caused me to rush out of my corner and straight into harm's way. Or, if it was just blind panic. Rocky and I collided head on and I accidentally stepped on his foot as I threw a punch. With the fluke of the century it smashed into Rocky's face and he landed heavily on his back, the crowd exploded. What a great dramatic finish that would have been - the beaten underdog scoring the monumental upset. But unfortunately Rocky got up at the count of 4 and beat the living crap out of me. If Jean's theory was correct all the perverts in the Booth got more than their money's worth that night. I lost count of how many times I had to drag myself off the canvas before the bell sounded to herald the midway point of my annihilation. Again, Mad-Dog followed me into my corner and before I had chance to say a word he said.

"Shut up Taffy and listen to me. You're not going to get any more than 3 quid whether you carry on fighting or not. Get your stupid arse out of the ring right now - if you quit now you'll be fit to fight next week. Stay in the ring with that idiot and you're going to get murdered!" I blew bloody bubbles out of my mouth as I slurred my reply,

"Fuck off Mad-Dog." The bell sounded to start round 4 and Rocky was in my face before I could heave another breath into my pain wracked lungs. His heavy punches hammering and thudding into my ribs caused me pain that I find impossible to describe. Every time I've seen a boxer training on the heavy bag since that night it makes me cringe. Every punch that caught me on either side of my ribcage sent an involuntary gasp hissing and whistling out of my throat. The sound of the bell was a relief, but not from the pain, that I took back into the corner with me. I don't know if I was relieved or not, to find that instead of following me to my corner Mad-Dog had gone to the neutral corner. I looked over at him, he just gave me that resigned look and shook his head in despair. Even he it seemed had given up on me. 'Oh yeah,' I thought, 'I'll show all of you.' Where the energy came from I don't know. But as the bell sounded for the 5th and last but one round I rushed out once more and collided with Rocky in the centre of the ring, and accidentally stepped on his foot again. And again caught him with a simultaneous punch which sent him flying back and sat him on his arse, almost back in his own corner. I chased him and hit him with a barrage of punches before he could get up and before Mad-Dog could prevent me from doing so. Mad-Dog pushed me back giving Rocky the opportunity to get to his feet. I brushed past the ref and purposely stepped on Rocky's foot before letting loose with all I could muster from both fists. Down Rocky went again and in dove Mad-Dog between us to prevent me from diving on top of Rocky before he could once again find his feet. The whole Booth was shaking with the volume of noise issuing from every throat around the ring, and I was gratified to see blood pouring from Rocky's mouth. His gang of cronies was almost beside themselves with fury as they screamed their encouragement at their bloody hero. He turned from them to face me his jaw set with renewed determination. I rushed to meet him and again attempted to stomp on his foot as I threw everything into one almighty punch. He avoided it handily and handed me a blow in the guts that must have bruised my spine and almost caused me to throw up all my vital organs. That was just an appetizer for the rest of the round. Punch after punch thudded into my ribs, punctuated by a hook or a roundhouse to the jaw that sent me sprawling to the canvas.

"Ah one - ah two - ah stay down you fuckin' idiot, ah three!" Chanted Mad-Dog. The sounds of the screaming punters seemed to surge and ebb in my head and ears in time with my pulse with a force that rivaled Rocky's devastating punches. When the bell rang to end round 5 I found I was conveniently sprawled in my own corner. I began the monumental task of dragging myself up the ropes to my feet after which, in order to avoid Mad-Dogs eyes I turned and looked across the ring to watch my opponent. He was shadow boxing and doing an exercise in fancy footwork for the benefit of his entourage. Just to show them he was still in fine fettle. I held both my gloved hands up in front of my face and glared with hatred at those huge pads that cushioned my fists. 'If I didn't have these fucking things on my hands all those screaming punters would be seeing a far different spectacle than the one they were witnessing now.' I thought. I became so angry and frustrated that I wanted to tear them off with my teeth. One more round to go, three more minutes of sheer agony standing between me and the 3 pounds I was determined to earn. The bell was startlingly loud,

"Fuck it!" I shouted at no one in particular, "You do what you wanna do, I'll do what I wanna do!" As Rocky came hurtling in for the kill I grabbed him, turned him upside-down and smashed him headfirst into the unyielding, unpadded canvas with all the strength I had left. Mad-Dog had made a preventative dive, but as the move was totally unexpected he was a mite too late. We ended up in an involuntary mutual bear-hug which I think was the only thing that held me up. What was left of Rocky was crumpled at our feet. Mad-Dog began to laugh, and barely managed to choke out between his chuckles,

"Sorry Taffy, that's not Marquis of Queensbury's rules, you're disqualified!" I wanted to laugh with him but the pain in my chest soon put pay to that. By then the shock of what I had done to their hero had dissipated. Rocky's furious followers began scrambling up onto the ring's apron their intent was obvious. Mad-Dog flew across the ring, I followed as fast as my pain wracked body would allow and by the time I caught up, Mad-Dog had thrown 2 lightning fast punches which resulted in 2 Rocky worshipers somersaulting back into their friends behind them. I punched one more who managed to hang on to the top rope and kicked another in the face who had just scrambled through the two lower ropes. Mad-Dog smashed the rope hanger into orbit with one mighty punch, as a fight erupted outside the ring between some of my fans and Rocky's gang of Pikeys. Now due to the excitement that ensued below us we were suddenly no longer the centre of attention. Mad-Dog took advantage and hustled me back across the ring.

"Let's get the fuck out of here, while we've got the chance Taffy!" he told me and after we'd stepped over the still prone Rocky, he Shepherded me safely out of the ring. As injured as I was, I still made a B line for Pricey with my hand out for my 3 pounds before making our way back to the bus with a concerned Jean in tow. It may not have been an honorable way to finish a fight. But for me it was as acceptable as circumstances would allow. I may not have won a boxing match in the eyes of anyone who had witnessed the fiasco. But, in the end I was the one who walked away and Rocky was the one laying on his back. That was victory enough for me, thank you very much.

"I'll see you in a bit." Mad-Dog told me, and was about to leave the bus after helping me into one of the seats and unlacing my gloves. His exit was interrupted by Rocky who slipped quietly onto the bus in order to retrieve his belongings. He looked at us apprehensively, before picking up his clothes, pushing them into his gym bag and leaving without uttering a word. Fortunately, there was no sign of any of his friends. Mad-Dog still chuckling, left right behind him. Now I had the painful task of trying to undress then put my jeans on after Jean had unlaced and removed my wrestling boots. Struggling into a snug T-shirt, with my ribs in the state they were in was excruciating. I was hurting so badly by then that if Jean hadn't been there, I think I would have cried with the pain. Something I had not allowed myself to do since I was about 11 years old. When I got out of the bus I didn't see Pricey, or any of his boxers outside the booth. So Jean and I left the fairground without ever saying goodbye to any of them, and with her help I hobbled 4 miles to the nearest Hospital. Upon arrival we made our way to the out-patient casualty ward. I explained to the night nurses who were on duty, that I had broken all my ribs. I must have presented a sorry spectacle with my eyes all blackened and bruised, my nose swollen to twice it's normal size and dried blood caked into every crevice on my face. They asked me how I came to be injured and

I made the mistake of just saying, I'd had a fight. With the amount of violence that was going on in that area of London at that time, and with the Race riots in full swing. They obviously misconstrued what I meant and they unsympathetically told me that they couldn't do anything for me that time on a Saturday night. If I wanted an ex-ray, as I had asked for, I should return on Monday morning. Which was what I ended up doing. I was very lucky under those circumstances that none of my broken ribs were penetrating anything vital. If they had been, I might not have been alive to have returned to the hospital 2 days later.

Well, I had learned yet another valuable lesson; - my body was not made of steel.

It was almost impossible to train with weights with the state that my ribs were in never mind how carefully I tried. Even breathing was pure agony and as you can well imagine wrestling was right out of the question. So wisely, though very reluctantly, I gave myself and the Foresters a rest for a while. My time now was split between gazing out of my window, looking for a job and taking Jean to the cinema or out to eat. She was painfully shy in public places, in a restaurant she would prefer to sit in the dimmest corner and was still paranoid that everyone in the place was watching her. She could on the other hand, be very amusing and would sometimes say things that I found shocking as well as funny. Like the time we were in a cinema and I was trying to fiddle about as the first movie ended. The interval started and the ice-cream Lady began walking down the aisle with her tray full of goodies, and Jean asked me,

"How many fingers have you got up?" As shocked as I was by her question, I answered, "Only one, why?"

"Well put two in," she replied, "I want to whistle for some ice-cream."

****

I had earned more money in so short a period of time, than I had ever earned before in my life, but it was evaporating fast. Alone, too injured to work-out and bored, I would often spend the afternoon going from one cinema to another. Jean and I had been going to the movies almost every night, plus bus and train fares spent in my quest for work were also taking its toll. I was suffering multiple frustrations not being able to find a job, lift weights, or wrestle. I was being sexually stimulated to the gills by the almost daily antics of the 'Lady in the window' and couldn't get past the moderate petting stage with Jean. Even though I was still a virgin I thought I could remedy that now, if she only gave me the opportunity. But no dice. I started going to the Forester's again, even though I was still unable to do much with the weights and just watch impotently as the wrestlers crunched each other on the mat. It didn't help my mood very much. Or Jean's either as she had been spoiled by too much attention lately and now seemed to resent the time I was spending in the gym. She thought that it could have been better spent with her. When I left the Forester's one night to go and meet her, I found her talking to her friend Maureen. Unbeknown to me she had been winding Jean up about not seeing so much of me, now that I was once again going to the gym. Instead of her usual welcoming smile as I approached, she shot me a glare that would have done credit to Medusa - Bad timing, I needed cheering up, not aggravation.

"What's with the face?" I asked her, rather than beat around the bush.

"I don't know why you don't live in the Forester's," she replied, "It would save you paying rent." As I said, I wasn't in the mood so diplomacy went out the window.

"It may come as a surprise to you," I told her, "but I didn't leave Wales and come to London just to meet you. I came to be a wrestler, and that's what I'm trying to do!" She was obviously aware of her 'friend' Maureen's supportive snigger at my abrupt retort. So she turned and began to walk towards her own house further up the road, and called angrily over her shoulder to me,

"We'll have this out in private, let's go!" Maureen caught my arm, and said,

"Let her go, stay here with me." - 'If you have friends, you don't need enemies.' I thought for the thousandth time. But, as I detected a carnal promise in Maureen's request for me to stay with her, I did just that. Plus, the way Jean had barked an order at me, guaranteed that I wouldn't comply with her request. Unfortunately for Jean and myself, we were both in the same boat. She would lose face if she'd had to come back for me, just as I would have if I'd followed her. So that was the end of that. It turned out to be a bad deal all round. I got a lot less out of Maureen than I'd been getting with Jean, plus she was much less attractive. I had liked Jean very much, I missed her company. Maureen couldn't fill the bill and I began looking elsewhere. The fact that I now had more time on my hands, meant more time window gazing at my very attractive and mostly naked neighbor. That did not help the disposition of a bored horny boy. The lovely Lady's performances ended as abruptly as they had began. So, just when I thought that things couldn't get much worse, I lost my only source of free entertainment. One evening I was so desperate for company I thought I'd go to Coffeeville and see if Bridget might be about. I was sitting at a table by myself waiting for her to come in and sipping my second cup of coffee, when I noticed a man sitting at a nearby table staring at me. I gave him that, 'who the fuck are you looking at?!' look. But he got up and left his table. Coffee cup in hand and sat himself down without invitation in one of the vacant chairs at my table.

"Are you a boxer?" he asked me in way of introduction,

"No, I'm not!" I answered indignantly, but was secretly pleased that someone had given me the chance to say, "I'm a wrestler!"

"Oh, you're not a boxer," he said, his eyes were wide, with what looked to me like fright, as he added, "but I'll bet you can punch hard?!"

"Yes I can," I assured him and I added, "You wouldn't want to find yourself on the end of one for a start." His quick intake of breath seemed to confirm my last statement. But he surprised me when he answered excitedly,

"Oh yes I would!" I looked at him more closely, but my original assessment still stood. He seemed to be trying to pick a fight but he didn't look like my idea of a fighter at all. He was very well dressed and very ordinary. But I also appreciated that appearances could be very deceptive, still I told him,

"Oh no you wouldn't!" He began panting, as though he had just ran a marathon.

"I would like you to punch me, as hard as you can!" He insisted. He was starting to piss me off, but I forced myself to answer him in a very calm almost friendly manner.

"Listen to me, you are not physically equipped to deal with the kind of danger that kind of talk will put you in. So, if I were you, I'd shut up and fuck off." He was gasping as though I had already punched him and I began to think he wasn't right in the head.

"I'll pay you to punch me." He hissed in a hoarse whisper and brought out a wallet from which he produced a 5 pound note which he pushed across the table, followed by another one, as I stared at him in disbelief. 'Now I know he's not right in the head,' I thought. "Are you fucking nuts?" I asked him, "You wouldn't survive one of my punches!" My last statement stuck in my throat as a third 5 pound note crossed the table and my mind was thrown into turmoil. With my fast dwindling resources, I wanted the money he was offering me. But, as young and inexperienced as I was I also knew there was no Santa Claus, no Easter Bunny, no Tooth Fairy. And if something sounds too good to be true - and so on and so forth. What was this idiot's angle? I was obviously being set-up for something. I thought of what had happened to The Mammoth from Perth, Big Bill Verna in this very same café. I couldn't figure out why anyone would want to do that to me. Mind you, I never did figure out why someone would want to do that to Ray Hunter, who Big Bill Verna had been mistaken for.

"Come on - come on, take the money!" The idiot insisted, so I did.

"Where do you want to go?" I asked him.

"We can go around the back of the café." He told me. Now I was certain I was being set up. But I'd taken his money and now it was time to earn it. The alley was just what I had expected. Plenty of hiding places for the ambushers that I was sure would appear any minute. The idiot seemed nervous, I knew I was. I wondered how many attackers there would be and whether or not they would be carrying weapons. Pictures of Big Bill's torn, bloody face kept flashing through my mind's eye. Unlike Big Bill at least I was ready for them. But if there were a lot of them being ready wouldn't really make much difference. 'I'll smash this bastard first,' I thought, 'at least he won't get away with setting me up.' I stuffed the money I had got from him further down into my jeans pocket. The very worst case scenario that I could think of was that I would not only get the shit kicked out of me. But that I'd also get robbed of the only reason that had lured me into this dark alleyway and the very probable danger in the first place. The alley stank of garbage. Most prevalent was the sweet, sickly combination of fish and rotten fruit. Even though we were only a few dozen yards away from the noisy hustle and bustle of London's West-end, which surrounded us in every direction. It was quiet enough where we were to hear the eerie echo of both our foot-steps as we walked deeper into the site of 'Adrian's last stand.' The scratching and scuttling sounds of Rats or Cats, behind, or amongst the trash cans and cardboard boxes piled with rubbish pricked up my ears and prickled the back of my neck. But still no signs of an attack. The idiot stopped, turned towards me and said with a trembling voice,

"This will do, we can do it here." My survival instincts snapped into high gear. Adrenaline fizzed through my veins like a nest of Irish Fire-Ants on St Patrick's Day. 'Here it comes!" I thought - as I waited for an armed thug to leap out of every dark corner. But nothing happened, it seemed that we were alone.

"Come on, - come on!" the Idiot demanded, "What are you waiting for?"

It's amazing to think of how many times I had found myself in this same situation in the past. Especially in Wales where fighting and brawls seemed to be part of our culture. But I had never faced anyone who just stood pathetically in front of me with his hands dangling helplessly by his sides, demanding that I punch him. I felt like a spare prick at a wedding. It was as though I didn't know what to do. He'd pissed me off, but not to the extent that I wanted to resort to violence.

"What are you waiting for?! The Idiot yelled at me, and did a comical, shuffling little dance of frustration. "Do it – come on, do it!" He screamed. The noise he made tightened my already shredded nerves another notch, and I began to shuffle myself. I tried to position myself into the best stance to deliver the blow he seemed to crave. But everything seemed strange, unreal even. I had never thought about positioning myself to begin a fight before. I just attacked when I saw an opportunity, or responded as best I could to defend myself when I was being attacked. This was awful.

"Where do you want me to punch you?" I asked him almost timidly.

"Don't ask me that!" He screamed at me, "In the face, hit me in the face!" I didn't let myself think. I just let loose and threw a punch that caught him smack under his left eye. I had expected him to disintegrate, but the force of the blow only succeeded in staggering him back a few steps. He just stood there looking at me. Now that really pissed me off. As a boxer it was pretty rare for me to land a good punch. But if I did -----! I stepped forward and my whole weight, rage and general frustration at the World at large went into a blow that exploded his face. It lifted him right off his feet and deposited him upside-down in the heap of trash cans and rubbish behind him. I looked at his shoes, now pointing at the starry sky and was brought out of my reverie by the sound of the Idiot's muffled voice calling to me from his bed of garbage,

"Oh, thank you - thank you!" He cooed. I was out of that fucking alley like a bat out of Hell! I apologize to my readers for such an anticlimax, after a suspenseful build up. But that might give you a better idea of how I felt at the time. I didn't know what to think, and didn't want to try. In order to block my thought process I came up with the perfect solution as I rushed back around the corner across the road and into the 2 I's Coffee Bar. There a hot froffy coffee and a mega-dose of loud, bumping, thumping music, proved to be the perfect poultice for my scattered thoughts. I should have stayed there, but I didn't.

Late the following Monday morning, I crawled out of bed wondering what day it was. I tried to think what the Hell had happened since I went out Saturday evening. I remembered everything after the incident with the Idiot. Going in and coming out of the 2 I's, that's when I had first noticed that one side of my ribs, my neck and shoulder were really giving me some pain. Punching that crazy Pratt was the first serious exertion I had inflicted on myself, since I had injured it in the first place. But I didn't begin to feel it till an hour or so later as I was leaving the 2 I's. I walked back over to Coffeeville and found that in the meantime Bridget had arrived there, but was working. She introduced me to a couple of friends of hers, a girl and her boyfriend, who invited me to go and have a drink with them in the nearby Stragglers club. Bridget said she would join us there later after she had finished her shift. So off we went. It would be the first time I had drank alcohol in ages, but I remembered thinking that a couple of stiff drinks might deaden the pain in my chest. That was the last thing I remembered that night with any clarity. Jumbled images of some lady sitting on a stool near me at a bar. Opening the fur coat she was wearing to show me that she wasn't wearing anything else. Some guy pulling me backwards off my stool, saying something about a Police raid. Running with him and some others out of the back door of the club and through some of Soho's dark alleys. Watching some other Lady in some other club perform an exotic dance. Then walking in the middle of a road in the drizzling rain, with traffic sounding their horns and whizzing past either side of me. While I wove back and forth narrowly missing vehicles that made nasty noises. Then dropping and smashing a bottle of something I hadn't realized I was carrying until I'd dropped it. I remembered getting out of bed some time when it was dark to take a piss. But couldn't really remember which night that was, or even where that was. After a soak in the bath my head shrank back to its normal size and I began to feel a healthy pang of hunger. I found that all I had to eat in my bed-sit was some sour milk and a few spoonfuls of porridge. But an extra spoonful of the last of my honey disguised the sour milk taste and at least put something in my stomach before I went out. I had been thoroughly disgusted with myself after counting what was left of my money. I decided I was going to do something meaningful with what was remaining. First I rejoined the YMCA. My chest didn't feel too bad at all. But I only used moderate weights to start my comeback. After which I walked purposefully downstairs and watched Alf Jacobs and Frank Nottingham grappling each other on the wrestling mat. They both seemed as delighted to see me as I was in seeing them. They took it easy with me when I pulled around with both of them in turn on the mat after I had related my injured ribs story. My chest was still tender but bearable and I did as much as I could until I got too hungry to do more. I showered got dressed and went straight into Soho. Not to the 2 I's, but to an 'Angus Steak House'. They would cut a steak to the customer's specifications and cook it likewise. When I explained how thick I wanted my steak to be, I was told that it would be a very large and expensive steak. I told them to go ahead and cut it anyway. The steak weighed 2 pounds 2 ounces and I ate it blood red. The meal cost 2 pounds, 10 shillings, by far the most I had ever spent on one meal in my entire life. I savored every mouthful, knowing it would be the last meat I would eat until my luck changed. The money I had spent re-joining the YMCA and eating 'the mother of all steaks' had cost me almost everything I had left. From now on it would be back to a diet of porridge made with water for breakfast. 2 slices of bread and raw spinach for lunch and a few spoonfuls of jelly before I went to bed. After I left the Steakhouse I walked all the way from Soho to the Forester's. I had another workout with the weights, joined the other would be pros and wrestled with them until the Forester's closed. That was my new lifestyle for the next few months. Early Thursday morning I would collect my 2 pounds 10 shillings, from the unemployment office. Then from morning till the afternoon 6 days a week I would lift weights and wrestle in the YMCA. Then I would walk to Hyde Park where I would sit and eat my bread and spinach. Then I would continue my journey to the Forester's where I would lift weights and wrestle, which I did five nights a week.

When I first arrived in London I had weighed 179 pounds. As everyone told me I was too small to be a professional wrestler, I had decided to try to increase my weight to 200 pounds. But as you can imagine training on the weights and wrestling on the mat eleven times a week, on a starvation diet was hardly compatible with weight gain. Instead of bulking up to 200 pounds as I wanted to my bodyweight dropped to 144 pounds, so instead of gaining 21 pounds I lost 35. When the weather turned warmer I would swim all day Sunday in the open air swimming pool in Roundwood Park, so I had no day of rest at all. In the YMCA I found that during the day many professional wrestlers trained there. Ray Hunter, Prince Kumali and 'Iron Man' Steve Logan, just to name a few that I became acquainted with at that time. I remember standing and looking up enviously at the size of both Ray and the Prince. Both of them were around 6 foot 4 or 5, and I said to them,

"Damn, when are you two guys going to stop growing?!" Ray

looked down at me from his great height and replied,

"Damn, when are you going to start?!" I suppose 144 pounds was pretty small. But I wasn't carrying an ounce of fat, my waist measured 27 inches and my chest 47 inches and every muscle in my body showed. I bumped into Bobby Selsden again one evening as I was going to the Forester's and he was on his way to his gym. As we walked along together, he told me that I was looking fantastic. I complained bitterly that with things the way they were it was impossible to gain any weight.

"Why would you want to?" He asked me, "With a physique like you've got you could earn money posing for muscle magazines." I can't tell you how much that sentence got my attention. - EARN MONEY! – POSE FOR MUSCLE MAGAZINES!

"How - where - what do I have to do?!" I asked him, "Do you really think I'm good enough?!

"I've done it, and you're in better shape than I am" he told me, "I'll give you some names and phone numbers." The first number I called was belonging to Bill Jones, who took photographs mainly for 'Modern Man', 'Man's World and Reg Parks Journal.' Under the pseudo name 'Mark'. How exciting I thought. I remembered seeing dozens of pictures in those magazines which I had been buying for years, with 'Photo by Mark' accredited to the photographer. Bill's studio was on the top floor of his home in Cheyne Walk. The front of his house faced the River Thames. I was still worried that I might not measure up to the standards of bodybuilders deemed worthy of appearing in the hallowed pages of such a prestigious 'Muscle Mag'. But Bill Jones assured me that I would do great. He was correct. As from the first batch of photographs Bill took they were all accepted by and featured in 'Man's World and Reg Parks Journal.' And that's not the best part, one of them was featured on the front cover. Bill was ecstatic in all the years he had been taking photos for physique magazines, none of his photos had ever made the front cover before.

"We must celebrate." He told me and invited me to join him and his friend Gary to dine with them in the very posh, Cumberland Hotel, near Marble Arch. Things were definitely looking up. The easiest money I had ever earned, 5 pounds for a half hour of doing what I like best - showing off. Being featured on the front cover of my favorite British Bodybuilding magazine. Then dinning for free in the Cumberland Hotel – and eating meat, large lumps of blood soaked meat! 'Damn,' I thought it can't get much better than this!" But it did.

Amongst the other professional wrestlers I came in contact with in the YMCA was Chic Osmond. I found him to be a very friendly fellow who advised me to drink a pint of olive oil every day. As he said he did, if I wanted to gain weight. I couldn't afford regular food let alone pints of olive oil. Although Chic used to train with the weights, he didn't really have much of a physique to show for it. I invited him to wrestle with me on the mats, but he declined and told me that he wasn't interested in wrestling amateur style only pro. That was great I assured him, I only wanted to wrestle that style myself. He explained that it wasn't a good idea to practice pro style where 'Queens parks' could watch and learn the tricks of the trade.

"Queen's Parks?!" I asked him, "What are you talking about?"

"Wrestlers have their own way of communicating," he told me, "it's based on the old Cockney slang invented by London's Costermongers - Queen's Park, is what you say, 'cos you omit the part that rhymes with what you are actually saying. What you mean is, 'Queen's Park Ranger', which means stranger."

"What?!" I said, then it dawned on me, as I had heard Uncle Fred come out with that sort of thing. Especially when he was with his Greyhound fancying friends. "Oh, you mean like, 'my trouble is up the apples counting her bread' - my 'trouble and strife' - wife, is up the 'apples and pears' - stairs, counting her 'bread and honey' - money."

"That's right," he said with a delighted beam on his face, "you've got to use your loaf and don't rabbit in front of Queen's Parks."

"What?!" I said, again he translated,

"You've got to use your 'loaf of bread' - head, and not 'rabbit and pork' - talk, in front of 'Queen's Park Rangers' - strangers."

"Oh," I said, still a little bewildered. But I soon got to get the hang of how it went much to my amusement, as I found most of their way of 'rabbiting' quite hilarious.

But getting back to the wrestling. There was a small room adjacent to the main gymnasium hall that was used for storing gym equipment. Including the wrestling mats when they weren't being used in the main hall. That is where Chic and I used to practice our wrestling. Away from everyone else's prying eyes and he would explain everything he showed me in the wrestlers version of rhyming slang,

"Look," he would say, "this is the way I would take your chalk, 'chalk farm' - arm. Or I'll dive down and take your left scotch - 'scotch egg' - leg. I'll spin you around into a full Nelson and work on your Gregory - Gregory Peck - neck." It was all very enjoyable, as well as extremely educational. But as I said the best was yet to come. It came one day when he told me that he had received an offer from Dale Martin's.

"The only problem is," he explained, "that I had agreed to wrestle for a new independent promotion and I've got a series of matches lined up for them. But if I wrestle for Dale Martin's they won't allow me to wrestle for anyone else."

"Independent Promotions?" I queried, "I didn't know there were any Independent promotions."

"Oh yes, there are a lot of independents," he assured me, "and I don't like burning bridges with any of them," he continued, "so do you think you could do me a favor and take my bookings for Johnny Child's promotion?"

What!!! I would let Dad himself shave off my sideburns and make Brian Gore and Hairy the Gypo my best friends for a quarter of half a chance to take his bookings!

"At least go and talk to them," he asked me, "that way they'll know that I didn't just leave them in the lurch." Chic explained to me that among the venues that Johnny Childs ran was 'The New Addington Hotel' which was in a suburb of London. He told me the best thing for me to do was to go along to the next show they were promoting there. Introduce myself, as the young wrestler that Chic Osmond had recommended to replace himself on their future wrestling shows.

"Better for them to see you," he explained, "you're in great shape and that way you're not just another voice on the phone." So that's what I did. When I arrived at the show, I watched the first match before I went back to the dressing room. I knocked on the door then walked into the first professional wrestling changing room I had ever been in.

"Queen's?" One of the wrestlers asked, the others with eyebrows raised, as I was first spotted entering their private domain. I stepped into a crossfire of suspicious, unfriendly eyes. Chic had warned me that that would be their most probable response and he also told me how to react to it.

"No, I'm not a Queen's Park," I told the inquirer, "I'm a wrestler like you and a friend of Chic Osmond. He sent me to 'have a rabbit' with Johnny Childs, the promoter about replacing him, now that he's working for Dale Martin's."

"I'm Johnny Childs," said a large pear shaped man, who came up to me with his hand extended. He had a fat, red face that was dominated by a red nose, that would have done credit to a Toucan. I shook his hand with what I thought was appropriate firmness for a professional wrestler. He winced and said, "ease up mate, what's yer name?"

"Adria---, er a, Kid Jonathan." I told him, as that was the name I had used as a boxer and the name I had told the physique photographer 'Mark' that I wanted to use.

"You look like Tarzan," accused Johnny Childs, as he flexed his fat biceps in emphasis, "waddya say yer name was again?"

"Kid Jonathan." I replied, Johnny looked thoughtful,

"What about Tarzan Jonathan?" He suggested,

"Kid 'Tarzan' Jonathan." I compromised. I thought that as I had already made the

name 'Kid Jonathan' at least a little bit famous from the few bodybuilding magazines I had appeared in, it would be a shame to waste it at that stage of my career.

"Yes, I like it!" Announced Johnny Childs, "Give me your phone number and I'll give you a ring and tell you when I can use you."

"I don't have a phone," I admitted, "but I'll keep phoning you until you tell me where and when you've got me booked."

"Give me your address then," he said, "and I'll let you know when I can work something out - Kid Tarzan Jonathan, yes, I think I like it."

'Yes,' I thought, 'I like it too. It's got that Don Leo Jonathan ring to it and he was one of my all time favorites.' A little later, I went back into the small hall where the wrestling was going on to watch the main event. One of the opponents was already in the ring pacing back and forth waiting impatiently for his adversary who seemed to be taking forever to enter the ring. All at once the crowd began booing and I saw a royal blue head bobbing up and down, as the masked mystery man from Austria, 'The Blue Baron' approached and entered the ring. He spun around theatrically and threw off his matching royal blue cape, serenaded by the jeering fans. He stood proudly in the centre of the ring, as he flexed his fat biceps. He was a large pear shaped wrestler and even the royal blue mask, didn't disguise the fact that the wearer had a fat face. But the most striking feature was the huge red nose protruding out of his royal blue mask that would have done credit to a Toucan - Who is that masked man I wondered?!

Just a few days later I received a package in the post. It was addressed to Mr. A Street, AKA. 'Kid Tarzan Jonathan'. I rushed upstairs to my bed-sit and with my hands trembling with excitement. I opened the package and pulled out a large folded wrestling poster. I unfolded it and laid on my bed in order to try to imagine it pasted to a wall and the first impression a passing wrestling fan would get. And to see if my name would prove to be noticeable amongst all the other wrestlers names that would be appearing on it. I staggered back as though I had just received a dropkick in the chops. Printed in large block letters, right across the whole top width of the poster was, Main Event - Kid 'Tarzan' Jonathan versus 'Gentleman' Geoff Moran. Then I panicked, what was I going to wear? I had nothing suitable and no money to buy anything. I looked at the poster again, an 8 x 5 minute round contest. WOW! The best I had done as a boxer was 6 x 3 minute rounds. I really felt as though I had arrived. Then I panicked again as I noticed for the first time what was printed under my name in smaller block letters, 'WELTERWEIGHT CHAMPION OF WALES.' Damn, how could I be Champion of Wales or anywhere else for that matter. I'd never had a professional wrestling match before in my life, let alone won a championship. 'Maybe they've got me confused with someone else?!' I wondered. Well if they don't mention it I certainly won't. At least not until after I'd had my 'Main Event' professional wrestling match. Then if they realize their mistake I will have already had my chance to show them my tremendous talent and sensational skill. I checked my wrestling boots and decided there was no way I could possibly wear them for my pro wrestling debut. Apart from the fact that they were the only pair of wrestling boots I had ever owned and were amazingly scuffed. Even after taking into consideration that I had owned them since I was barely fifteen years old. They had really met their Waterloo during my booth boxing days; where every day they had been soaked in someone's blood, mostly my own. I needed money and I needed it fast. My first professional wrestling match was just 3 weeks away and a 'Main Event' wrestler needed to make a great impression. Especially as it was also going to be his first impression. I scoured the West-end for ideas. What would Kid Tarzan Jonathan wear, and more to the point, how would he pay for it? I called Bill Jones and asked him if he wanted me to do some more modeling for him. His affirmative answer and another half hour posing session netted me another 5 pounds towards my war chest. Next I tried a new number that Bobby Selsden had given me; it belonged to John Graham who lived in Knightsbridge. Bill Jones would only take 12 photographs at each session and would pick 8 of the photos he liked best and those he would submit to the muscle magazines. In contrast John Graham would snap dozens of photos and submit as many as would be accepted, by any magazine that he could interest in them. I must have posed for over 2 hours the first time I modeled for him and was then disappointed with the 3 pounds I received for my efforts. After questioning him on the subject, John explained that Bill Jones was a wealthy man who only took physique photographs as a hobby. Where as he relied on it as a major part of his livelihood and therefore couldn't afford to pay top dollar. To be honest I would have been more than happy to do it for free. Not only did I get a tremendous kick out of appearing in the same magazines that I had been buying myself for years. But I figured, that the publicity I gained by appearing in them could only do me good in my quest to gain fame as a professional wrestler. Be that as it may, I still wanted more money. I rang a third photographer, who was known in the muscle mags as 'Lon of London' when he took photos for British magazines. And he told me 'Lon of New York' when he took photos for American magazines. Although that turned out to be a lie, as he had once worked with the real Lon of New York, and then ripped off the title. I found out after I met him, that he was American and his real name was Dominick. In spite of the French beret he always wore on the side of his head Lon, looked like a dainty, mini version of the Chicago Gangster, Al Capone. Complete with a scar right across one cheek. But there the resemblance ended, as Lon didn't look as though he could have fought his way out of a wet paper bag. I thought he had something wrong with his legs, as he took swift but tiny little steps. I wondered if I should recommend some good leg exercises to him, to help strengthen them. I thought better of it in case he might be self-conscious about it and I wouldn't have wanted to embarrass him.

"Oh, Kid Tarzan Jonathan," he seemed to shriek, as he opened his apartment door to my knock. "I've seen your lovely photos in 'Man's World' Mark really did a lovely job on you. Oh, come right in," he invited, "and meet my Baby, Christopher. Look who's come to see you Christopher," he shrilled, "it's that gorgeous Kid Tarzan Jonathan." I followed Lon into his studio and shook hands with his 'baby' Christopher who turned out to be a very fluffy black and white Cat. I said,

"Hello Christopher, as you're only a cat you can call me Adrian."

"Oh, he's such a clever Cat," crooned Lon, "I've even taught him to play the piano, haven't I Christopher?!" I noticed that he had already set up his studio, lights, cameras and even a display of fake marble pillars, which made a set that resembled something from Ancient Greek Mythology.

"Try one of these on," he said, offering me a handful of tiny posing trunks, "they're my new line. I have them made in New York and I advertise them in 'Adonis' and 'Body beautiful' magazine. If you like them I'll let you keep them." I undressed and tried on a few of the trunks. I thought they were very nice, though a bit on the brief side, even for me - I also hoped they weren't a little transparent, as they were made of a very thin, silky fabric.

"I'll be going over to New York again, this weekend," he told me, "and I'll be bringing back my new line, very exciting."

"Are these okay?" I asked, showing him the trunks I was

wearing.

"Oh, totally delicious!" he exclaimed, "Here let me put some of that oil on your back!" He took the bottle of olive oil out of my hand, that I was using to spread liberally over my chest, arms and shoulders. He began to smooth the oil on my back and I found it really unpleasant, as it felt more like a slow caress.

"You have lovely skin, Adrian," he told me, "you must eat a lot of fruit." He made me feel uncomfortable, then he suddenly shrieked which made me jump about 3 feet in the air,

"Oh Adrian, you've got the most gorgeous long eyelashes!" I winced away from him as he tried to touch them, "Oh, they're so long and they all curl upwards, they're absolutely perfect!"

'What's up with this twat?' I thought, 'I've come here to have photographs taken for muscle magazines and all this bloody fool is on about is fucking skin and bloody eyelashes. By the time Lon finished taking photos, I felt as though I had been in his studio for a month and he had taken a thousand pictures.

"Well I think that will have to do for today Adrian," he said, "can you come back tomorrow and we can finish off? I won't be able to take any more photos after that until I get back from New York."

'Damn!" I thought, "after all the photos he'd already taken, I wouldn't imagine he'd ever need me to pose for him again for about 10 years.' But he handed me a 5 pound note so I said, "Yes, I can make it tomorrow, thank you very much." Before I left he offered me a glass of 'Welch's Grape Juice' which I had never seen or tasted before, it was absolutely delicious,

"I get it in New York," he told me, "would you like a bottle to take home?"

"Would I ever?!" I exclaimed, "It's bloody gorgeous!"

"Just like you, Adrian." He purred.

I purchased a pair of white satin trunks that had wide burgundy colored side stripes and then took a trip to Borovik's near Soho Market to find some matching fabric to make a cape. My cousin Margaret, had promised to run it up for me. In Borovik's I found some satin that matched the white and burgundy perfectly, white for the outside of the cape and burgundy for the lining. But I had to settle for blood red velvet ribbon, which Margaret used to make the block letters which were sewn on the back of the cape to spell 'Kid Tarzan Jonathan'. Boots were another matter. I visited 'Lonsdale's' in Beak Street and the only boots they had in stock were not only more expensive than I could afford at that time, but were too boxing and not enough wrestling in their style. They told me they could have them custom made to my specifications. But that it would take more time than I had left and also more money than I had left. So I decided to take advantage of my nickname 'Tarzan' and wrestle barefoot, until I could afford to buy new boots. Now I was all set to take the Wrestling World by storm. I began running barefoot around Wormwood Scrubs Common to toughen my feet. But I was always only too happy to interrupt my exercise and explain to anyone the reason why I was doing it.

"I'm a bare foot wrestler." I would begin and then go on to relate my life story.

THE PROFESSIONAL WRESTLER

"Ah, here's my new main event," called Johnny Childs, as I entered the dressing room, I really liked the sound of that greeting, "come and meet your opponent, 'Gentleman' Geoff Moran." He continued. I walked over to where Johnny and the 'Gentleman' were sitting down facing each other and nodded my own straight-faced acknowledgement to my future first opponent. I sat down in the chair that Johnny had just dragged around to face them both.

"This is 'Gentleman' Geoff Moran and this is Kid 'Tarzan' Jonathan," introduced Johnny, "you two should have a great match." The 'Gentleman' nodded at me, so I nodded again. "What do you think Geoff? Johnny said, "I think the Kid should go over."

"No, I don't think so," replied the 'Gentleman, "I've got a big reputation in this hall, so I think I ought to win."

"I think the Kid should win." Argued Johnny, I felt instantly endeared to Johnny Childs. As it sounded to me as though he had faith in my ability to prevail, in my first pro match even though he had never seen me perform.

"No," said the Gentleman, "It would ruin my reputation here and you know that I'm the best thing you've got."

"And 'The Blue Baron'," agreed Johnny, "but I still think the Kid should win."

"Well I don't," stated the Gentleman adamantly, "he hasn't got the experience." 'We'll see about that.' I thought.

"Okay," sighed Johnny Childs, he turned to me and said, "do two, one in 7."

"What?" I replied, I didn't have a clue what he was talking about and I thought he must be using a series of wrestler's Cockney slang I hadn't learned yet.

"Do two, one in 7," he repeated and seeing my puzzled expression, added, "do 7 rounds." I was livid; I felt that I had just been demoted from an 8 round match to a 7 round match just because my braggart of an opponent had finally convinced the promoter that I wasn't good enough to do 8. I couldn't believe how quickly he had changed his opinion of my chances, then knuckled under and even knocked a round off my match. One minute he seemed to have great faith in my ability to win, the next he didn't even think I could last 8 rounds.

'I'll bloody well show you!' I thought.

"Well you two sort it out yourselves," said Johnny with a sigh, "I've got some business to see to." Then to everyone in the dressing-room he said, "if I'm not back in time to watch my friend 'The Blue Baron' in action, I'd appreciate you all telling me how well he does!" And with that he disappeared out of the dressing room.

"Main event match is on third." The Gentleman told me. I just nodded my head.

"I'll take my first fall in the third round and then a submission in the seventh," he told me. I looked at him in disbelief, not only did this bloody idiot think he was good enough to beat me. He was even telling me in which round he was going to pin me and make me submit in. Well I'd been playing the intimidation game since I took my first breath, 'talk is cheap,' I thought. 'We'll see what you can do when we get in there.'

"I'll take my fall in the third with a double-leg nelson," he continued, "and then I'll take a submission with a step-over arm-bar on your left arm in the seventh round, after I've worked on it for a while."

'This twat is unbelievable,' I thought, 'never mind it'll be a bigger shock for him when he comes face to face with a little bit of good old fashion reality.'

"I'll probably start working on your arm in about the fifth round," he said and then added, "What are you going to do?" I didn't realize he was asking me to tell him what I wanted to do in order to take the second and equalizing fall on him. When he asked me, "What are you going to do?" I thought he was saying 'I'm going to pin you and make you submit in the round I choose to do it in. And what are you going to do about it?'

"You'll see when we get in there." I told him and walked back and sat in the chair where I'd put my wrestling gear. I noticed that everyone had gone quiet, including the Gentleman. I was getting some strange looks from everyone. 'Jealous of the new main event,' I thought. By the time I had undressed and donned my new White and Burgundy wrestling trunks the first match was in the ring. By the sound of the screaming and applause coming from the small but packed hall, they were having a very good match.

'Wait until they get a load of me!' I thought, 30 years before Jack Nicholson said it. I laced up a pair of red string sandals that I would wear to the ring and remove before the match started and would then wrestle barefoot like Tarzan.

The way wrestling shows were presented in Britain was first there would be a preliminary match to warm the crowd up. Then next the semi main event, which would be the second most important match on the card. That would be followed by an interval, usually about 15 minutes and then it would be time for the main event. Which mostly featured a Hero against a Villain. It would probably have a very controversial result designed to bring the crowd back in droves for the next show in order to see revenge meted, justice served and good prevail. Then the last match which would be a preliminary match and usually designed to send the fans home happy. After already pissing them off with the controversial end to the main event. I had already warmed up by doing a couple of hundred push-ups and oiled myself by the time the second and semi-main event match began. I crept out of the dressing room and stood quietly in the shadows at the back of the hall. There I could watch the Blue Baron in action again without being seen by anyone in the audience myself. I wanted their first sight of me to be when I marched to the ring to do combat, in tonight's main event. As I watched the Blue Baron with the huge red nose sticking out of his blue mask. Huffing and puffing around the ring. I thought, 'now why doesn't it surprise me that Johnny Childs hasn't got back in time to watch his 'friend' the Blue Baron doing battle?!' However, he did arrive back in the dressing room towards the end of the interval. His red face and nose was even redder and sweaty. His hair was wet and disheveled. But most noticeable were the patches of blue dye all over his face.

"Oh no," He moaned, "Don't tell me I missed watching my

best friend the Blue Baron wrestling again, how did he do?!" he asked, hoping for a complimentary answer.

"He was fuckin' awful!" Replied the Gentleman. I didn't know whether to admire him for his honesty or hate him for his meanness, but I had to laugh all the same.

Now it was time for my match and as 'Gentleman' Geoff Moran walked past me to exit the dressing room and make his way to the ring he smiled at me and said,

"Good luck, Kid." I nodded and replied,

"Thanks, same to you." And thought, 'you're going to need it!' As soon as the wrestling fans in the hall spotted the 'Gentleman' swaggering arrogantly towards the ring they began to jeer and boo for all they were worth. 'So he did have a reputation.' I thought as I prepared to follow him. I walked to the ring, sure that I was having a wonderful dream. I couldn't believe that this was really happening to me at last. Any second now I was convinced that I would wake up disappointed, as I had done countless times before. To add to the unreality of what was happening, I swear I couldn't feel my feet touching the ground as I got closer and closer to the ring. And my first professional wrestling match. The audience was cheering me like crazy and the Gentleman was leaning over the ropes raining insults down on my head. Saying something about "hurry up and get in the ring, as he wanted to watch a soccer match on TV that started in 10 minutes. And he wanted to finish me off quickly so he wouldn't miss the beginning." But I was in my own dream world and what he was saying hardly penetrated my brain. The fantastic reaction I was receiving from the fans amazed me and I wondered if many in the audience had seen me boxing on the booth, or were bodybuilding magazine fans. In time I would learn that if an opponent was hated enough, as the Gentleman was. The crowd would cheer themselves hoarse for anyone who opposed him, whether they recognized them or not. By the time I climbed onto the apron and then into the ring, the fans were hysterical. As I held out my arms to spread my cape they hit a crescendo, that made me want to laugh and cry at the same time - I was here, this was it, it was really happening. I disrobed and unfastened my red laced sandals and slipped them off, as the MC introduced the Gentleman. Then myself and surprised me by announcing that it was an 8 five minute round contest. 'Perhaps Johnny had forgotten to tell the MC that he had changed it to 7 rounds,' I thought. 'Or better still, changed his mind about changing it.' Anyway the MC had announced 8 rounds so as far as I was concerned that made it official. With the Introductions complete the bell rings to herald what I had longed for. Trained for. Prayed for. Sweated and bled for, and I rushed out of my corner to begin my new career and my new life. I stopped short of the centre of the ring, as the Gentleman was still in his corner and hadn't moved an inch. He gave me a hateful sneer and instead of coming out to meet me face to face, he suddenly dove out of his corner and began rolling head over heels, around and around the ring. 'What the hell is he doing?!' I thought. Convinced that he had some elaborate strategy planned and that his strange antics were designed to sucker me into doing something dumb. I backed back into my corner and just watched him rolling around and around. 'I'm not going to fall for whatever he's got in mind and he's got to stop rolling eventually,' I thought. He did – and the strange, slightly bewildered look he gave me as he got back to his feet, convinced me that my assessment of his tactics had been well founded. Pleased with my intuition I advanced smugly towards him. He made a grab for me, but I countered with the swiftness of a mongoose, and as soon as I secured an arm-bar, I threw both my feet into the air and with the whole weight of my body drove the Gentleman face first into the canvas.

"FUCK YOU!!!!!" He screamed, as way of submission. The referee dived down to separate us and that was the end of my first professional wrestling match. At first the audience were stunned to silence. But they soon recovered and the Gentleman, who had predicted my demise. Even to the extent of foretelling the rounds in which it would occur, was lying at my feet with a badly dislocated shoulder. I absorbed the cheers from the fans which hit a volume never before achieved in that hall. As my opponent was unable to continue, I was announced the winner of the contest. And surviving a chronic anticlimax of too easy a win. I stood proudly in the centre of the ring, as the referee raised my arm in victory. On my way back to the dressing room, I signed my first autograph books as a professional wrestler and enjoyed the congratulations I received from my fans on my win.

"We've bin waitin' fer more'n a year to see that bleed'n Geoff Moran get what's comin' to 'im!" I was told. I entered the dressing room like Julius Caesar entering Rome in triumph, after he had conquered and subdued Gaul.

"When am I going to get my first Championship match?" I roared at J Childs.

"What the fuck do you think you were doing out there?!" he countered. Every eye in the dressing room was focused on me and there wasn't a friendly pair amongst them.

"What do you mean, I won didn't I?!" I asked, taken aback by his attitude.

"Do you think people are going to be happy, paying good money to watch a main event that doesn't even last two fuckin' minutes?!" He demanded.

"Get me some better competition!" I suggested, "What about a championship match or something?" Johnny opened his mouth to retaliate, but before any sound came out of it, a Woman's voice screamed right into my face.

"You fuckin' stupid, clumsy bastard!" It was 'Gentleman' Geoff Moran's Wife. Helping a very distressed 'Gentleman' Geoff, back into the dressing room. She continued, "Tarzan my fuckin' arse, you're more like a fuckin' mad Ape. They should put you back in you're fuckin' cage, you fuckin' bastard!" For once in my life I was almost speechless. I had never been spoken to like that by a Woman before.

"If you were a man, I'd punch you in your filthy mouth!" I managed to splutter. I thought of something more appropriate to say, but it stuck in my throat, as both she and the Gentleman suddenly started to cry. I looked first at Johnny Childs, then at the other wrestlers in the dressing room for help. But was met only with looks of embarrassment, or hostility. I picked up my bag and clothes and took them into the furthest corner of the room, out of everyone's way and sat down. The last match went into the ring and an ambulance came for the Gentleman, and thankfully his wife went with him. No one spoke to me or even looked in my direction. I went to the washroom, cleaned up, returned to the dressing room. I got dressed before the last match ended and the wrestlers came back to change. Just then Johnny Childs came back from phoning the hospital to find out how the Gentleman was faring.

"Well, he'll probably be out for a while," announced Johnny to everyone. "His shoulder is dislocated." The announcement caused everyone to glare at me once again and I just pretended not to notice. I would have been happy to have left already, but I hadn't been paid yet and I figured that I couldn't count it as a professional match unless I got money for doing it. And I'd been promised 2 pounds 10-shillings. It was as though Johnny Childs had read my mind and he came over to me and spoke to me in a much gentler tone of voice than he had just after my match.

"I can't give you 2 pounds 10-shillings for that Kid; I'll give you 2 pounds instead and think yourself lucky I'm paying you anything." He took a wad of cash out of his pocket and peeled off 2 pound notes which he handed to me,

"You're gonna have to help me out Kid," he said, "I've got 'Gentleman' Geoff billed to wrestle all over South London and now you've fucked him up. You're gonna have to stand in for him."

"You can count on me!" I told him valiantly, while pretending not to notice the blue dye that had now dried on his face.

"And try not to fuck anyone else up!" He added, looking at me as though I was something he'd just scraped off his shoe. "But if you can't help yourself make sure you don't fuck anyone up until you have given the fuckin' marks at least half an hour!"

"Marks?!" I queried.

"The wrestling fans!" He supplied. "Listen Kid," he added with a sigh, "Go and see Johnny Kilroy, he's a good friend of mine." He began writing down an address, "he's got a good wrestling club, down near the Elephant and Castle. Tell him Johnny Childs sent you and tell him I said, 'to teach me to die'." Well according to all the wrestlers and officials present, who witnessed my pro wrestling debut, I was a total fuck-up. But I consoled myself with the fact. That in spite of what Johnny Childs had said about the fans not getting value for money, due to the short duration and the very abrupt finish, to my match. Many of them had expressed enormous satisfaction at seeing 'Gentleman' Geoff Moran dispatched so easily and decisively.

An added and even more satisfying consolation, was that I

got a few more professional matches out of my faux-par. Which unfortunately for the 'Gentleman' was at his expense. 'Okay,' I thought, 'things might have started out rough, but they could only get better.' And get better they did, at last I got a job! But first I had to take a medical examination to make sure I was fit enough to do the work, which I was pre-warned could sometimes be quite strenuous.

"If I can't do it no one can," Was my reply. The Doctor who examined me told me to strip off, and he did all the usual stuff. Finally he weighed me and measured my height and informed me that I might be a little heavy for my height. He recommended that I should watch how much I ate and do some exercise. I just looked at him in disbelief and managed with great effort not to say one single word. I was 5 feet 7 inches tall. I weighed 144 pounds of muscle and bone. My waist was a rock hard 27 inches, my chest was a rock hard 47 inches and I didn't have one ounce of fat on my entire body. I had been working out on the weights and on the wrestling mat, for an average of about 7 hours a day, 6 days a week and I swam all day on the seventh. All on a starvation diet and this fucking quack, is advising me to diet and get some exercise to lose weight!

****

Anyway, as heavy as I was for my height, I began working for the Railway as a van-boy in Paddington Station, on the following Monday. I was paired with a driver named Bill Waller. The day I started coincided with Bill having to double for another driver who was on holiday. So for the first two weeks of my new job we had to make deliveries to Bill's regular route and then continue on to the absentee driver's route. I remember Bill not being very happy, with a double territory to cover and a rookie van-boy, who didn't know the ropes to help him cover it. I had to work for 2 weeks in hand before I received my first weeks pay.

There was a Greengrocers shop next to the Paddington depot, that sold crusty cheese and salad rolls to die for. They were absolutely delicious and now that I could at last afford to eat, I would buy 2, 3 or sometimes 4 each day. One day I noticed they were selling the largest fresh peaches I had ever seen and while they were in season, I could devour at least a half a dozen a day. I would usually buy a dozen when I finished work on a Saturday and they would barely last me until I could re-stock on the following Monday.

As usual, I was at the swimming pool one Sunday and I found that I was down to my last 2 peaches of the week, which I had brought with me to sustain me between laps of the pool. While I was sitting down eating the first of my precious peaches, I locked eyes with a very pretty girl. I think what attracted me most about her was her enormous tits. She came up to me and said, "Hello," and as she had the most enormous pair of tits, I offered her my last whole peach. We chatted away between bites of our juicy peaches while standing next to the pool. When all of a sudden some boy rushed past me and pushed the girl, who had told me her name was Pauline into the water.

'How rude,' I thought and then, 'what a waste of a lovely peach.' Pauline had disappeared under the water and I watched as she slowly resurfaced, said something about not being able to swim and then sinking back below the surface. I had heard what she said, but being mesmerized by the sight of her big buoyant breasts wobbling in the water. It didn't penetrate my preoccupied brain. Until some other guys jumped in and saved her from drowning about 4 feet away from where I was standing. Still enjoying my peach and the view. It wasn't until they dragged poor Pauline out of the pool, all embarrassed and bedraggled that I realized I had just lost an ideal opportunity. Not only to appear as the hero of the hour, by saving her life. But to also cop a feel of her great big tits while I was doing it. Damn! I gave myself a hard time over that one. But she didn't seem to hold it against me, so we decided to get dressed leave the swimming pool and take a walk around the park. We had found a nice grassy knoll where we soon came to grips and were cuddling nicely. When a large shadow suddenly blocked the sun and an all too familiar voice said,

"Is this the reason you haven't been down to see me lately?!" We looked up and there silhouetted against the blue sky was a very angry Maureen.

"I haven't been down to see you because I haven't wanted to." I answered irritably. I had been enjoying what I was doing and resented being disturbed by anyone, especially Maureen.

"Aren't you going to introduce us?" asked Pauline stiffly.

"Yes," I said, "This is my Girlfriend Pauline," I told Maureen and was gratified not to be contradicted by Pauline, "and this is my ex-girlfriend Maureen." I told Pauline.

"We'll talk about this tomorrow night after you've finished working out in the Forester's club." Stated Maureen.

"We've got nothing to talk about." I replied.

"I'll see you tomorrow." She insisted.

"Not if I see you first." I told her lamely. Maureen walked off in a huff and Pauline and I just lay on the grass for a while in silence. Our former mood bent out of shape by the untimely and unwelcome interruption by my now former girlfriend. I was trying to think of a line to get us back to where we were, when Pauline asked me,

"Can girls work out at your weightlifting club? I'd like to build up my muscles."

"Well we can always ask," I replied, "maybe I could teach you to wrestle too." I added, as I eyed her bosom. And that being the line I was looking for, we got back to practicing a few holds in advance.

****

It had taken me longer to find Johnny Kilroy's professional wrestling club, than I thought it would. As a result, when I marched in most of his members were already practicing their wrestling prowess. The suspicious and angry Buzzard looks I got as I entered unannounced, unheralded and uninvited into the hallowed and secret world of wrestlers, would have reduced a lesser man to ashes. I asked for Johnny Kilroy and after he identified himself, I recited Johnny Childs' message, 'teach me to die.' I hadn't known what it meant, but I relayed it perfectly.

"Oh, you must be Tarzan," chuckled Johnny Kilroy, "the one who fucked up 'Gentleman' Geoff Moran, yeah, Johnny Childs told me to expect you."

He was interrupted by all the other wrestlers who had gathered around and were demanding to know if I had already had a professional wrestling match. My affirmative reply seemed to dismay and shock them and they bombarded me with more questions,

"What promotions have you wrestled for?!" – "What's your name?!" – "Who have you wrestled?!" – "When are you wrestling next?!" - "What's the phone number of your promoter?!" I said bombarded with questions. But they were more like accusations and were delivered in a very hostile manner. The raw hostility and unfeigned jealousy displayed by Johnny Kilroy's wrestlers was quite disturbing. They almost fought amongst themselves to be the first to try me out, I ignored most of their questions and stepped through the ropes into the ring and spent a very hectic and eventful evening. I was soon aware, that my time spent as my brother's punch bag. My rough and tumble street-fighting days in Wales. My boxing on a fairground booth. Most of all my daily marathon workouts held me in good stead. And no one got the better of me that night as hard as they all tried. By the time I left I had earned the very reluctant respect, but not the friendship of Johnny's boys. Only two of which present that night ever made a name for themselves as professional wrestlers. The first was 'Iron Jaw' Joe Murphy, a pudgy bombastic Irishman and Tony Scarlo. I had completely forgotten about the message I had delivered from Johnny Childs, to Johnny Kilroy until I was on my way back home. I began to wonder if I had 'learned to die,' that night - Probably not, I concluded as I was sometimes a very slow learner.

Not always though. As soon after we were back to Bill Waller's usual delivery route, I had learned my way around the Holloway, Highgate, Camden Town, Finsbury Park, Islington and Hampstead Heath area, almost as well as Bill. Who had been doing it for years. Two or three times a week we would deliver packages to Holloway Women's Prison. Bill never told me what to expect the first time he sent me in there. As it was summertime, I would only wear boots and jeans when delivering, as I never missed a chance to work on my tan. I often got complaints from some of the managers of posh shops, especially in the Hampstead Heath area. As they didn't think a half naked muscleman marching back and forth with packages, added a lot of class to their premises. I never had any complaints however, when delivering packages to the Women's Prison. All I can say is thank Goodness for the guards. But even they seemed highly amused by the reception I received from all those male starved ladies. Much to Bill's delight, even after I had got used to it, I never left the Prison without a face as red as a Baboon's arse.

When we sorted our packages in the station depot and loaded them into the van each morning. Bill had it down to a fine art. He knew exactly what part of the van I should place each package in, and as I was following his instructions, he would work out our best route in his mind. As a result we usually finished our whole days work well before lunch. Bill had a mysterious part time job, working I suppose as a driver for the owner of a breaker's yard. The owner's name was Ted Flock, who, Bill told me used to be known as a Gangster with a very violent reputation. Now supposedly retired from his life of crime he ran a 'legitimate car breaking business'. How legitimate it really was, I can only guess at. As there were many speculative incidents that occurred from time to time. Starting with the fact, that I was never ever to learn where Bill went for the rest of the day after he dropped me off at Ted's yard. In order to keep me occupied in Bill's absence, Ted gave me a part time job working in his yard breaking vehicles with a sledge hammer. An instrument I was very familiar with. There were a few other men who worked full time in the yard, including Ted Flock's Nephew and heir, Albert. Who in spite of being named manager would receive the most belittling and embarrassing putdowns from Ted for any tiny thing, real or imaginary that Ted thought was wrong. The only thing I found more nerve rending than the bollockings Albert received, was Albert's whining voice when making his excuses to his Uncle Ted. Oh - here I'll correct myself, there was something else that I found more nerve rending. And as a result I quickly taught myself to break any vehicles I was instructed to, without really looking at them in the process. The reason for that was, my mistake in expressing my horror one day at the sight of the inside of the cracked windows of a car, that was covered in blood. The other breakers were delighted by my aversion to it, and told me stories that curdled my guts. About teeth they often found imbedded in the dashboards of vehicles. Bloody pieces of scalp or flesh hanging from jagged pieces of shattered glass or jagged metal. Severed limbs and even eyeballs amongst the twisted, broken bodywork of the wrecked vehicles that we all worked on. And blood, blood and more blood. I suspected even then, that a lot of what they told me was exaggerated, if not outright lies. I also realized, that at least part of the reason they told me the gory horror stories, was to keep me from joining in their ghoulish habit of searching through every square inch of the inside of wreckages, for any valuables they could scavenge. To me their greed and avarice would make the filthiest, most rabid Hyena angelic by comparison. I was also surprised at myself, at genuinely being horrified by so much blood. When it didn't bother me at all, if it was coming out of someone who I had inflicted the injuries to, that had caused the blood to flow in the first place.

****

Pauline did come and train at the Forester's, but only for a short time. I don't think she had really been interested in lifting heavy weights in the first place. But wanted to keep her eye on me, knowing that I had to pass by Maureen's house every time I finished training. The funny thing is, that after I had finished going with Maureen, Jean called to me one evening as I was on my way to workout. She said to me,

"Hello Street, aren't you talking to me anymore?" I remember looking at her suspiciously and replying,

"Yes, if you like, what do you want to talk about?" But after a bit of awkward banter we were soon chatting away merrily. Even though I was still going out with Pauline I began to look forward to sharing a bit of gossip with Jean whenever I passed on my way to and from the gym.

Between having a full time job with the railway, a part time job on Ted Flocks' car breakers yard. Sporadic professional wrestling matches. Well paying muscle posing sessions, I was earning more money than I had, since I finished boxing on the booth. But I wasn't saving very much of it. The reason was, that in an effort to regain my bodyweight I was eating and drinking like a pig. But my metabolism must have been racing like a rocket as I couldn't seem to gain a pound never mind what, or how much I ate. Pounds of steak, chicken, cheese, fruit, salad, gallons of milk and raw eggs by the bucketful didn't succeed in making me any heavier. But it certainly made my pocket lighter. On the plus side, I had noticed my strength increasing, very, very dramatically. What I put it down to at the time was the vast amount of red meat I was consuming, after so many months of starvation. I am sure that was half the reason. But what I didn't realize at that time was, that marathon sessions in the gym, 11 times a week were far too much. Overtraining was something that I had never heard of, and like many more young bodybuilders in those days mistakenly thought that more was better. The fact that I now had a full time job didn't only give me more money for food, it also gave me less time to train. Without really appreciating it, not being able to go to the YMCA through the week was extremely beneficial. As it almost cut my training time in half. If I was lucky enough to wrestle professionally as many as 3 times in a week, that would cut my remaining time in half. But in those days, I was usually lucky if I wrestled more than once a week. As strong as I became on most of my lifts, for some reason a 200 pound bench-press still alluded me. Even though I could do a few reps with 190 pounds, put 200 on the bar and I couldn't budge it off my chest after lowering it. Looking back on it, I don't think my Neanderthal training methods helped. I would do dozens of sets of every exercise I liked every time I went to the gym.

In spite of his dislocated shoulder 'Gentleman' Geoff was soon back in action.

"I had to get back in the ring as soon as I could," he told me, "my bleed'n shoulder didn't only stop me earning money for wrestling. It messed up my own business as a window cleaner too."

"No wonder your Wife was upset with me." I responded.

"Oh, I'd keep well out of her way if I was you," he replied, "she'll have your bleed'n guts for garters." I had began wrestling against Geoff as soon as he had returned to the ring. Instead of bearing me a grudge for injuring him, he seemed to take me under his wing by helping and advising me on anything that would help me improve. But whether it was due to friendship, or self-preservation, I never really figured out. I told Geoff that my ultimate goal was to wrestle full time for Dale Martin.

"You're not good enough Kid," he told me bluntly, "and probably never will be. Why don't you stick with me and Johnny Childs? I can guarantee that you'll earn over a 100 pounds a year, on top of what you're earning working for the railway. Look at it this way," he explained, "you've got a nice little number here, with me'n Johnny and we'll make sure you wrestle main event, nearly every match. Can you honestly ever see yourself wrestling main event for Dale Martin's?"

"Yes!" I replied without a second's hesitation. Geoff sighed in exasperation.

"I'll tell you what I'll do for you Kid," he said, I'm wrestling up in Birmingham in a few weeks time for Tony Ansel's promotions. I'll give him a ring and ask him to put you on the card and we'll travel up there together, waddya say?"

"Great!" I replied enthusiastically, 'WOW!' Birmingham was about 100 miles north of London and would be the furthest I had ever traveled to wrestle.'

"You won't be main event though," Geoff explained, then added smugly, "That will be me against Captain O'Rourke of the Royal Canadian Mounted Police."

"Never heard of him." I replied.

"Don't tell Tony Ansel that." He warned me.

In the meantime, I wrestled for 'Dropkick' Johnny Peters in Sheerness. To get there, I had been told to take the underground tube train to the Oval Station and meet in a café. The only wrestler I recognized at the meet was Tony Scarlo, who I was wrestling with that night. I always watched as much of the other matches as I could, to see what was getting the best reaction from the fans. And also to see if there was any neat move I could 'borrow' and mould to my own style. The second match on the card that night was a spectacle that I would never want to borrow anything from. It featured 'Lucky' Bert Lamb against a snide villain named 'Slip' Waterman. Bert Lamb was a bulky, powerfully built wrestler, whose nickname 'Lucky' came as a result of him taking up wrestling after recovering from a nasty bout with polio as a child. It had crippled his left leg and left it as skinny as a toothpick. And a few inches shorter than the other one. So that he had to wear a thick built up boot on his left foot. I admired his guts and determination almost as much as I was sickened by the sight of his little white matchstick of a leg. I wondered why he didn't wear some long thick padded wrestling tights. To at least cover, if not disguise his disfigurement. I was soon to learn; in contrast to him wanting to hide his gamy leg. It turned out to be his gimmick. Or what set him apart from other wrestlers. It was also the main character in the story line his matches always took. First there would be the sympathy from the fans. Who would get behind a natural underdog. That would make it very easy for his villainous adversary to build up hate against himself by taking unfair advantage of poor Bert's impediment. If Bert's leg sickened me, you can imagine my reaction to his opponent, who, after being introduced slid out of his thick wooly dressing-gown. To reveal a tall, white, scrawny body who's back and neck was covered with huge red and yellow throbbing boils. I watched in horror and disbelief. I didn't think that I would ever see anything more revolting in a wrestling ring again. I was proved wrong within a few minutes. After Bert had shown that in spite of 'the leg' he had the wrestling skill to outmaneuver his opponent. Who, I had already christened 'Pus-in-Boots.' Was outclassed by a smarter wrestler. He soon began to resort to foul tactics and concentrated his aggression on 'the leg'. He bent it, twisted it, bit it and kicked it, until the wrestling fans were screaming the arena down. Then he viciously used it to take a submission on. Which gained the bad guy the first fall. As it was the best out of 3 falls the match then continued in the same vain. With Bert's leg getting twisted like a stick of liquorish. I didn't think the match could get any more disgusting, but that just showed how much of a novice I was. Eventually poor crippled Bert got his second wind and mounted a triumphant and spectacular comeback. And to the delight of the howling fans he did it by squeezing out the throbbing boils all over Slip Waterman's neck and back. The crowd loved every scream that accompanied each jet of bloody, yellow pus that their valiant hero squeezed out for their sadistic pleasure. I was ready to throw up and totally freaked out by the thought that I would soon be wrestling in the same ring that was getting messier by the minute. The climax of the match was, after Slip had appealed to referee Billy Barber, for the thousandth time to stop Bert from squeezing any more boils. Instead of sympathizing with him. Billy the referee simply lifted up his grubby T-shirt. And showed Slip and the audience a bunch of boils hanging out of his armpit that looked like a bunch of plum sized grapes. They made all of Waterman's now deflated boils pale into insignificance. The frenzied fans cheered Billy Barber's prize sized boils until they were hoarse. In fact his boils stole the show. For once I was happy that I was not main event. They had to follow Bert and Slip into the ring, and hopefully use their big sweaty bodies to mop up most of the mess before Tony Scarlo and I had our match.

I had been disappointed when I saw the wrestling posters outside the venue. As not only was I wrestling in a 6 round preliminary match. But they had me billed as King Jonaphone from South Africa.

"I thought you were Black!" a disappointed Johnny Peters told me when he first saw me. I checked in the dressing room mirror to make sure.

"No I'm not," I agreed, "but I do have a good sun-tan." I had that problem with a few promoters in those days as I also found myself billed as King Johnson from Jamaica and Kid Jensen from Sweden. My first contact with them had been by phone and I suppose that my Welsh accent must have thrown them. Well I wasn't black and the closest that I had ever come to it was when I worked in the coal-mine. But I was the living proof that White men can jump. I was so agile that one of my Tarzan like maneuvers, was to jump so high when I delivered a dropkick that I could easily land on my feet. And be ready to deliver another one with seconds to spare, as soon as my opponent regained his feet after receiving the first one. I could take one step towards my opponent and jump up so that I had his head trapped between my thighs in one motion. I loved it when the referee of my matches was really tall. If he put himself between me and my opponent. All I had to do is slap him on top of his shoulder to measure him and I could leapfrog right over his head while he was standing fully erect and then land on my opponent the other side of him. In my match I had thrown in most of my little tricks and a few more that I snatched as opportunity presented them to me. Tony Scarlo had done the same, as we both thought that we had a lot of making up to do if the fans were going to get their money's worth that night. Especially after the embarrassing fiasco in the second bout. Towards the end of the match I caught Tony with a terrific Monkey-flip and he flew upside-down right across the ring. He bounced up just in time for me to catch him with another one and off he sailed again. But as he bounced up again and I attempted to repeat the maneuver for the third time, he caught both my ankles and as he dropped back against the ropes. He threw both my legs over his head into the air behind him and now it was my turn to fly upside-down, but it wasn't across the ring - it was right out of it! I landed in the audience about 4 rows back and took out about 7 or 8 chairs and their occupants. By the time I managed to untangle myself from the melee of bodies. Arms and legs of both humans and chairs, clamber over the heads of the 3 rows of them to get back to the ring. I was just in time to hear the referee count to 10 as I hauled myself back onto the ring apron. When the promoter told me earlier that night, that I was to go over, I don't think that that was what he meant. But it got a standing ovation from all the fans that were still standing and decided to keep that sequence in the back of my mind for future reference.

****

Meanwhile at the Forester's I had been getting steadily stronger on most of my lifts and I began to concentrate on the strength sets as we called them. They consisted of, first arm curls, then bench-press and finally the squat. The undisputed heavyweight King of the Forester's was Les Clark from Barbados. At 5 foot 9 inches tall he weighed in at 266 pounds. He possessed the broadest, thickest shoulders I had ever seen on a human being up until that time. The Light heavyweight champion, Phil Woods was also from Barbados he was about Les's height but weighed in the region of 185 pounds. He like Les was inhumanly strong. The Lord of the Middleweights was Tommy May who was the only White man in the Forester's team. He was about my height and he weighed around 165 pounds, but was a virtual pocket-sized Hercules. Both his curl and bench-press lifts left mine in the dust. But when it came to squatting, I could even give the powerful Tommy May a real run for his money even though he outweighed me by 20 pounds. I couldn't perform a curl with what I considered to be a respectful weight to save my life. It was the Forester's weightlifting coach who encouraged me to concentrate on the strength sets with the aim at threatening Tommy May's middleweight dominance. Although I think his true motive was really designed to push Tommy further ahead of any minor threat that either of them thought I might possess.

I knew I wasn't going to be main event when I debuted for Tony Ansel's promotions in Birmingham. But I still felt an air of importance at the thought of being transported 100 miles north of London, just to do my thing. AND I was also told that I would be receiving 5 pounds for my services. Which was twice the amount I normally got paid by Johnny Child's organization. Johnny Peters had been paying me 4 pounds a match, and I had been paid 5 pounds once before by 'Black Butcher' Johnson when I wrestled for him in West Bromwich Baths Hall. I also learned another lesson when dealing with 'Black Butcher.' When I met him in the dressing room the night I wrestled for him the first thing he asked me was,

"How much did you say you weighed?!"

"About 175 pounds." I lied.

"You wouldn't weigh 175 pounds if you were wearing a diving suit, complete with lead boots!" He retorted.

"It would be a good gimmick though, wouldn't it?" I responded, while trying to smile disarmingly as I changed the subject. 'The Butcher' scowled and walked off, muttering something about, "No place in wrestling for fucking midgets!"

'Where can I get a diving suit?' I thought, then I began revising, 'if I knew where I could find a diving suit I doubted if I could afford to buy one. And even if I could, I don't think I could wrestle in one even if the promoters allowed me to.' But an idea germinated that I thought might help me out. I gathered my scanty savings counted it. Went to the nearest public phone and rang all of the photographers so that I could do the rounds and earn a little extra. I even posed and was interviewed, for a schoolgirl's magazine called 'Boyfriend.' And was chosen as the 'Boyfriend of the month' in their next issue. When I had what I considered to be sufficient cash, I purchased a pair of black Cowboy boots with heels that gave me at least 3 extra inches in height. To match it I added a pair of skintight black leather trousers. Then I bought a thick black leather jacket which was decorated with leather fringes around the shoulders and down the sleeves. It made my already large chest and shoulders appear even larger. To complete my ensemble, I added a couple of shiny black satin shirts that actually looked like leather. The black leather belt I had made for myself when I was 13 still fitted my waist on the same notch. So I was all set to make a good first impression on any new promoters I might wrestle for. And make a new good impression on any of the old ones. I believe that the average height for men in Britain in the 50s was about 5 foot 8 or 9. At 5 foot 7, I was just an inch or two shy of average height. But with my new Cowboy boots I was now at least 5 foot 10 inches tall. With the extra height and the added bulk afforded by my black leather outfit, I must have added about 30 pounds cosmetically to the way I looked. Thanks to my love of history and my fascination with the costumes and uniforms worn by warriors of the past. They were often designed to make the wearer appear much larger. I was now able to duplicate their idea, and use it in my own cause. Helmets with horns, wings, spikes, plumes and horse hair crests, could make a warrior look as much as a foot or two taller. The same as the feathered war bonnets of American Indians and the feathered headdresses worn by the cannibals of New Guinea and dozens of native tribes in Africa. Breastplates, shoulder armor and even epaulets. Although designed mainly for protection against enemy weapons. Were often made in a way that made the wearer appear much more impressively built than he really was. Alexander the Great may have only been 5 feet tall, but stick a 2 foot high Hoplite helmet on his head and slap an embossed bronze breastplate on his chest. And you'd be looking at a very physically impressive warrior King. Then I began to think about what would happen in the dressing rooms after I stepped out of my Cowboy boots to enter the ring barefoot and suddenly become as short as I could possibly get. Even if I was wrestling someone, who like myself was only 5' 7", while he was wearing his wrestling boots and myself barefoot, he would still top me by an inch or two. I decided that I needed to take advantage of any means at my disposal, never mind how minimal the results. I would begin by giving up the barefoot gimmick and wearing boots. I never liked wrestling barefoot in the first place. I would always hurt my feet in spite of all the toughening exercises that I had subjected them to. Plus, I didn't think it looked right. So that was it, I'd wear boots from now on and kiss the bare feet goodbye. But after all my very extravagant recent purchases, my coffers were once again as slim as I was, without my new outfit. So instead of shopping for wrestling boots, I bought a can of high gloss white paint and splashed a thick coat of it over my old scuffed black ones. When they finally dried they looked bloody awful. The dark patches showing through the white paint made the boots look worse than before. Undeterred, I gave them another coat of high gloss white - then another and another and then another. In fact I lost count of how many coats it finally took to make those scruffy black boots into a shiny snow white. But in the end they looked a treat. Even though they had gained double their weight and were now as stiff as a board and had set solid to the contours that my feet, ankles and lower calves. Still they looked great, even though they were as solid as a pair of wooden Dutch clogs. Their color matched my White satin trunks and cape perfectly. They would give me at least a little bit of height and a lot of protection for my long suffering trotters.

"Gotta try'n save on the expenses for the promoter," explained 'Gentleman' Geoff as 5 wrestlers attempted to squash their bodies into the seats of an average sized car. 'If he doesn't have to pay too much for our petrol he'll be more likely to use us on his cards more often." Well at last we were off to Birmingham to wrestle for Tony Ansel's promotions. A 100 miles in Britain in those days, with the condition of British roads, it would take us hours to get there and hours to get back. Take into account that there were 5 heavily built men stuffed like sardines into something not much larger than a sardine can. And you'd guess right if you thought we were in for a very long and uncomfortable trip. I didn't mind one bit. To me it was an adventure and not very many years would pass before I would appreciate that things could be a lot worse in the wrestling business. On the long trip north I was reminded by Gentleman Geoff not to tell Tony Ansel that I had never heard of Captain O'Rourke of the Royal Canadian Mounted Police. AND, it would also be wise not to mention Chinook in his presence. This evoked roars of laughter from all the other wrestlers, so naturally I was intrigued. Which made me very popular as there is nothing that wrestlers like better than to find a pair of ears that are still virgin to a good story. Tony Ansel, like most other wrestlers had similar dreams of becoming a Grappling Superstar. But also like many others he didn't really have the appearance or the talent to achieve his dreams. With the result he found it very difficult to get promoters to book him. If you don't put arses on seats you don't get booked very often. And even when you do, it's just to make up the number of wrestlers it takes to fill the card. Not a very satisfying position to be in. So Tony like a few other wrestlers in the same situation, began promoting his own wrestling shows. He obviously booked himself on his own shows in prime position and would promote himself as main event. But even on his own shows Tony found he couldn't draw a crowd. So he hit on the idea of creating a new and much more colorful character for himself by dressing up in a mountie outfit and re-dubbing himself as 'Captain O'Rourke of the Royal Canadian Mounted Police'. He even bought himself a beautiful, snow white German Shepard Dog, and named him Chinook. Chinook would accompany the gallant Captain O'Rourke to the ring and the fans loved it. If the truth be told the real star was Chinook, but both the Captain and his furry friend were a great team. For the first time in his wrestling career the crowds would cheer at the first sight of the Captain, as they knew he would be accompanied by Chinook. The usual scenario would be for the Captain's opponent to enter the ring first and he would always be a villain. He would prowl and scowl his way around the ring, snarling at the fans and provoking their boos and jeers for all he was worth. Then a loud fanfare of something like 'Rose Marie,' would erupt to herald the entrance of the fan's new hero and his faithful sidekick Chinook. The crowd would go wild. The Captain was in seventh heaven, recognition and appreciation at last. After he and his dog had entered the ring and been introduced, the Captain would strip off his scarlet tunic and get ready for action. Chinook would be taken ringside in the charge of the Captain's ring second. At first the villain and the Captain would wrestle clean. But as time went by, the Captain proved to be just too slick and clever for the villain.

The villain would begin cutting corners and getting rougher and more spiteful. This would provoke a response from the Captain, where he would proceed to give the villain an attitude adjustment. It would always backfire and cause the villain to declare all out war. From then on the poor Captain would be ragged, bagged and shagged. The nasty villain would proceed to do a shithouse shuffle all over the battered and bruised body of the fallen hero to the sound of the booing fans. Then just as the villain slammed the Captain down onto the mat and covered him for the winning pin fall. The Captain with his last dying breath would manage to sound a loud piercing whistle. That would bring Chinook, who had obviously seen every Rin-tin-tin movie leaping into the ring. Barking and snarling at the villain as it jumped and scampered around him. On cue the villain would be terrified which would cause him to leap off the Captain's prostrate body a second before the dreaded 3 count. Backing away and waving his arms about in total confusion. Encouraged by the screaming, cheering fans the Captain would suddenly come back from the dead in a way that would make Lazarus look to his laurels. Taking full advantage of the villain's bewilderment, he would quickly turn the tables on him as he'd slam him down for the 3 count and the victory. Everyone would go wild, except the defeated villain. He would slink back to the dressing room with his tail between his legs while Captain O'Rourke and his furry sidekick Chinook, would evoke the thunderous applause fit for two conquering heroes. This was to become Tony Ansel's tried and tested recipe for success. He would have probably been happy to have milked the scenario until he had used up a succession of as many Chinooks as Roy Rogers had used up Triggers - Until the night he wrestled Big 'Bully' Pye. Bully was the younger Brother of the legendary Jack Pye. A household name in Britain long before wrestling was made even more popular by TV. Bully had a similar attitude and temperament to Bert Assirati. But without Bert's subtlety or charm. On this night, everything had gone great until the very end of the match. When Bully, after subjecting the Captain to a mauling that would have done credit to Genghis Khan. Had finally slammed him down for the pin-fall that would afford him the victory and the gallant Captain his first defeat since before he became a Mountie. But of course, everyone knows what happens next - a loud whistle from Captain O'Rourke - Enter Chinook, leaping and barking - shock, terror and total panic on behalf of Big Bully. Thus giving the Captain those few precious seconds he needs to recover and turn the tables and the decision of the match in his favor. WRONG! Not this time. The devastated Captain whistles, but there's no sign of Chinook. He manages to whistle even louder - same result. Except, now all the fans instead of booing or cheering were laughing. 'What the Hell is happening?!' thinks the Captain. As Bully Pye, not famous for his patience drags the Captain off the mat and head buts him in the face as hard as he can. As the Captain hits the canvas he whistles again. No one knows for sure if he's doing it on purpose to attract his Dog or if it's the sound of the air leaving his body with the force he hits the deck. The fans are not just laughing now, they are roaring. The Captain is still trying to whistle even louder while he's still got teeth in his head to whistle through. Bully, who thinks the fans are laughing at him gets rougher and more dangerous to be around by the second. But still the fans keep laughing. Finally the bully's patience is completely exhausted. He grabs the Captain, hurls him into the mat like a sack of shit. Grabs both of his ankles under his own armpits and turns the Captain over into a Boston-Crab and sits into it so violently that he finds himself sitting on the back of the Captains head. Instead of using his dying breath to summon his Canine savior to the rescue. The Captain used it to submit before his spine is snapped. Still the fans laughed. A totally embarrassed Bully hardly stayed in the ring long enough for the referee to raise his arm in victory. Before he rushed back, red faced to the sanctuary of the dressing-rooms. The Captain was laying face down with his head under the ropes near his own corner and wondered if he would ever be able to walk again. 'This isn't real,' he thinks, 'I must be dreaming. Or I've hurt my head and I'm imagining things.' But the fan's laughter hadn't abated one bit. 'What are they all laughing at – and where's Chinook?' He spots Chinook and now he knows he's dreaming. He shakes his head and tries to refocus his eyes, but the image of Chinook doesn't change. About halfway through the Captain's match with Big Bully a lady who was sitting in a ringside seat near the

Captain's corner, had taken off the fur coat she was wearing and laid it on a vacant chair beside her. It caught Chinook's eye and it was love at first sight! Captain O'Rourke could have whistled till his front teeth melted and it still wouldn't have distracted his Dog. And now as he lay in agony under the bottom rope he watched Chinook in disbelief as it humped away at the lady's fur coat like there was no tomorrow in rhythm to the hysterical laughter of the Captain's faithful fans.

"So now you can see why you can't mention Chinook to Tony Ansel," chuckled Gentleman Geoff, "he fired the fuckin' dog the same night!"

I remember thinking the story was hilarious and everyone in the car was laughing. Even though everyone besides me had heard the story before. "Now promise me you won't forget yourself and say something to Tony about Chinook," Geoff persisted, "'cos he'll probably guess I told you and I don't want to piss him off." A worried frown crossed Geoff's brow, when I replied,

"If Captain O'Rourke doesn't mention my size - I won't mention his dog." I was hoping that Chinook might have been reinstated as I would have liked to have seen him. But after we at last arrived at 'The Atlas Ballroom' I found that there was no chance of a reconciliation between Chinook and Captain O'Rourke. Tony Ansel had even fired Captain O'Rourke and was once again wrestling as Tony Ansel. I always thought he had made a dreadful mistake, if he'd carried on regardless I think that they would have become a bigger draw than ever. Tony Scarlo and I were the first match that night and I remember how strange it felt walking to the ring while wearing boots for the first time as a professional wrestler. 'At least my feet are protected now,' I thought. The match started and was going great. The fans were really receptive to both our fast and furious styles. Although I was still conscious of the strange sensation of wearing a pair of stiff, solid, unyielding boots. I knew that in time I would get used to them. We were still in the first round when I saw an opportunity to throw one of my patented, 'landing on my feet after delivering a rib crunching dropkick.' I leapt into the air like a coiled spring with both my feet exploding into Tony's chest and hurling him backwards across the ring with enough impetus for me to land easily on my feet. But unfortunately, the fact that my boots were so stiff, solid and unyielding they caused me to land on the tips of the toes of each boot. My knees collapsed beneath me and my arse hit my heels with all the force and weight of my body behind it. The impact was so powerful that it completely tore both the soles of my boots away from the stiffened uppers. It felt as though I had broken every toe on both feet. I was sitting on my heels in the middle of the ring and couldn't even move enough to get off them. As I couldn't get back to my feet unaided the match was called to a halt. But even when the referee and my second helped me to my feet I still couldn't walk. I managed, with help to get to the ropes and a huge wrestler who was due to wrestle in the second match came down to ringside to help lift me out of the ring. The fans gave him a great cheer for appearing to be such a good Samaritan, and the silly sod got carried away with himself and attempted to carry me away too. All the way back to the dressing room draped over his shoulder like Santa carrying a sack full of goodies. All I wanted him to do was to put me on my feet and help support me as I limped, hopped or dragged myself along. I found it extremely embarrassing hanging over the shoulder of this stupid, bloody Man Mountain, who was only interested in showing the fans how strong he was. I told him to put me down but as he refused. I began to struggle for all I was worth to push and wriggle my way out of his grasp.

"Stop struggling or I'll drop you!" He growled.

"Put me down and let me walk!" I snarled, but he would not relinquish his hold on me as he plodded on. So I put one hand on his shoulder the other hand on his head and levered myself upright with all of my strength - Just as he walked through a doorway that lead to the dressing room. The top of the doorway hit me in the back of my head and almost decapitated me. As I slumped back down on his shoulder I almost threw up my lunch. I didn't know which end hurt the most, only that I was in bloody agony. Later, in the dressing room after finally succeeding in removing my feet from the solid restrictions of my wrestling boots. My toes all expanded to double their former size and were already turning color. I dressed after washing myself in a hand basin but found that I couldn't put my Cowboy boots on. In order to get to the car after the show was concluded I had to lean on 2 wrestlers while Geoff carried my wrestling bag. The trip back to London seemed to take three times longer than the one to Birmingham had. After a nightmare of monotony, cramped muscles, aching head and neck and throbbing toes we finally drove into London. The nearest spot to where I lived on their way home was the West end. They dropped me off on the corner of Tottenham Court Road and Oxford Street. I had already learned that most wrestlers wouldn't go one yard out of their way for anyone, whether they were injured or not. They had left me about 8 miles from home. I must have stood on the corner for 20 minutes, looking at the other side of the road before I attempted to make my way there by putting one foot in front of the other. It was agony crossing the road. Once I made it I just stood and stared towards Oxford Circus, before attempting to continue my painful journey. I had my wrestling bag in one hand and my Cowboy boots in the other. Even though I was hobbling along in one of the greatest cities in the world, when it was late at night in the 50s you could often walk about in the middle of the West End without hardly ever seeing a single soul - or in this case a taxi. I was loathe to spend my hard earned money on taxi fares. I would always walk home when it was too late to get on a bus or ride on the underground. There were buses that would run all night and occasionally I would be lucky enough to catch one. But they ran so infrequently, that I very rarely bothered with them. But tonight I needed a taxi and the only place I thought I was fairly sure of getting one was at Marble Arch. Which was at the very opposite end of Oxford Street from where I was now limping along. My feet were becoming more numb with pain every time I took another step. Even though the night was chilly, by the time I reached Oxford Circus I was bathed in sweat and my feet were just two lumps of pain. I crossed Regent Street and gritted my teeth as I carried on towards my destination. It felt as though hours had passed by the time I finally reached Marble Arch and hobbled painfully across Park Lane towards 'Speaker's Corner',

"Hey Tarzan, are you still trying to toughen your feet? I thought you said you were going to wear wrestling boots from now on!" Shouted a loud screeching voice. It was Becky 'Big Tits'. One of a number of 'Night Ladies,' that I would usually stop and chat to at this stage of my journey. I told her the whole story of my plight. When I finished, to her delight went on to tell her of the Captain O'Rourke and Chinook saga. By the time I finished the story I was surrounded by close to a dozen of Becky's mates.

"That bleed'n Chinook sounds like some of my bleed'n clients," observed Becky, "Show 'em a bit of fur and they can't bleed'n control themselves!" All the Girls and I laughed which encouraged more randy banter from some of the others. I was suddenly aware of the fact that I had been standing on my bare feet, chatting away with the Girls for quite a while. And although they were still in agony they actually felt more bearable than they had since before I first hurt them. The Girls were just the distraction I had needed. Now that I had once again become aware of them I realized I needed to get home.

"I've got to get a taxi," I told Becky, "thank goodness it's Sunday tomorrow and it'll give my feet a bit of time to recover before work on Monday."

"Come back to my place," invited Becky, "I may not be able to cure 2 feet, but I can certainly take care of a few inches!"

"You live up my way don't you?" asked one of the other Girls, "I've had enough for one night; we can share a taxi if you like."

"WOOOOO!" Said all the other Girls in unison, as the Girl called a taxi and after we informed the cabbie of our destinations, I held the taxi door open for her.

"Hey Tarzan, yer want to be bleed'n careful of that bleed'n Maggie, she can swallow little wrestlers whole!" Shouted Becky Big Tits. "It's 'im yer want to be careful of," shouted one of the others, "bleed'n Welsh are all the bleed'n same - Men's cocks an' Boy's bleed'n pocket money!" I must have heard that saying every time I stopped and talked to these Girls. I wondered if that was standard, or if they had a different one for the English, Irish or Scots. Talking of Scots, I found that the Girl I was sharing the taxi with was named Margaret and was from Glasgow. She now lived just off Portobello Road, about 4 miles from my bed-sit. In contrast to Becky Big Tits, Margaret was quiet and a bit more sober. But as the Taxi pulled up in front of her flat she asked me,

"Do you want to come up for a bit?" and smiled to emphasize her innuendo.

"Not tonight, thank you Margaret." I answered and as she took out her purse to pay the taxi driver, I added, "That's ok Margaret, I'll get the taxi."

"Are you sure?" She asked.

"Positive." I told her.

"Okay," she replied, "I owe you one, are you sure you don't want to come up?" In spite of the feet, I was becoming tempted, but I answered,

"I think I'd better go home and try to relax for a couple of days."

"Well I live in the front flat, second one down from the top floor, come and see me when you're up to it." She said as she got out of the taxi.

"You could have got a bleed'n freebie there!" The taxi driver shouted back to me, as we pulled away from the curb. Not missing a chance to talk about me, I told the taxi driver the reason for my reluctance to partake of Margaret's kind offer.

"She'd a soon took yer bleed'n mind offa yer bleed'n feet!" He retorted unsympathetically. To change the subject, I went on to tell him the Chinook story and must have sat in the taxi outside my bed-sit for another 10 minutes to finish it. When I stepped out of the taxi and paid the fare he told me again,

"You could have got a bleed'n freebie, there yer know!"

****

By the following Monday, although my feet were still very painful the swelling had subsided enough for me to wear my working boots and walk carefully. On the Wednesday of the same week after Bill and I had finished our deliveries, he had gone off driving for Ted Flock. I had been left to mind Ted's office, as both Ted and most of his workers were out collecting wrecks. I was sitting on Ted's chair near the office door, eating peaches out of a large can. I had my feet elevated on Ted's desk, when all of a sudden the door burst open with such force that it hit the side of the desk where I had put my feet and almost knocked me backwards off my chair. I was surprised it hadn't flown off its hinges. It bounced off the desk, flew back and would have slammed closed. But someone outside kicked it, and again it smashed back into the desk. I looked up as a tall heavy set man, walked into the office as though he owned it. I was really pissed off, as I hadn't heard him coming up the stairs from the Street below. The suddenness of his violent and noisy entrance had almost made me jump out of my skin. He looked down his nose at me and it wrinkled as though I stank like a skunk.

"Where's Ted Flock?!" he demanded.

"Why don't you knock and wait to see if you're invited in, instead of kicking the fucking door?!" I challenged and his expression turned to one of fury.

"Do you know who I am?!" he thundered.

"No," I replied, "and I don't want to, so fuck off!"

"I'm the Chief of Police!" he informed me.

"I don't care if you're Chief of the fucking Indians," I told him, "if you want Ted, he's not here, so piss off back to your reservation and phone for a fucking appointment!"

"Do you want to get yourself nicked?!" he threatened.

"For what?" I replied, "You're the one who likes breaking and entering!" He puffed himself up like a Bullfrog and gave me his most vicious glare, I said,

"If you're going to fart, would you mind going outside, I'm trying to eat!" I carried on eating my peaches as though he had already gone. After a brief hesitation he marched out of the office, but once again swung the door back into the desk to punctuate his exit. I don't know how Ted Flock got to hear the story. He could only have got it from my unpleasant visitor. But he came back to the office less than an hour later and wanted to hear my version of what had transpired. I began my account of what had occurred just as Bill returned. So Ted stopped me and asked me to begin again for Bill's benefit. I didn't know if I had done wrong and Ted was mad at me, but I told them both exactly what happened and what was said. To my surprise and relief, Ted laughed so much, I thought he was going to have a heart attack - if he didn't choke first. He kept trying to talk, but was prevented from doing so by renewed fits of giggling. When he finally recovered enough, with tears running down his cheeks he pulled out his wallet, opened it and handed me a 5 pound note.

"Oh you make me bleed'n laugh you do!" He said, "Nah promise me, you'll stay outa 'is way an' if yer see 'im ag'in don't say nuffink!" I knew exactly what I was going to do with that 5 pound note. The very day before, Bill had dropped me off at my favorite kosher bar near Leicester Square for a salt-beef sandwich, while he went off to take care of some private business. We had finished our deliveries for the day and Bill didn't have any more use of my services. So I told him that I would be happy to make my own way back to Paddington Station in time to clock off. Which would save him having to come back and pick me up later. It also meant that I wouldn't have to hang about in one place waiting for him. After I had eaten a couple of sandwiches, washed down with a couple of glasses of hot steaming coffee. I left the kosher bar and hobbled painfully along to Piccadilly Circus, I turned left into Regent Street and came across a Sports shop that I had never noticed before. Very few sports shops carried wrestling boots in those days. Even if they did, it would probably be the little short amateur style. Some of the pros wore them, but I liked the higher, more American looking style. Always the optimist I walked into the shop and asked the first assistant that I saw if they carried wrestling boots. Much to my surprise he told me that they had just 3 pairs left and much to my astonishment, the only pair he showed me that was my size, was white with red trim. They couldn't have matched my cape and trunks better, if I had had them custom made. But of course I couldn't afford them. Not until today anyway. Bill once again agreed to drop me at the Kosher bar while he went off to do whatever it was that he did. Now I owned a new, comfortable pair of boots I could be proud of. In spite of my injured feet I could hardly wait for my next pro match to show them off. I would still wrestle barefoot when I practiced in the Forester's club, as these boots were too precious to me, to risk getting them scuffed. Nevertheless, I took them with me that night when I went to the Forester's just to show them off. After I had finished working out with the weights, I tied the laces together, draped the boots over my shoulder and casually strolled into the wrestling hall. The mats were already in place and liberally speckled with grapplers. Kneeling on the first mat I approached was Bill Smith talking to a face I had seen before but never in the Forester's club. The great Olympic Bronze Medal winner of 1952, Ken Richmond. I could tell that Bill was as thrilled with the presence in our club, of such a famous celebrity as I was with my new boots. But when he said to me in way of introduction,

"Hello Adrian, are you up to a match with Ken Richmond?" I couldn't resist teasing him by looking down my nose at Ken and replying in my haughtiest voice,

"No thank you very much, I'm a professional wrestler - I don't play with amateurs!" Ken Richmond's smile vanished and he came off the mat and after me in a flash - I vanished faster than Ken's smile and much to my relief, found that with all his wrestling prowess and fame he still couldn't run as fast as I could, even though my feet were still very much under par. By the time I snuck back into the wrestling room, I found Ken and Bill still laughing. When Ken spotted me he changed his expression to one of mock menace and shook his finger at me threateningly. I responded by adopting my best imitation of the 'Nature boy' Buddy Rogers' strut.

My bodybuilding and weightlifting was going very well and although I still couldn't come close to the 12 stone club champion, Tommy May's bicep curl or bench press. I was matching him on the squat pound for pound and rep for rep, even though he was the champion and outweighed me by over 20 pounds.

When I had wrestled for Johnny Peters in Hove Town Hall the last time. I had been approached after my match by a short, dark, stocky built Girl. She told me that she had won Black Belts in various styles of Martial Arts and wanted to put her skill to good use by becoming a professional Lady wrestler. She said her name was Chi-chi Dahleb and that she came from Algeria. I was flattered that out of all the wrestlers she had seen performing at Hove. That it was me she asked to teach her to wrestle. Even though I was flattered, I wasn't really interested in teaching anyone as it seemed I still had a lot to learn myself. But I told her where I trained and added that if she was ever up that way I would be pleased to give her a few pointers and even a lesson or two. I had had similar conversations with any number of aspiring young guys who expressed a desire to become wrestlers. Even though Chi-chi was the first Female who had approached me on the subject, I thought no more about it. I would have entirely forgotten the encounter, if not for one night, when I turned up at the Forester's and to my surprise, found her there waiting for me. After we had both changed into our training wear I began teaching her some basic bodybuilding exercises. I noticed with envy, that even though I had very large and muscular legs for my size. Chi-chi's legs were much more massively built than mine were. As it was obvious that I was instructing as well as training we were soon joined by Archie the postman. He was always picking my brains for some magic workout schedule. Never mind how hard he trained, or whatever he did, nothing seemed to work for him. Archie was an extremely hard-gainer and like all the rest of us in those days, he thought that more was better. He worked out harder than a hive of Japanese Beavers on speed but didn't have the slightest hint of muscular development to show for it. His skin was the color and texture of porridge oats and his body was skinny, scrawny and angular. I had told him that the only way to force his muscles to respond was to use heavier and heavier weights. He did, but nothing happened. Then I noticed that he didn't like training his legs and thought that might be part of his problem, so I told him,

"Squat and squat heavy!" He swore he was going to give it all that he'd got. On the night that I was training with Chi-chi, I noticed as he approached that Archie had a thunderous frown on his face and his mouth was set in a thin red stripe.

"Fuck you!" he said in way of greeting.

"That's very nice of you, Archie," I replied, "especially in front of a Lady." Archie gave Chi-chi a double take and then said,

"Er, a – sorry missis." With Chi-chi having such a thick muscular body and very short black hair, it was easy for Archie to mistake her sex at first glance. Especially in a club that was normally men only.

"What's wrong with you anyway?" I asked him, as he was still glaring at me as though I had just kicked him in the shins.

"You and you're bleed'n heavy squats," he replied, "you nearly got me killed!"

"Why, what's wrong, what happened?" I asked him, unable to suppress a smile, as the usually meek and gentle Archie looked so uncharacteristically hostile. Archie told me that he had taken my advice so seriously that he decided to squat as heavy as possible on an everyday basis. On his rounds as a postman he had noticed a road works in progress. Workmen had put up barriers across a number of upright stands, to prevent anybody falling into the holes they had dug in the road. Archie thought that a pair of the upright stands would make an excellent set of squat racks. He could set it up in his back garden, load them with a very heavy barbell and have them at his disposal any time he was at home. So later that night when no one was about at the road works, Archie crept around there and 'borrowed' a couple. He took them home, set them up and was in the squatting business. Soon his legs would be rippling with huge, firm muscles, or so he thought. He told me that he loaded the barbell with over 300 pounds. For me that would not have been heavy. But for Archie's long, skinny, scrawny legs, it was ridiculous. He got his shoulders under the bar and with great effort he managed to lift it off the stands. But as he attempted his first rep he realized that he had vastly overestimated his strength and squatting ability. As he was attempting to replace the heavy barbell back onto the stands, a neighbor's dog ran into Archie's back garden and watched his efforts with interest. Archie was wearing a pair of baggy legged shorts – and they must have been short! Because as he struggled to rid himself of his very heavy burden, his balls that were dangling about a foot below the hemline of his shorts attracted the dog's attention. With tail a-wagging, it trotted up and started licking them. Archie screamed and tried to kick the dog away. But the dog would not be denied and once it got a taste it kept coming back for more. Soon poor Archie was performing a very strange looking dance. In his attempt to kick the dog and rid himself of the heavy weight he accidentally knocked one of the stands over with one end of the barbell. Now there was nowhere to put the weight. Archie panicked and began to scream. But the dog, who must have thought that they were having a very jolly game, alternated licking Archie's balls with barking and snapping at them. Archie danced faster and screamed louder, but the louder he screamed the louder the dog barked. So no one seemed to hear Archie. Finally exhausted he fell flat on his back while still holding the weight and claimed that his neck landed across the barbell and knocked him out. His wife came out of his house to call him for his dinner, just as he was regaining consciousness.

Poor Archie had to try to explain to her, why he was laying on the grass with his legs wide apart allowing the neighbor's dog to lick his balls.

I had felt more than a little embarrassed by Archie's vivid and very detailed description of his adventure in the presence of Chi-chi. But she responded by saying,

"I hope it was a girl-dog Archie!" My own advice to any aspiring bodybuilder is - don't be a hard-gainer - unless you are particularly fond of dogs.

Later on the wrestling mat, I found that I had to calm Chi-chi down, as she proved to be downright dangerous. I explained to her that if she wanted me to teach her anything it would be better for both of us, if she wasn't trying to snap my fingers or sweep my legs from under me while I was doing it. After I had succeeded in at least tempering, if not curbing her enthusiasm, Chi-chi proved to be an excellent student. And to my surprise and delight, showed me a few moves that were entirely new to me. So 'me' teacher - 'you' student, actually evolved into a trade off and I ended up learning as much as I taught Chi-chi. Although the hold she demonstrated that made its greatest impression on me at the time, proved to be of little use in a real fight. Due to the fact that it would be extremely difficult to maneuver someone into a position, where you could apply it in the first place. But that fact alone turned out to be the greatest lesson I had learned so far in my quest to become a great wrestler. It made me realize that it doesn't matter how many holds, or throws you know. Unless you have mastered the art of positioning an opponent, you can't apply them in the first place. So I realized that the art of wrestling is the art of positioning. Then I realized that that must also apply to many other martial arts type sports, including boxing. In my short but eventful pro boxing career, even though I may have had more physical attributes than almost everyone I fought. I would put so much effort into thrashing thin air. While my skilled adversary would almost casually and effortlessly clean my clock. So it seemed that the art of boxing, was at least partially the art of positioning too, an art that I obviously hadn't mastered.

I took one of my frequent pilgrimages to Brixton to once again beseech Jack Dale that I was ready. I waited for and received the inevitable speech - "You are not old enough, big enough or experienced enough!" I had heard that every time I had asked for a start. It was now time to bring out the big guns,

"I am already wrestling professionally for the independent promotions, Mr. Dale," I told him smugly, "so I must be old enough, big enough and experienced enough."

"What the bloody hell did you do that for?!" Demanded Jack. I was taken aback, as that was not the reaction I expected, or had hoped for. "Now you can never be an amateur champion after wrestling for those bloody cowboys, you've lost your bloody amateur status you bloody fool!" I had wanted to lose my bloody amateur status as much as I had wanted to lose my bloody virginity. Leave bloody school and leave the bloody pit. But it didn't look like a bloody good time to mention it. Oh well, back to the bloody drawing board. I knew by now that Jack Dale, as well as being impressed by amateur champion wrestlers admired both champion bodybuilders and weightlifters. When I had visited Brynmawr that November in 1958, for my Brother's wedding I heard that there was an upcoming 'Mr. South-Wales' and a weightlifting competition being held in a town close to Brynmawr. So I decided that Kid 'Mr. South Wales' Jonathan might just be the thing to redeem me in Jack Dale's good books. On the day of the contest I was accompanied to the hall by my Brother Ter and my old training partner the former Mr. South Wales, Colin Thomas. And just like old times we all had a workout together in the dressing room, where weights had been supplied for a pre-contest warm-up for the contestants. While warming up I had the opportunity to check out the opposition. After fair and careful scrutiny I came to the conclusion that if there had been a phone handy, I would have been justified in calling Jack Dale and informing him that I was now Mr. South Wales. No one came within a mile of my physical condition. When the show began, they started with a pre-contest line-up. Everyone was compared with each other by standing on stage facing the audience and the judges. Then turning to the right, then to the left, then with our backs, while we were judged in a relaxed stance. Later would come the individual posing routines. Lesser physiques would be eliminated and the rest would go on into the finals. To break up the pre-contest line up from the posing section, they would have the weightlifting contest. Then to break up the individual posing routines from the Mr. South Wales final, there would be a posing exhibition by guest poser and former Mr. Wales, Albert Williams. He was in terrific shape and in my opinion the only person in the building that night who could have given me a run for my money. At first, with tensions running high, none of the contestants had wanted to talk to each other. But after the pre-contest line up had concluded and we were all back in the dressing room everyone seemed to relax. Almost all of them began to gather around me and vie for my attention. It was as though they had already agreed with my assessment and conceded that I was the favorite. But true to form - I always have to go the extra mile, to justify the attention I was receiving. I was soon showing the other contestants my photos in the bodybuilding magazines, that 'I just happened, to have with me.' And then boast that I was a professional wrestler. When the weightlifting began I excused myself and went to join Ter and Colin, who were already in the audience watching. As I sat down a man sitting directly in front of me turned around and said to me,

"You look great, you've got it won." I gasped, as I recognized him and was gratified to see a very prominent and ugly scar between his lower lip and his chin.

"Hello Sean," I replied, "do you still work in Acton Bolt Factory?"

"Yes," he said, "I'm a foreman now." Sean and I had never spoken to each other again after I had kicked him in the mouth. I had often caught him staring at me while we were at work, but he had never said a word and neither had I.

"What are you doing here, are you in the weightlifting competition?" I asked,

"No," he answered, "I'm here to support my training partner who's lifting in the heavy division, he's gonna be hard to beat." We both went back to watching the competition. Occasionally Sean would turn around and make some comment related to what was going on, on stage. When the heavyweight contest began Sean pointed out which contestant was his partner and then really got into it. He must have strained harder than his training partner did as he performed his lifts. By the time the contest was over Sean was bathed in sweat and totally exhilarated by his friend's victory. He whooped and hollered, shook hands with Colin, Ter and myself as though he had won himself and he had us to thank for his success. Sean didn't seem to be a bad chap at all. But I couldn't help wondering what would happen, if I had related the story of what had occurred between Sean and me, outside the Bolt Factory to Ter, while Sean was in range of Ter's wicked left fist. When I returned to the dressing room to prepare for the individual posing which would determine who would advance to the finals, I had a group of officials and judges waiting for me.

"We have reason to believe that you are a professional wrestler," Accused their spokesman, "and as you should know, you can't compete in an amateur competition, if you are a professional athlete." It would be one of the hardest things for my ego to tolerate. To plead not guilty to being a professional wrestler and a professional athlete. But I looked the accuser straight in the eye and lied,

"No, I am not a professional wrestler yet, but I'm going to turn professional after I've won the Mr. South Wales title."

"You told the other contestants that you were already a professional wrestler." Insisted the spokesman.

"They must have misunderstood what I said." I insisted right back. I could tell they were not convinced, but they still allowed me to remain in the competition. When it was my turn to go on stage and perform my posing routine I was surprised how out of place I felt. I loved showing off while I was in the ring wrestling. But here on stage in a bodybuilding contest where I was supposed to be showing off, I felt like a spare prick at a wedding. After I ran through a series of poses and couldn't think of anything else to do, I smiled at the audience, shrugged my shoulders and walked off the stage.

"You should have bowed to the judges, before you left the stage!" I was reminded gleefully, by one of the other contestants as I passed them in the wings. When the posing was concluded I was gratified to see the disappointment on all the other contestant's faces when my name was read out as one of the 8 finalists. I made sure to watch Albert Williams' guest posing routine to see whether it would give me a few last minute pointers, before I rushed back to prepare for the big showdown of the day. Where I would be crowned the new Mr. South Wales. Well actually, I wasn't crowned the new Mr. South Wales. I did place, although I wasn't told officially what place that was. I didn't come first, second or even third. The winner was as soft and smooth as a Babies arse, with no muscle tone at all. In spite of my disappointment, I had to laugh at one of the other contestants when he commented, that he had looked exactly like the new Mr. South Wales - before he had ever began bodybuilding. He had started training with weights because he didn't like being 'a big fat bastard'.

"You should have won!" I was told by another disappointed contestant and suggested that my failure was probably due to my lack of post posing etiquette. Personally I think it was due to my big mouth and overly inflated ego. If I had left the bodybuilding magazines in my bag and kept my mouth shut about professional wrestling, I would have been a certainty to win. I have always enjoyed watching bodybuilding contests and I've attended dozens of them since that time. But I was never tempted to enter another one myself.

****

Out of the blue, I got a letter from Dad, to say he was coming up to spend a long weekend with me. I met him off the train after I had finished work for the day, on a Friday evening. Dad said he would be staying with me until the following Tuesday, it would be a very long weekend indeed.

"I've come to check and see how you're getting on." He told me. A cheap holiday would have been a lot closer to the truth. Normally, Dad would have stayed with Auntie Pat, but he would never be forgiven for 'the letter'. So I had to suffer the consequences. It was bad enough that I had to smuggle him into my bed-sit, as I was not officially allowed visitors. But as Dad entered my bed-sit for the first time with his suitcase still in his hand, he just stood and gazed around the room. His face etched in exaggerated horror and said,

"Uh! And you left home for this?!" I felt like saying, "No, I left home for two reasons, one to become a wrestler and the other to get the hell away from you!" But I bit my lip and didn't say a word. At bedtime, Dad got undressed and asked me if I wanted to sleep at the top or at the bottom of the bed. As that was the only way we both would have been able to fit. I told him that I would sleep in the chair.

"There'll be plenty of room if you sleep at the bottom." He argued, but I was adamant. I hadn't slept in a bed with another person since I was 7 years old and had shared a bed with my Brother, before we had left Queen Street. The thought of sharing a bed with another man was totally repugnant to me. Even though the man was my Father. Or in this case, especially as the man was my Father. I slept as best I could sitting upright in an uncomfortable wooden chair, for the 3 nights that Dad stayed in London. Saturday after work I took Dad to The British Museum, which is a place we both enjoy very much. My favorite section contained the Elgin Marbles, Dad's favorite was the huge collections of items from Ancient Egypt, from giant stone statues, to mummies, to jewelry and Scarab Beetles. This of course, gave him the excuse to get on the subject of Moses and Israelites in the house of bondage -

"With all those mummies about, don't you mean the house of bandage?" I suggested, hoping my flippancy would divert another sermon. But Dad being Dad, he wouldn't be diverted. So, as we left the British Museum, I devised another plan to try to change the subject. Dad had professed that he'd wanted to see how I'd lived since I'd left home, so I decided to show him. A cup of coffee in the 2 I's would be nice, and at least if we were still on an Exodus I wouldn't be able to hear about it in the noisy confines of the Rock 'n' Roll dungeon. We had just got to the bit about the sinful idol worshiping Israelites drinking ground down golden calf dust. When in desperation I purposely lead Dad into an ambush,

"Hello Guv' wouldga like a good time?!" Demanded the tall Redhead with the short black leather skirt. Dad staggered back as though he had been bludgeoned as the girls began to surround us and try to cut us off at the pass. As he recovered, he seemed to press his chin into his chest, hunch his shoulders and plough forward through the Valley of Death, pummeled with cries of,

"Two quid fer a short time, or, I'll give yer a hand job fer ten bob!"

"Oh, terrible - terrible!" I heard Dad say, as he quickened his pace to a trot. I was really tempted to tell him, that the prices the

Ladies had quoted were not terrible - terrible at all, but was the going rate in Soho. He may have said 'terrible - terrible' again, while we drank our coffee in the 2 I's. But with the incredible noise going on all around us I was blissfully oblivious. Regent Park Zoo the next day must be a nice change from the Tabernacle, I thought. I think Dad enjoyed it, but as it was a Sunday he made sure that he didn't show it too much. Monday I had to go to work while Dad shopped for presents for Mam and Pam. Tuesday morning with a sigh of relief I said goodbye at Paddington Station, before walking further down the end of platform one, to clock in. I remember thinking, how much I appreciated getting my bed back and also remembered how much I had appreciated that same bed the first night I had ever slept in it after spending a few nights sleeping rough.

One night in the Forester's, after I had finished with the weights I went over to the Wrestling room and found that the few wrestlers present were sitting on the mat talking. I said hello to everyone in general and a couple of them nodded a response, but were caught up in an argument about something or other, so I basically got ignored. Butch seemed to have the most to say. I walked away from him and the others and practiced break-falling with the hope that I might attract one of them to come over and wrestle with me. As no one did, after I had been throwing myself around the mat for about 20 minutes, I got bored and decided to have an early night. I walked over to Butch and the others and asked them if they wanted me to help them put the mats away, before I left. I made a point of directing my offer to Butch, who carried on talking as though I wasn't even there.

'How rude.' I thought, but said, "Oh well, if you don't want my help, you can do it yourselves." And I left to have a shower. I had finished showering and was sitting down on a bench drying my feet with my towel when Butch burst into the dressing room and got right into my face and screamed,

"How come you left me on my own to put all the wrestling mats away?!!!!"

"I didn't leave you on your own," I protested, "you had some of the other wrestlers with you, and I asked you if you wanted me to help you. But you ignored me and just kept on yapping with the others!"

"Don't give me that," he roared, "you never spoke to me once, and then I saw you sneaking out of the wrestling room while I was on my own putting all the mats away!" As that was the most blatant untruth I told him, "You are a fucking liar Butch - I - OUCH!" I never got a chance to finish what I was going to say as Butch's big fist exploded right into my face. It slammed my back into the wall behind me. I used it as a rebound and exploded myself right off the bench, and took the 230 pound plus, Butch with me across the room where I smashed him into the wall opposite. I grabbed him by the throat with my left hand and hammered punch after punch into Butch's big fat, unprotected face. Hands reached for me from all sides as other members who were in the dressing room, tried in vain to halt the storm of blows that was battering the helpless, hopeless Butch. I shrugged them away and continued. I was hardly aware of someone leaping on to my back in an attempt to stem the violence I was handing out. And I launched myself backwards into the wall behind me to rid myself of my new assailant before diving forward with renewed vigor to punish Butch. I tore him up and flung him into a corner, where I crashed down on him and again began battering his face. This time alternately with both fists. He was screaming like a girl until he lost consciousness. Then I lost interest and got off of him. Only to find most of the members helping the Gym instructor up from where he had also been laying unconscious after I had slammed him into a metal radiator to shake him off my back. I was very sorry about that as he was a nice guy, but I didn't even remember doing it until after I was reminded later. I walked into the shower room and gave my hands and face a quick swill, before going back to recommence dressing. I had no sooner sat down when Butch walked by and stopped near the exit and said,

"You haven't heard the last of this, I'll get you again!" I looked at him; he was clutching his clothes to his chest and hadn't even attempted to wash the blood off that was all over his face, and now dripping on the clothes he was carrying. I had heard what he said, but I asked him again in a loud voice, so that no one present would blame me if I belted him again.

"What did you say?!"

"You heard," he replied, "I'm going to get you for that!"

"If you'll just wait until I get my kicking boots on, I'll come with you right now," I told him, "but I hope you do better next time, or you'll be wasting my time you useless, pathetic pussy!"

I'll see you again!" He insisted and left. By the time I had dressed and left the Forester's Club Butch had had plenty of time to make tracks. I did take a halfhearted stroll in the direction that he normally went when he left the gym, but I didn't see him and I didn't really care. He had proved much to my surprise to be a very poor fighter in spite of his size and formidable appearance. Just as Jack, the giant Gypo had a few years earlier. I puzzled for days for a reason why Butch, who I normally got on great with would suddenly get so fractious. I was sure I hadn't done anything to him. The only thing I could think of was the amount of enthusiasm I had displayed when telling everyone about my best friend Peter. Of how we used to practice wrestling for hours. The fact that he would soon be joining me in London and the plans we had made to Work, train and wrestle together. I had in the past said that Butch, was my favorite wrestling opponent in the club. Maybe now that Peter was coming to join me in London Butch was becoming jealous of being usurped. A couple of months went by before I saw Butch again and when I did, it was when he once again began attending the club. I knew him for many more years to come but never once in all that time did he ever even mention the incident I have just described. It was as though it had never happened. But even though everything seemed to go back to normal, I never really felt right about him again.

In the meantime I had met Johnny Milo one Saturday afternoon in the YMCA. I told him how much I had enjoyed his match with Johnny Kovacs in Newport, during the first live wrestling show I had ever seen. He told me that he and one of his Brothers Tommy Milo, who was also a wrestler owned a small Mexican style restaurant nearby and invited me to join him there later after I had finished my workout. 'The Acapulco' was in a little side street on the other side of Tottenham Court Road, and Tommy greeted me as I entered as though he was expecting me. Tommy was a slightly larger version of his Brother Johnny. I was sitting with them having a chat over coffee and they told me of their oldest Brother Milo Popocopolis. Milo had been known in

Britain as 'The Golden Greek'. They also told me that Milo was now a wrestling promoter and that I should pop along to his restaurant which was in Soho Street and introduce myself to him. They didn't need to tell me twice. I thanked them for the coffee and their advice and was on my way. I asked a waitress if Milo was about as soon as I entered the restaurant, and after checking with her boss, she ushered me upstairs to his office. Milo was a larger version still of his two younger Brothers. He stood up from behind his desk and offered me his hand before inviting me to sit down. I liked him right away. In spite of an air of aloof dignity he proved to be very friendly and chatty when the subject of wrestling came up. After telling him about the match I had witnessed featuring his youngest Brother Johnny, he asked me whether I had ever seen him wrestle. Reluctantly, I had to admit that I hadn't. But he soon remedied that by setting up an old 8 mm movie projector, and rolling some old silent black and white films of himself in action. The style of the wrestling seemed fairly slow in comparison with most of the wrestling that I had experienced. But very enjoyable all the same, and even more so, due to the fact that I was able to discuss what we were looking at with one of the participants. Milo seemed to be very impressed by my knowledge of American wrestlers. Especially the early ones and he called to the waitress that had brought me to his office to serve us both coffees while we talked. Before I left him he gave me a match on an upcoming show he was promoting in Hastings.

I can't remember who drove the car I traveled to Hastings in. But two of the other passengers were Gunga Singh, a Sikh from the Punjab and Mike Dimitri, a Greek wrestler and friend of Milo's. I vaguely remembered Mike Dimitri being a bit on the aloof side when I introduced myself to him. After we had reached the venue and I had began changing Gunga, who was sharing the room with, asked me what I had ever done to Mike Dimitri that had made him so hostile towards me.

"What do you mean?" I asked him, "I've never met, or heard of him till today." Now it was Gunga's turn to look surprised and he told me,

"Do you remember when we stopped for refreshments?"

"Yes of course," I replied, "Why?"

"When you got out of the car and began walking towards the café," Gunga told me, "Mike said to everyone who was still sitting in the car - look at him, just look at him. The arrogant, cocky little upstart who the hell does he think he is? Look at the way he's dressed, all that black leather - just look at him! One of the other wrestlers said to him, "He's okay Mike, just a bit young that's all." Then Mike said, "Young! He wouldn't have got to be as old as he is if he were my kid, I would have drowned him at birth!"

I was as mystified as Gunga, but I certainly wouldn't lose any sleep over it.

"I haven't got a clue why he doesn't like me, Gunga," I told him, "and I couldn't care less, most people I've met don't like me. But at least they usually get to know me well enough first, so I can give them a good reason." Gunga thought that was funny but it made me realize, that I had never been bothered whether people liked me or not. I've always liked myself enough to compensate for that. I wrestled a guy they called the 'Irish Whip' that night, his name was Peter Kelly. He was an absolute riot, he had me laughing so hard in the dressing room before the match that I was almost afraid to get into the ring with him. I would only have to look at him and I would laugh until my stomach hurt. I had to literally beat the living crap out of him in the ring just to keep a straight face.

****

When we got back to London that night, I was dropped off at the Oval Station but too late to ride the Tube, so as usual I began to walk home. I reached Marble Arch, where I took a break by chatting to Becky Big-Tits and company,

"Oi Tarzan," she shrilled, as she saw me approach, "Where've yer bin tonight?"

"Hastings," I replied and then quickly added, before one of them got it in, "earning some boy's pocket-money."

"Got any yer wanna spend?" she inquired.

"No, not tonight thank you, Becky Big-Tits." I replied, "I've been physically abused enough already trying to earn it." As the bawdy banter continued we were suddenly interrupted by

Margaret, who had been talking to another girl a few yards away,

"C'mon Tarzan," she said, "It's my turn to get the taxi tonight."

"That's right, piss off then," shouted the other girl at Margaret, "can't stand the fucking truth can you?!" A taxi pulled up in front of us and I was whisked in before I could protest or consent and as the door was slammed behind us I looked through the window in time to see the other girl giving us both, a farewell two finger salute.

"What's wrong with that silly bitch?" I asked Margaret.

"Oh Cassie's okay," answered Margaret, "she's just a bit young that's all."

'Where have I heard that before?' I thought. When the taxi stopped in front of the building where Margaret lived I wasn't asked if I wanted to go upstairs with her, she just stepped out, paid the cabbie and said to me, "Come on!" So I went. I wondered what kind of flat a Girl of Margaret's profession would live in. It turned out to be quite nice but nothing spectacular. One main room - with a bed. A tiny separate kitchen and what I liked about it best, was a small private toilet and bathroom. In both of the bed-sits I had lived in so far the toilet and bathroom had to be shared with other people who lived in the house.

"Want something to drink, Tarzan?" She asked me as she took off her coat.

"A coffee would be nice." I replied, I took her coat and hung it on the door.

"Sure you wouldn't like something stronger? She asked, as she slipped her skirt down, stepped out of it and threw it on a chair, "I've got some scotch."

"No thanks, coffee will be fine." I said, trying my best not to stare. Margaret smiled that knowing smile and began unbuttoning her blouse, as she turned and gave me a chance to admire her backside as she walked into the kitchen. Her high heeled shoes, stockings and knickers, were as black as Margaret's long hair and her thighs were a contrasting milky white. She caught me in the act of ogling and she said smiling,

"Make yourself comfortable; take your clothes off if you want to." That statement caused me a little brain turbulence, as I didn't really know what to expect. Did she think of me as one of her clients or was she offering a freebie, as the cabbie had suggested on the last occasion I had shared a taxi with Margaret? Either way, I wasn't totally comfortable with the offer. I wouldn't pay money for sex for two reasons. Firstly, if I had to pay for it that would mean that the other person would be doing it for the money, not because she really wanted to, and my ego won't except that. Then secondly, I would be too mean to want to pay for it anyway, as money was too hard to come by. If she was doing it out of gratitude, in my books it would amount to the same thing. There was also a third reason, but at that time I hadn't really admitted it to myself. I was jolted out of my reverie by Margaret, who called from the kitchen doorway,

"Why don't you make yourself comfortable?!" I caught my breath as I saw she was only wearing her shoes and stockings. 'Maybe I should have chosen the scotch'. I mused. 'Whatever I do next is going to be embarrassing,' I thought, 'if I'm standing here naked when she comes out of the kitchen, or if I'm still fully dressed. - 'I know what I'll do, I'll strip down to the briefs I'm wearing, courtesy of Lon of London.' In fact the only underwear I owned I had been given by Lon, the physique photographer and I knew I looked good in them. So what was I worried about? Margaret would not be the first girl that I had shown them to. I undressed and sat on the arm of a chair and was posing furiously, while trying to look relaxed as Margaret walked in carrying my coffee. She stopped gave me an appraising look up and down, smiled and gave me a low Wolf whistle. At first, that gave my ego a tremendous boost. But then I had to spoil it for myself by wondering if that was one of her stocks in trade. Did she really find me appealing, or was that just a part of her professional act? Instead of handing me the coffee she placed the cup on a bedside table, between a large brass alarm clock and a small bedside lamp. She turned it on before walking to the entrance of the bed-sit to turn off the main light. 'She knows I like to watch her walking around the room,' I thought, 'I wonder if that's an instinct they develop?'

"Come and get it!" she called, as she walked back towards the bed.

'I hope she means the coffee!' I thought.

As I was walking home later, I felt utterly disgusted. Not with

Margaret, but with myself. I had been sitting with her on the bed sipping my coffee, when she put her hand on the front of my briefs. I almost jumped through the window, and Margaret came very close to wearing the coffee. I'd felt as though she had electrocuted me.

"What's wrong?!" She yelled, "Did you hurt it wrestling?!" The only thing I was not ashamed of in retrospect, was the fact that I didn't take advantage of the excuse she had just handed me, by pretending that I was hurt. although my excuse was just as feeble.

"No, I'm not hurt - you just took me by surprise that's all!" All the way home I kept on thinking, 'what a bloody ludicrous statement - I'm almost naked, sharing a bed with a naked Lady and I had told her 'I was taken by surprise' – oh God, what an idiot, what must she be thinking now?' I had then claimed that I didn't want to impose on her. I realized that she had been working all night. And now she would probably prefer to relax rather than indulging in what she did for a living. But she assured me that she did want to indulge. Although I had never been interested in any kind of sex with someone who wasn't willing. I didn't mind trying to coax someone if I thought that they really wanted to, even if they initially said "no." Most Girls I found in those days would pretend not to want to indulge at first, until you gave them the excuse to consent. Now I was being coaxed and I was desperately trying to think of an excuse not to consent without hurting Margaret's feelings.

"You've been doing that all day," I told her gallantly, "Wouldn't you prefer to take a rest, I would imagine you're sick of it by now."

"It's not the same thing," she assured me, "that's just business. You should see the state of some of the prats that I have to put up with, and I don't enjoy what I'm doing unless I take a fancy to someone." I can't say that attempting to imagine 'some of the prats that she had to put up with' did very much for my libido - There you go, I'm making excuses again! But we carried on talking in the same vein, until eventually she gave me a way out by saying that 'I was probably too tired after wrestling and maybe it would be best if I went home to rest,'

"But don't be a stranger," she made me promise, "and come

back when you feel better and in the right mood."

'I could never be too tired for sex.' I told myself. But as I obviously hadn't proven it, I wasn't really convinced. I got dressed and as I was about to leave, Margaret came with me to the door, gave me a friendly kiss on the cheek and said,

"I really do fancy you, you know, so please come back soon."

'Yeah, and then what?!' I thought. As I walked on I thought of my two fears as a child. My terror of heights and my embarrassment and fascination with sex. The first I tackled head on by forcing myself to climb the most dangerous and daunting cliffs and ravines. I never got used to it and I never, ever lost my fear, but at least I did my best. I could force myself to climb a cliff. But how could a boy who didn't have the experience, the guts, or the confidence to go all the way, force himself to have sex? My answer all these years, had been to lie to all my peers until I had made myself into a sexual legend in their eyes. And in so doing, had managed to put reality to the back of my mind so successfully, that I had come to believe my own lies and my own fake legend. Now I felt sick to my guts. I realized that I was still trying to make excuses to myself when I was, in fact just an empty braggart. A loud mouthed buffoon who was all talk and no action, when it came to what was important to me. As if I could hide my inferiority from the only one who really cared - me! 'If a little child can overcome his terror,' I thought, 'I can do the same now.' And I did go back to the foot of the mountain - namely to Margaret's flat. But unfortunately with the same result, I was a no go. What I came to realize and finally admitted to myself was, that with Margaret I felt that I was totally out of my depth. Here was a Girl who was having sex with God knows how many men, God knows how many times a day. Men who knew what they were doing, and I with no experience. What the Hell could I possibly do, to make an impression on her after that?! I found out, that Margaret had given birth to a Daughter when she was barely 15, who was now being looked after by her parents in Glasgow. And that Cassie, the Girl that Margaret had been arguing with, was Margaret's younger Sister. Cassie was an unpleasant and spiteful person. Very snide and arrogant. How Margaret could put up with her constant sarcasm I'll never know. But I also knew, as in my own case that Margaret could be very patient. I was walking around Portobello Road Market one Saturday afternoon, when I met Margaret on her way to do some shopping further up the road. I asked her if she wanted me to accompany her and help her carry her groceries, but she said,

"No, I won't be out long, why don't you go up to the flat and wait for me?" So I did. I let myself in and began to walk across the room when I almost collided with Cassie, who had just come barging out of the bathroom. Her hair was done up in a towel turban. I almost didn't recognize her at first as she had beautiful long black hair like her Sister Margaret. That was the only resemblance between the two sisters. Margaret was very neat and petite, where as Cassie was quite statuesque. Margaret always had a ready smile while Cassie seemed to have a permanent scowl.

"Hello Cassie," I said, "fancy almost bumping into you."

"My name is Cassandra!" She snarled, deepening her scowl.

"Named for King Priam's most beautiful Daughter no doubt." I replied in an effort to avoid any conflict.

"What the fuck do you want Tarzan? She scowled, "Maggie's not here!"

"I know," I told her, "I just met her on her way to the shops and she asked me to come up and wait for her." She just grunted and walked over to the electric fire and turned it on. Then she stood a wooden clothes horse in front of it before going back into the bathroom and returning with some damp underwear, which she placed on the clothes horse to dry. I pretended not to notice what she was doing, but I caught my breath and she caught me catching it. As I couldn't help noticing the size of the bra that she had just placed before the fire. To say I was impressed would be an understatement and then some. I had never noticed until now what a spectacular figure Cassandra had. As if reading my thoughts she let the grey silk dressing gown slide apart enough to confirm what the triple D sized bra suggested. Just then Margaret walked in. The look on her face would have done credit to Cassandra on a bad PMS day. But in spite of that I found it impossible to tear my eyes away from Cassandra's huge tits. Cassandra must have read Margaret's expression the same way I did, as she said to her with the most beautiful, but mischievous smile,

"Don't worry Maggie, nothing's going on. Don't you know that your Tarzan is a bleed'n Wooly Woofter?!" I burst out laughing. I had never heard that expression before and thought that once again my Welsh heritage was being made sport of. 'Wooly Woofter' indeed. I could just picture myself as a cross between me as a kid and a little furry Marmot like creature scurrying all over the rocks on the wild Welsh mountainside. Rather than a majestic Welsh Mountain Goat that I had been referred to as in the past. Margaret's expression didn't soften, in fact her frown deepened to the extreme and that made me laugh even more.

"You do like Girls don't you?!" Pleaded Margaret anxiously. 'What the fuck has that got to do with it?' I thought, but all I could do was laugh. I looked at Cassandra who was laughing as hard as I was. She had taken the towel from her hair and as it framed her face she looked absolutely gorgeous. The transformation when she laughed from her usual angry scowl was almost as astounding as her now fully exposed naked breasts that were wobbling with mirth. 'What a shame she's such a fucking bitch,' I thought.

As my infrequent visits to Margaret became less frequent still. I found myself spending more time talking to Jean after I left the Forester's each night, and eventually we began going out together again. I probably would have asked her out sooner, but once again she was being heavily chaperoned by her 'friend' Maureen. Although it was a huge sigh of exasperation accompanied by a roll of Jean's eyes. As Maureen was approaching us one night, that made me realize that Jean was as frustrated by Maureen's continual presence as I was. That prompted me to risk rejection and make a move on her. I was welcomed back with open arms, which unfortunately for me were not the limbs I was most interested in opening, but nevertheless I persevered.

****

I was within a few blocks of home very late one night, after an evening of lifting weights, wrestling and spending time with Jean. Suddenly my nostrils twitched and the back of my neck prickled as I picked up a scent that I recognized but couldn't readily place. I had only been very vaguely aware of a few men who were walking up the road ahead of me, and in the same direction that I was heading. I was gradually overtaking them, due partly to the fact that I was a fairly fast walker and that they seemed to be having a heated discussion, and were continually stopping to make some point. A few seconds before I recognized the culprit, I remembered where I had smelled that overpoweringly sickly scent before - Joseph Mackey! I had forgotten until that moment that Mackey always reeked of some foul, sweet smelling deodorant that he must have continually bathed in. If he wore it to mask an unpleasant body, or foot odor it certainly worked well. But how much of an improvement it made had to be in question, as I found the stink quite revolting. There were four of them and by now I was close enough to detect by their accents that they were all Irish. I knew without a doubt that if I was recognized by Mackey there would be trouble. How I wished that he had been on his own. I could have easily avoided any risk of contact with them by either slowing my pace a little. Or by turning left down any one of the side streets that would have taken me the opposite way around the same city block and wouldn't have lengthened my journey by any more than a few yards. In fact, for a change it wasn't unusual for me to do that anyway. But me being me, I knew I couldn't take the easier and safer way out. If I was lucky enough to walk by them without Mackey noticing, or recognizing me that would be fine, I could live with that. But it was not in my nature to alter what I was going to do, even if it meant escaping aggravation. I have been that way all my life. A prime example was walking to Sunday school as a young kid. There were two ways I could go there from home, one way was just a little shorter distance than the other. On the shorter journey I would often find myself face to face and threatened by a big, black Giant Schnauzer, who would rush towards me whenever I passed the house it lived in and bark and snarl right into my face. Which in those days was only a little above the level of the slobbering, noisy jaws of the vicious looking dog. I would be lying, if I said that I wasn't frightened of the dog. And on the odd occasion that I passed by the house and the dog wasn't about, I would be both relieved and happy to go on my way unthreatened. No one would have been any the wiser if I had chosen the safer route - except me! Mam may have raised an idiot, but not a coward. There was a fair chance I thought, that Mackey might not recognize me. Due to the fact that the last time we had faced each other I had weighed 35 pounds more than I did that night. But I had hardly drawn level with the four Irishmen, when Mackey turned and shouted at me, "Hey, you!"

"What do you want Mackey?!" I demanded, matching his expression with a disgusted grimace of my own.

"I've been looking for you!" He roared and surprised me by marching aggressively towards me. I dropped my gym bag and turned to face him, which stopped him immediately in his tracks. But he stood his ground and seemed to raise himself on his toes above me, trying to make himself appear even larger than he was.

"Well you've found me now, so what are you going to do about it, you stupid Irish twat?! I answered.

"Hey, we're Irish too!" Barked the largest of his companions and all four were now gathered in a semicircle in front of me.

"Your problem, not mine," I told him, "anyway; I'm talking to him not you!"

"Well it's your problem now," he growled, "and we don't take kindly to you English badmouthing the Irish!"

"Hey, I won't take kindly to having to spend the rest of the week picking Mackey's teeth out of my fist." I replied, "But that's life - mind you, I suppose I'll have to catch him first. He's good at picking fights and then either running away, or getting someone else to do his fighting for him." I looked Mackey in the face to see if it had started doing the itchy-twitchy tango. 'No go yet,' I thought, but I was just warming up.

"Carol certainly had you pegged, Mackey," I sneered, "you are a creepy bleeder." 'Was that a twitch I detected?' I thought glaring at him. 'Yes I'm sure of it.' So I ploughed right on. "Poor Mackey," I said, addressing the other three Irishmen, as though Mackey wasn't even present. "He fell madly in love with a girl named Carol, but she told me that she wouldn't piss on him, even if he was on fire. - But, judging by the way he smells tonight she must have changed her mind." One of the Irishmen began to laugh at my quip. But a deadly glare from the other three shut him right up. I looked again at Mackey and I wasn't disappointed in fact he could have got his name in the 'Guinness Book of Records' for furious face twitching. "Have you lot seen the state of this idiot's face?" I asked the others, then I laughed out loud as one of them took a closer look. Then I added, "Thank goodness there are no young children about this time of night; he'd frighten them to death." I knew full well that if I carried on talking in this manner, it was only a matter of time before one of them threw a punch and suddenly I panicked - Not at the thought of someone throwing a punch. I had just remembered that my precious white wrestling boots were still in my gym bag and the thought of losing them in a scuffle with these morons was unimaginable. I turned quickly and grabbed my bag, an immediate plan already formed. If they start throwing punches, I'll have my bag to hold up in front of me for protection. While I'd go on the attack below my bag with my heavy boots into their shins, knees and ankles. Well so far a punch hadn't been thrown, but my new priority was to get my gym bag containing my boots home to a safe haven. I continued my verbal harassment of Mackey while I sauntered slowly towards the corner of Scrubs Lane. They all followed at the pace I set. I would purposely stop from time to time, in order to defuse the chance of any of them getting the idea that I was attempting to escape. But bit by bit I got closer to my bed-sit. Now I reached the crucial spot - The corner of Scrubs Lane. The four Irishmen had obviously been walking home north on the Harrow Road. We now stood about 100 yards from my bed-sit. The last house away on the very opposite end of the block. Would I be able to coax them to follow me closer to my wrestling boot sanctuary and further away from their own destinations - or would the showdown start on the corner?

"Listen," I told them as I made a definite move into Scrubs Lane. "Why don't the rest of you go home and leave Mackey and me to settle our score in peace? We'll both pop off further down this road find somewhere quiet. Then when I've finished with him, I'll leave what's left on the corner where you can pick it up in the morning."

"There's a perfect place where you can settle it by the canal," the big guy claimed, "and we'll come along to make sure there's fair play."

'They must live somewhere close by,' I thought, 'to even

know that the Grand Union Canal passed under the road just a little further down Scrubs Lane from where I lived - Well at least we're going in the right direction.'

"The canal is a good choice," I agreed, picking up the pace. "But it will be a complete waste of your time, to come along to make sure there's going to be fair play - because there isn't going to be any - I'm going to do things to that twat that's even going to make me feel squeamish."

"No," replied the big guy, "I'm going to make sure that Joe gets a fair fight."

"And who's going to see that I get a fair fight?" I asked. Although I wasn't much interested in his answer, as we were now level with my bed-sit front door. "Excuse me," I told him politely. I fished out my keys, walked up the short path, opened the door, placed my bag inside where it and my boots would be safe. I closed the door then turned and walked back down the path to face them. As I said, Mam may have raised an idiot, but not a coward. If I'd chosen to I could have simply stepped inside, closed the door behind me and gone to bed in complete safety. Leaving these morons with no other choice but to go home. They would probably soon forget that this incident had ever occurred and no one else would ever know the difference - except me!!! And I would have to take it indoors with me. I would take it to bed with me and I would have to live with it for the rest of my life. I may have failed to be a man with Margaret but that was sex - This was violence, something I knew a little bit more about! Our argument dragged on. There was no way I was going to accompany them along the banks of the Grand Union Canal. I wasn't the brightest knife in the cutlery set, but I wasn't the dullest either. I knew that I wouldn't stand a chance of defeating four men at once. Especially as even the smallest of them was larger than I was. I would surely end up in a bad way, maybe even floating face down in the bloody canal. Losing patience I said to the big guy,

"Listen Paddy, if you are determined to interfere with something that doesn't concern you. I don't mind fighting with you first. As long as I get a crack at Mackey after I've beaten you. But I'm not going to fight you all at the same time." The big guy seemed to have taken charge and determined to set the rules.

But eventually my determination seemed to have worn his patience down. And he agreed that Mackey and I should go off on our own and finish what had started over a year before. I looked at Mackey his face almost a blur of twitching. He had been very silent and I knew he didn't relish his friend's decision. But I suddenly saw a glimmer of hope appear in his eyes and knew that he had received some look or signal from the big guy who had taken advantage of the fact that I was no longer looking at him. I lead the way and Mackey followed a pace or two behind. I walked around the corner into Waldo Road, left into Letchford and right into Riggley.

"Hurry up!" I barked at him. I wanted to put as much distance as possible between the two of us and Mackey's friends because I knew that I wasn't going to remain alone with him for long. Sure enough we had hardly turned the corner into Riggley when I heard the thumping of fast running feet. 'Fortunately,' I thought, 'they hadn't seen us turn the corner and they weren't sure where we were. Will that give me the time I need?' Unfortunately it didn't. As I charged at Mackey the other three came hurtling around the corner behind me and as I made a grab for twitchy they must have all crashed into me from behind at once. Again, as happened in the first installment of the Mackey saga. I collided with a wall, but this time it was the side of a house. I ended up lying on my side, with my back wedged up against the bottom of the brick wall. The four of them lay into me with their boots. I put my hands on my head my forearms in front of my face, which also protected my upper chest with my elbows and I brought my knees up to my elbows which protected just about everything else. I had just turned into a tortoise. I was still feeling the impact of their vicious kicks, but they were unable to reach anything vital. Plus, they were all getting in each other's way. Mackey must have been the first of them to appreciate their dilemma, and I recognized his voice as he shouted at the big guy.

"Pull his hands down so I can kick him in the face!" And straight away the big guy attempted to comply. He began struggling to pull my hands down. I struggled to keep them where they were. But as he had placed both his hands around both my wrists in an attempt to tear my protection away. He had unwittingly placed himself in a very dangerous position. I took full advantage of it by biting his right thumb and hanging on to it with my teeth like a rabid Bull Terrier. The big guy began to scream like a locomotive's whistle and I bit down harder. "He's bitin' me fuckin' thumb off!" He screeched. One of the others made a grab for my wrist and tried to pries me off his friend which resulted in me biting harder. The big guy screaming louder. I grabbed the other's wrist with one hand and his middle finger with the other and snapped it back until it touched the back of his hand. While still keeping the big guy's thumb firmly fixed between my teeth. As they both tried to pull away I allowed them to use their agony and energy to pull me into a more upright position, from where I could stand up when I was ready to do so. It also made me a little more vulnerable to attack from the two others. As one of them made his move, by snatching a handful of my hair I let go of the wrist and finger of my last attacker and grabbed my new attacker by the balls and squeezed with every ounce of strength I could muster. Now I heard screaming in stereo. And as I squeezed and chewed it sounded like a fucking farmyard. In his frantic attempt to escape my last assailant pulled me from the ground all the way back to my feet. Both of which I began to employ immediately with deadly accuracy, as I kicked furiously at every shin, ankle and knee within range. I released both thumb and balls so that I could add maximum impetus to my kicks. But as soon as I did, all four of them took off up the road as though all the Banshees from hell were snapping at their arses. I tore off in pursuit but only succeeded in covering a half a dozen paces before stopping dead as a result of a badly sprained ankle. I could never decide if I had injured it as a result of the kicking I had received. The kicking I had dished out, or from stepping awkwardly off the curb as I began to chase them. Which was also the first time that I became aware of it. Although I wouldn't have turned down the chance of inflicting as much more injury to any of the four Irishmen as I could, especially if it happened to be Mackey. My main objective in following them was to find out where each one of them lived. So that I could settle with them one at a time at a later date. Unfortunately my ankle put pay to that. By the time I had limped as far as the Harrow Road, there was no sign of any of them. I knew that I had really hurt three of them and I suppose that as a result I should have felt pleased with myself. But I wasn't, the reason being that I didn't know whether Mackey was one of the three I had injured, or the one I hadn't. As I never met him again it will forever remain an aggravating mystery. They say that bad things happen in three's. My visit from Dad. My bust up with Butch. My failure with Margaret and the confrontation with Mackey and friends. That's bloody four I thought?! Then I received a letter from my best friend Peter Inge telling me that he had given in his notice to Shiver's Garage where he worked and would be arriving in London next week end. I knew my bad spell had finally run its course, until I arrived at work that day.

"They're going to transfer you to a different driver," Bill told me as he started the van, "Do you remember the other driver's territory that we had to cover while he was on holiday?" He asked,

"Yes." I replied.

"Well, that's the same route and the same driver that you'll be working for, from the week after next." Bill said.

"Why me?" I asked, "I like working with you on this route."

"It seems that you are the most eligible." He told me.

Why am I the most eligible?" I demanded, "I only did the bloody route for 2 weeks, I'll go and tell them I've completely forgotten it after all this time."

"That's not the reason you're the most eligible," Bill replied, "apparently this will be the third of his van boys that Tom McBride has beaten up and every one of them have quit their jobs as a result. They figure that if he tries that with you, he'll bite off a bit more than he can chew."

"Why don't they fire him then?" I asked.

"Well good drivers are hard to find. While van boys like you, are a dime a dozen." He said teasingly, "Tom McBride may be known as the 'Mad Irishman' but he's also known as a good driver."

"Now I know you're full of crap," I told him with relief, "you really had me going there for a minute." I had told Bill, the full Mackey's Irish gang saga. Starting with our first confrontation in the Factory. Up to what had happened just a few days earlier, after he had asked the reason for my limping and my bruised and scratched hands. Now Bill was ribbing me, as he knew at that time, Irishmen were not exactly my favorite people. At least that's what I thought he was doing. Unfortunately I soon found out that he wasn't kidding and after the following week I would be working with the 'Mad Irishman'. That would also mean that I would lose my part time job working in Ted Flock's breaker's yard. Ted was appropriately sympathetic when I told him and also appreciated that I would miss the work he had given me that I had come to rely on.

"I'll 'ave a word wiv 'Polish' Peter," he promised, "he likes wrestlers, Peter Rann and 'Mad Fred' the ear biter works fer 'im, 'e'll give yer a job."

I'd seen Peter Rann wrestling a couple of times in the Seymour Hall, but not 'Mad Fred' and I didn't know who 'Polish' Peter was at that time, until Bill filled me in.

"He's got property all over North-west London." he told me, "Peter Rann and Fred the ear biter work for him as enforcers and rent collectors. He's got whole gangs of toughs working for him doing the same thing."

"Who's Fred the ear biter?" I asked Bill.

"'Mad Fred' Rondell bit some black geezer's ear off 'cos he wouldn't get out of one of Peter Rachman's properties." Bill answered.

"Peter Rachman! Did you say Peter Rachman?!" I shouted.

"Yes, why, do you know him?" asked Bill.

"No, but I've heard Margaret, Cassie and Becky Big-Tits talking about him. I think he looks after some of them and finds them flats to work from."

"Yes, that'll be him," Bill agreed, "he'll buy a house cheap, 'cos it's full of blacks. Then he'll get his enforcers to kick them all out, do the place up and then charge prostitutes a fortune for rents." That was enough reason for me to shy away from Peter Rachman. I had seen too many adds for apartments that was 'No Blacks need apply' and 'Whites only' whenever I was looking for somewhere to live myself. The race war was still going strong in North-West London and I didn't want to be involved in it, in any way, shape, or form. As it happened, I found out later that Bill had only known a few of the facts and even those were a little jumbled. Peter Rachman didn't throw blacks out of flats; he'd put them in, like sardines in a can. And then charged astronomical rents into the bargain, after first using them to drive out sitting tenants.

Many properties in those days that had 'sitting tenants' - tenants who paid controlled rents. They became a 'white elephant' for their owners as it would often cost them more to own a house than they could make back in rents. They were not allowed by law to increase the rents, until the old sitting tenants left and were replaced by new ones. Obviously if a person was paying peanuts for a decent flat they would never leave it. So the owners were only too pleased to sell the property dirt cheap and 'Polish' Peter Rachman was only too pleased to buy them. Then when the property was his, he'd harass, threaten and frighten his sitting tenants away. He'd fill the place up with blacks who were happy to live dozens to a room at extortionate rents as they had nowhere else to live. Stubborn sitting tenants were at first offered a monetary bribe to leave. If that didn't work he'd move a tribe of rowdy West Indians in. They would party all night, break locks, smash toilets and threaten violence. He even had the roof removed off one Bayswater property in order to get his point over. In the end the sitting tenants would always move out. Polish Peter as well as having rough, tough rent collecting enforcers working for him. He also had a number of West Indian gangs that he used solely for harassment purposes. After they had completed their work and the sitting tenants had fled from one house, he would move the gang on to the next property he wanted cleared. This formula worked well for him, until one of his West Indian gangs decided that they liked living in one of the houses they had just cleared of the old tenants. When he told them he had another property for them to move on to, they refused the offer. They said that they decided they would remain where they were. So after many appeals and threats, Rachman had to send in the heavy guns. 'Mad Fred' Rondell. At first sight Fred was anything but an intimidating figure. He looked a little more dangerous than Benny Hill and unless one knew of his reputation they could be forgiven for not taking him seriously. He wasn't an exceptionally large man either. Except for his feet, hands and head, all of which were lethal weapons. His head, which was his most recognizable feature was huge and round, but with a very distinctive point in its crest. As it was also bald, it exaggerated its prominence dramatically. He wore a straggly beard and most often walked about wearing nothing on his feet but rubber flip-flops - even in the winter time. I remember Peter Rann telling me that he had seen frost forming between Fred's toes, without causing their owner the slightest bit of concern, or apparent discomfort. Peter Rann also told me what happened on the day that 'Mad Fred' went to evict the West Indians, who refused to vacate 'Polish' Peter Rachman's latest realty acquisition. A tall, athletically built Jamaican answered the front door to Fred's heavy pounding and stood in the doorway glaring down at him.

"C'mon, Peter's told you you've gotta move out." Fred ordered.

"Okay, mon," replied the Jamaican. He opened the door and stood back to make way for Fred. "You'd better come in and we'll talk about it." Fred entered and after the Jamaican had closed the door, he led Fred along the passageway and down a flight of stairs into the basement. Fred didn't suspect that anything was amiss. He knew full well that the West Indians would make use of every square foot of space in a house. There were always so many of them to share what space there was. They would often keep chickens and even goats in the basements or back gardens. The Jamaican had led the way down the stairs, but he stood aside as he opened the door of the basement, allowing Fred to enter first. Inside the basement was pitch black and as Fred hesitated the Jamaican hurled his weight against Fred's back, sending him sprawling into the darkness. An iron bar thudded down onto Fred's skull. I often wondered if that was the cause of the unique shape of his head. Punches and kicks rained on him from every direction. It was so dark, that Fred would have been unable to see his assailants even if they had been white. Even so, that did not stop 'Mad Fred' retaliating. His hands and feet shot out all around him and the sickening crunches and yelps of pain manifested to their effectiveness. Anything his hands could grab, he would crush, tear and rip pieces off. He pulled one of his attackers to him and ripped his ear right off his head with his teeth. The attack stopped as suddenly as it started. That gave Fred the opportunity to find and flip on the light switch, to reveal the sight of a bloody massacre. Fred was now the only man standing. The good news was, that the West Indians vacated the premises. The bad news was that Fred was arrested for assault and grievous bodily harm. When he appeared in court at one stage proceedings had to be halted, while Fred stood upside down on his head in the dock to enable him to collect his thoughts. He was a devout practitioner of some form of yoga. When asked by the prosecuting council, if he had any idea what had happened to the ear he had bitten off,

"I musta swallowed it," he replied - "I was too busy at the time to spit it out!"

I have seen him standing for an hour or more with his arms held out in front of him, parallel to the ground. In countless repetitions he would stretch his fingers open and then squeeze them into a fist, as though he was crushing rocks. This he told me was how he developed his inhuman grip. To engage Fred in conversation was like talking to a machinegun with hiccups. He spoke so fast and changed the subject even faster, sometimes mid sentence. A 15 minute chat was more than sufficient to send my brain reeling as though I was shell-shocked. As crazy as he seemed to be, Fred was an expert on horticulture. He also spoke several languages fluently including Hebrew. He was born in Berlin, Germany in 1927 and was the son of a prominent Jewish businessman. After his Mother died in 1934, 6 year old Fred was abandoned by his Father, who immigrated to Palestine with Fred's siblings, leaving Fred to fend for himself. A few years later, Fred was liberated to Britain, by the Kinder-transport system, from Nazi Germany, just before the war began. He was then sent to live in Manchester and was educated in a Jewish school, where he learned to speak English. He even studied to become a Rabbi in the Talmudical Collage.

I asked Peter Rann about 'Mad Fred's wrestling career. He told me that back in the beginning of the 50's, Fred just suddenly turned up one night from nowhere as a substitute for one of Assirati's many no show opponents. All he had in the way of gear, was an old pair of black trunks, which he carried in a paper carrier bag and he wrestled barefoot. As we all know by now, Bert could be excessively generous, when delivering pain and punishment. On the first night he wrestled Fred, his demonstration of raw violence seemed to know no bounds. When the match was over Fred seemed to be pouring blood from every natural orifice in his body, plus a few more that were newly acquired, courtesy of Bert. While collecting his scant earnings, Fred asked the promoter, Sammy King, where the wrestling was going to be held the next night. After being told he left the building. Most of the wrestlers thought that with the state he was in from the terrible beating he had taken, that he would probably go off and find somewhere to die in peace. But next night Fred was back, to collect a few more pounds wages and another savage mauling from Bert. Fred slept rough on park benches, where he had been working as a gardener. He wrestled 2 or 3 times in a week, often with Bert. Whenever he arrived at an arena his beard would still be matted with dried blood from the previous night, that had seeped out of his ears, or cuts around his eyes, mouth and nose. He seemed to take the excessively brutal style of Bert in his stride and took it for granted that that was normal treatment in the World of pro wrestling. Although he was born in Germany, wrestling promoters billed him as Vladimir Waldberg, 'The Polish Eagle' or 'The White Eagle.' I had heard the story that Fred's apparent 'Brain damage' was the result of a concentration-camp fight to the death. I somehow doubt that, as Fred was only 9 years old when he left Germany. If 'Mad' Fred did sustain brain damage during a fight I would be very tempted to attribute the cause of it to that gentle soul, Bert Assirati.

****

My best friend Peter Inge would be arriving Saturday evening, I just couldn't wait to see him. I was buzzing with excitement at the very thought of all I had to show him. The Forester's Club, the YMCA, The 2 I's Coffee Bar. All the wrestlers and promoters I would introduce him to. I remember laughing out loud at the thought of the expression that would appear on his face, when I subjected him to Becky Big Tits and company. She'd hit him with her line "All you Welsh are the same, Men's pricks and boy's bleed'n pocket money!" 'And talking about money,' I thought - After all the boasting and chest thumping I had done for his benefit when I was with him last, I would need to make as much as I could as quickly as possible. To be financially impaired at the offset of Peter's arrival, would hardly be conducive to the image I had painted of myself, as an up and coming grappling star. Also I would no longer have a part time job in the breaker's yard. So I picked up the phone and called Lon, as he never seemed to tire of me posing for him. All I ever had to do was give him a call and he'd schedule a modeling session. I had taught myself a very effective method of oiling my own back. I would pour it into one hand, place the back of the other hand onto the oiled palm. And then put my arm right up my back as though I was in a hammerlock. That way I could smooth the oil all over my own back with the back of my hand. When next Lon offered to oil my back I had triumphantly demonstrated my new patented method of doing it myself. I was puzzled that instead of being impressed by my ingenuity, he seemed a little miffed. In spite of the fact that Lon was almost always a reliable source of money whenever I needed any. I found him uncomfortable to be around. His flighty spastic movements, could sometimes be quite unnerving. And although I had almost got used to him by now nothing had prepared me for this modeling session. When I arrived at Lon's flat I saw that he had already arranged the backdrop. Decorated with an array of fake marble pillars all of varying heights. He gave me a tiny posing pouch to wear, my most un-favorite posing garment. All it consisted of was a pouch that barely covered the crown jewels, held in place by two thin strands of elastic that would pass around my hips and between my buttocks. I never liked wearing them and never liked seeing other bodybuilders in the muscle magazines wearing them either. I was always impressed and inspired by a well muscled physique, but there was a limit to how much of it I wanted to see. Anyway, there I was, scantily pouched, heavily oiled and posing away under the bright studio lights as Lon snapped gaily away, all of a sudden he shrieked,

"Oh Adrian, don't move!" I hadn't been moving anyway. Well at least not until he screamed, "don't move." After initially jumping about a foot, I was now waiting to see what was going to bite or sting me.

"Oh Adrian, don't move a single muscle," he repeated, "You look magnificent. Just let me tilt the pillar you're leaning on, so that it matches the symmetry of your gorgeous body!" I was leaning with both hands against the top of the pillar he referred to. Facing a black velvet curtain with my back turned towards Lon. He scurried around to the front of me and began to tilt the pillar to the angle he thought more suitable,

"Don't move, don't move, don't move!" he chimed. It seemed he was making a difficult job of it. Then he dropped to one knee in an effort to get it just right, at least that was what I hoped he was doing. I could feel his breath on the front of my thighs.

"Oh, Adrian!" He gasped, but this time it wasn't the pillar he was trying to tilt. His hands slid around the back of my thighs and he tried to bury his face in my crotch.

"GERRRROFF!!!!" I roared. My leg shot out and Lon flew arse first into the corner. He, or one of the pillars must have landed on an electric wire, as all his studio lights seemed to drop in a shower of sparks. In sequence like a stack of exploding dominos. Through the corner of my eye, I saw Lon's camera falling to the ground and instinctively my hand shot out and I caught one leg of the tripod, just before it made impact with the floor. I carefully placed the camera upright on its tripod and looked over at Lon who was whimpering in the corner,

"Oh Adrian, I'm so sorry," he sobbed, "I don't know what came over me."

"Well it isn't going to be me for a fucking start!" I told him, "Give me my money, I'm going!" he crawled out of the corner and shuffled across the room to get my wages.

"Oh yes, we'll call it a day I think," He agreed, "I don't feel very well - now you will come back soon won't you Adrian." He asked, as he handed me my money, I noticed that he was handing me two 5 pound notes instead of the usual one. I snatched them and left without saying another word. When I got home that night and undressed to get into bed, I first found that I was still oily and then discovered that I was still wearing the dreaded posing pouch. That episode bothered me – and not only because I had just lost another source of income. As Lon of London, New York, or anywhere else for that matter had definitely snapped his last shot of yours truly. But I succeeded in putting it to the back of my mind as Saturday came around and this evening Peter would be coming to town. 'Fuck Lon and his Cat Christopher.' I thought savagely. The day dragged on and on. As Bill and I usually finished work early on a Saturday, I would mostly go straight to the YMCA from work and then go home to eat. I went to the YMCA that day and was conscious the whole time I was lifting weights and wrestling on the mat, that the very next time I came here to train I would be accompanied by my best friend. Peter had obviously never seen me wrestle professionally and I knew that he, like me, couldn't wait to enjoy that experience. I hung about the YMCA that day as long as possible, willing the time to pass faster. Then I walked all the way to the rotisserie in Edgware Road, as that was fairly close to the Station. I ordered a large steak, half a chicken, a baked potato and coleslaw. Being a fairly slow eater, I thought that my meal would take a bite out of the time as well as take my mind off the waiting. I dawdled my way up the Edgware Road and down Praed Street to the Station, window shopping as I went. I arrived on the platform about 20 minutes before Peter's train was due to arrive. Those 20 minutes I thought was the longest I remembered waiting since I had stood on the bottom of the pit in Beynon's Colliery. Waiting for the cage to take me to the surface for the very last time. At last the train appeared and by that time, I was so pent up and impatient that I even resented the train slowing down before stopping to disgorge its passengers. As the passengers alighted and began to fill the platform, I hopped up onto a luggage trolley so that I could see all the passengers, and could be seen by them as they walked by me.

'Come on Peter,' I said to myself, 'I've bloody well waited long enough.' The torrent of passengers soon dwindled to a trickle. 'Come on Peter,' I said to myself again. 'He must have brought every single one of his Worldly belongings with him and he's waiting for me to go and give him a hand.' I walked down the platform peering into every carriage compartment as I went until I reached the very end; there was no sign of Peter. 'Maybe he's in the baggage compartment.' I thought, so I looked, but he wasn't there either. I walked back and checked every compartment again, no sign of him. I knew that he hadn't walked passed me. I concluded that somehow he must have missed the train. When I reached the engine, seeing the driver was still in there. I asked him when the next train would be coming in from Newport. When he told me he didn't know and that I should go and check at the ticket office, I glared at him as though it was his fault that Peter was not on the train. At the ticket office I was told that I had another 2 hours to wait until the next Newport train arrived. He would have to be on that one as it would be the last train from Newport that night. I was on tender hooks for the whole time. It did cross my mind to walk back to the rotisserie and claim another steak, but under the circumstances even my huge appetite had deserted me. My 2 hour wait seemed to last a little over 2 months, but with the same result. The train arrived but Peter didn't. He wouldn't be coming tonight. I couldn't phone Peter to find out what had happened, as his family like mine, had never owned a phone. All I could do now was what I'd been doing all day - wait. Wait for a letter, or wait for him to turn up at my bed-sit.

'How I'd love Mackey and his friends to be walking home tonight,' I thought as I passed the spot where I had encountered them not very long ago. 'Especially if Peter was with me – Damn it, Peter wasn't with me and I'm fucked if I know why not!' I refused to believe that Peter, like gutless Chewy and the treacherous Black Rat, would intentionally let me down. We had made too many plans and I would have trusted him with my life. There just had to be some other explanation to why he wasn't here right now.

Monday morning came at last and that was the day I would begin working with my new driver, the 'Mad Irishman' Tom McBride. 'I'm just in the mood for that kind of aggravation.' I thought belligerently as I marched towards the parcel depot after clocking into work. I had never knowingly met Tom McBride. But after Bill's description of him, I expected him to be some huge, bestial, Neanderthal type, as thick as two short planks. He turned out to be a very pleasant looking man, with bright blue, intelligent looking eyes and aged somewhere in his late twenties. He was only a few inches taller than me, but probably outweighed me by about 30 pounds. He didn't offer me his hand when we were introduced, so I didn't offer mine. We loaded the van together, but he never said a word that was unnecessary. Only what order the parcels and packages should be stacked in for delivery. As we drove towards our destination the only sound was from the van's engine. All the way to our first delivery neither of us spoke. Although I caught him looking at me, with what I interpreted as speculation, on a few occasions. Whenever I caught his eye, I held his gaze and raised my own eyebrows expectantly, but he would look away and the silence continued. We had very few regular deliveries that day, in spite of an almost full van. The bulk of our cargo was to be delivered to the depot in the Minories. After unloading most of what was left, we began loading again with packages for the depot near London Bridge Station.

"We'll deliver them after lunch and pick up another load from there, to take back to Paddington." McBride explained to me, 'there's a café down the road you can get something to eat there if you want."

"Yes, I know the place," I told him, "I've been there before." It was the same café where I had drank two cups of coffee with the last shilling to my name at the end of my second week working for the railway. Tom had told me to meet him back at the Minories depot at 3.30.pm. which gave me over 3 hours to kill. 'Great,' I thought, 'and I know exactly where I'm going to kill them.' After I had finished my lunch, it was just a short walk down the road to The Tower of London. I spent a good 2 hours in the White Tower, examining all the Arms and Armor at my leisure. This turned out to be an almost daily ritual and I found that I usually had anywhere between 2 and 4 hours, to explore one of my favorite places in all of London. Things were not looking so bad after all and then at the London Bridge depot, later that first day I hit pay dirt. No, unfortunately it wasn't another source of income. But almost as good. A number of businesses backed on to the depot, and one of them was a printers that put together glamour girl magazines. Every day there would be stacks of reject photos printed on large sheets, dumped outside their back entrance waiting for the garbage collectors. I wondered if the garbage men noticed, that after my discovery there would be very little trash for them to collect. While my rude, nude Girlie collection grew larger each day. Tom never began a collection of his own,

"I'm a married man," he explained, "My wife would skin me alive if I took anything like that home." But he did share my interest and he seemed to look forward to what I could scavenge as much as I did. A shared interest in Betty Page thawed the ice and Tom and I became good friends. We never ever discussed the reason why I had been paired with him. And in all the years that I was to know him, I never saw the slightest sign of his so called violent nature.

****

About that time, I once again bumped into Bobby Selsden. Someone I had been waiting to have a word with. He had been the person who had put me in touch with Lon in the first place. I wanted to tell him about my last encounter. And to warn him to be careful, as Lon was obviously not right in the head. As I recounted my experience, I was disconcerted by the ever widening grin on Bobby's face. Instead of the shock, disgust and disbelief, I had expected. By the time I had finished, I was the one who was shocked and disgusted, by Bobby's hysterical laughter. At first I thought that he didn't believe me. As even to me, the story did seem more than a little far-fetched, but between the gales of laughter Bobby managed to blurt out,

"C'mon Adrian, you must have known Lon is a Wooly-Woofter?!"

"No he's not, he's an American!" I argued. Bobby had been leaning on a street lamppost. Now he was on his knees, hugging the lamppost, while he simply screamed with laughter. Now I enjoy a good laugh, as much as anyone, but I couldn't for the life of me see what was supposed to be funny. As Bobby began at last to recover, I insisted,

"Lon isn't Welsh, he's American." And off Bobby went again. I thought he might die laughing. I would have walked away and left him hanging around the bottom of the lamppost, but I wanted an explanation and I wasn't leaving until I got it.

"A Wooly-Woofter is a poufter, a queer, an arsehole-bandit," explained Bobby at last. My blank expression, finally convinced him that I still wasn't following his drift. So he explained the whole thing right down to the last gory detail.

"I thought he was nuts." I muttered pathetically.

"He was," agreed Bobby, "nuts about you - or nuts about your nuts!" He roared with laughter again at his own joke. I cringed, as I remembered an incident that occurred not long after Cassie had first called me a Wooly-Woofter. I had been on my way home after a wrestling match and had stopped to talk to the girls as usual. When a client of Becky Big-Tits, upon hearing my accent had asked me where I was from. And I replied,

"Can't you tell mate? - I'm a Wooly-Woofter!" Cassie, much to my surprise was the only one laughing. Instead of the only one who didn't laugh at one of my witticisms.

Now I'm not saying that I had never heard of anything like that before, I had. But I never believed it. When I was a kid in Brynmawr, I remember a man who the other kids called 'Horace the bummer.' The stories they told about him, to me were totally bizarre. If there was any truth in them at all, then he must have been completely off his head. I thought him very eccentric and we did wonder why Eric Barnes' face blushed so red that all his freckles disappeared. When Horace once called to him as he passed us standing in the market square one day,

"Hello Eric, when are you coming around for tea again? You haven't been to see me for ages." Any boys that we thought weren't as daring as the rest of us, we would call sissies. But that was in reference to their courage, not their sexuality. Miss Hughes, the girl's gym instructor in the Grammar school, was reputed to have a preference for girls. But it was often beyond me, what a man was supposed to do with a girl, let alone how a Woman would manage it. That rumor faded when she got married to the Headmaster, Mr. Birchmore. But once again reared its ugly head, just a short while later after they got divorced. Birchmore resigned as Headmaster of the Grammar school under a cloud of speculation. Of course we all wanted to believe the worst, as we hated Birchmore a lot.

"They're all bleed'n irons," Bobby Selsden continued, as he began to recover, "well most of them anyway."

"Irons?" I queried.

"Iron hoof - pouf, its Cockney slang, like Wooly-Woofter - poufter, or Ginger, ginger beer - queer, they're homosexuals. Most of them are like that. That's why they like taking photos of blokes." I didn't like the sound of that at all.

"Well no one else has ever tried anything like that." I told him.

"Yeah, well perhaps they don't fancy you as much as Lon does," He chuckled, "Mind you, I think you're quite cute sweetie." He added, imitating Lon's funny voice, while he minced Lon-like around the lamppost.

"Bollocks!" Was all I could think of saying.

Bobby then asked me how my wrestling and weightlifting was coming along, and I was very happy to change the subject. Although, I had already made my mind up to clear the air with any of the other photographers I posed for.

"When are you going to come to my club for a workout?" He asked me, as he did every time I spoke to him. I had never bothered to take him up on his offer, simply because they had no wrestling at his club only weightlifting and bodybuilding. But this time for some reason, I agreed to go and workout with him on the following Tuesday. The club that Bobby trained at was in a school in Kensal Rise. When I arrived there that Tuesday evening, Bobby and a few of his regular training partners, welcomed me as though I was a famous celebrity. They wanted to know all about my wrestling exploits. Who I'd wrestled, where I'd wrestled, when I'd wrestled last, where and when I was going to wrestle again. And they seemed to hang on every word I uttered. I attribute the attention I received, that fanned my ego and made me feel important to my very impressive showing. We started with bench-press and after we had all warmed up with a moderately light weight. My turn came around again, I added a couple more plates to each side as my warm-up had been much too light. And I had a great fondness for heaviness when I lifted. I pressed the barbell up for 6 reps, without forcing myself too much and as I sat up to let the next guy have his turn, it was to a chorus of,

"WOW!" – "SHIT!" – 'BLEED'N' HELL!" But best of all. Bobby explaining what the fuss was all about, with one short sentence,

"Damn Adrian, I thought you told me you couldn't bench-press 200 pounds?!"

"I can't ---," I began, but Bobby interrupted me,

"Well you just did 6 reps with it!" I spun around on the bench and checked the barbell. And after adding up the plates, plus the bar a half a dozen times, found that he was absolutely correct. He wasn't playing a prank, as Bobby was so prone to do.

"Put some more weight on!" I ordered and succeeded in getting one easy rep with 220 pounds. I was ecstatic; I just couldn't wait to tell the guys in the Forester's club.

"Were you wrestling last night?" I was asked when I arrived in the Forester's the next night. As everyone there knew that that would be the only reason I would miss a night's training.

"No," I replied, gratified to see that all the guys that I regularly trained with were present, plus a number of rivals. "I went to train in a club up in Kensal Rise," Although I was buzzing with excitement. I forced myself to appear totally mundane. Then added as casually as I could, "I bench-pressed 200 for 6 reps and then got one with 220."

"Yeah, right, I'd like to see that!" Was their first response, with "Bullshit!" being a close second. "Some weights are not as heavy as other's! Added another of them.

"220 pounds, is 220 pounds!" I argued. But was very happy to see that none of them were convinced. 'Oh dear,' I thought, 'I suppose I'll just have to prove it won't I?'

"Load the bar!" I ordered, as everyone gathered around to see me making a fool of myself. I knew I responded well to positivity, but responded even better to negativity. Just try to convince me that I can't do something that I really want to. Then just stand back and watch. With the bar loaded to 200 pounds I easily got my 6 reps and really got everyone's attention. With the result in my attempt with 220 pounds I got 2 reps out, instead of only one, as I had done the night before.

"Let me try 230." I demanded and got one easy rep out of it. That very night the weightlifting instructor invited me to enter the upcoming club weightlifting competition in the lightweight division and I accepted his offer.

At last, I got my long awaited letter from Brynmawr, that would explain why my best and childhood friend Peter Inge, had not arrived in London on the evening he had promised to come. The letter was short and to the point. It seemed that Peter had a very valid reason for not turning up - He had polio. I had never in my life prayed for anything as hard as I prayed for Peter. Not even for myself. He had been my friend from the time we were infants and one of the very few people in the World that I totally trusted. It was Peter who had drawn my attention to professional wrestling in the first place. And then helped to develop and nurture my ever increasing interest. If not for him, I might not have been following my dream in London. While he lay in bed in Brynmawr, the victim of a horrible, debilitating and deadly disease. I knew very little about polio. I knew it could be terminal and even its luckier victims, who survived death could spend the rest of their lives suffering from crippling deformities. Peter had so badly wanted to become a wrestler. What chance could he possibly hope for now. A picture of 'Lucky' Bert Lamb kept appearing in my mind, with that ugly twig he called a left leg. That contrasted so sadly, with his powerfully built right leg. And as pathetic as he was, he was considered one of the fortunate ones. I found it impossible to come to terms with the fate of my friend. Still life goes on. I continued to pray and watched the mail for more news.

****

Since the first time I had gone to the Cumberland Hotel, as a guest of Bill Jones and his friend Gary Grant to celebrate Bill's first front cover success, with his photo of my favorite wrestler, Kid Tarzan Jonathan. I had been invited to eat with them, on an almost regular basis. Mostly it would be in some expensive restaurant and sometimes, Bill would cook himself in his home. I wasn't the only bodybuilder who posed for Bill, who would be treated this way. A few others including Sean Connery, who had placed third in the tall men's class in the 1953 Mr. Universe for instance. Sean, like myself posed for physique photographers to help pay his way, while pursuing his dream. In Sean's case it was acting. When Bill cooked, he knew that the favorite of most bodybuilders in those days, were big steaks. He had a butcher who would cut the steaks to Bill's exact specifications. Bill liked to encourage his models to develop very large upper arms, which he would measure and cook a steak for the owner which would match the upper arm measurement. If a model had a 15" upper arm, Bill would get his butcher to cut a 15 ounce steak, if the model possessed a 16" upper arm, he would get a 16 ounce steak and so on. When I had first arrived in London, weighing 179 pounds, my upper arm measured almost 17". But after losing so much weight I also lost inches from all over my body and it was always a very sore point with me, that at 144 pounds body-weight I could not get my arms to measure much over 15". I was therefore disqualified from receiving one of Bill Jones's famous 1 pound beef steaks. Bill and Gary's restaurant invitations were my first introductions to many gastronomic delights. Before I knew them, I had never even tasted a mushroom. In fact in those days, Mam wouldn't have known how to cook them. The only spaghetti I had ever tasted had come out of a can, courtesy of 'Heinz'. But after my first meal in Bill's favorite Italian restaurant I was totally hooked.

"Have you ever eaten Chinese?" Bill asked me, as a result of the enthusiasm I had displayed over a large steak. Accompanied by spaghetti, which was smothered in a rich Bolognaise sauce and sprinkled liberally, with a small mountain of Parmesan cheese.

"No I haven't", I admitted, "but it couldn't be better than Italian."

"Well next time we'll find out," stated Bill, "we'll all go to 'The Lotus House." On the night we ate there, I suggested - and Bill and Gary agreed, that they should order for me, as I didn't have a clue what was appropriate, to suit my uneducated palette. Soon the waiters were filling the table with dishes containing a myriad of Oriental delicacies, which smelled divine. My stomach growled savagely, with anticipation. Although, I eyed the shrimp mixed into a huge bowl of rice and vegetables with acute suspicion and apprehension. I soon forgot my worries after the first taste and was anxious to sample everything on the table. Which I washed down with glass after glass of the sweetest, coldest wine they had available in the restaurant. Bill and Gary had long since given up in their attempt to share with me their appreciation for fine wine. While they would go into raptures over a bottle of vintage Bordeaux. I would grimace and complain that I thought wine was supposed to be sweet. They would compromise and while they would share a bottle of Burgundy or Bordeaux between them, I would have my own bottle of Sauternes, or Muscatels. Which of course, made me feel very important. It must have amused Bill and Gary that I was such a complete moron, and were duly impressed by the amount of Chinese cuisine I put away, accompanied by 3 bottles of Sauternes. After the meal was complete, I declined the offer of a lift to my bed-sit in favor of a long walk, in order to clear my head and settle my overstuffed belly. It didn't remain overstuffed for long and half a mile up Harrow Road, I lost the lot. I was so sick that night I swore I would never go into a Chinese restaurant again, even if I lived in China. It seemed as though I had still not come to terms with Crustaceans. The very next time I was in Bill Jones's company after the Lon incident, I related the story to him to determine what his reaction might be. He like Bobby Selsden, seemed to think that it was very funny. Until he saw by my expression that I didn't share their sense of humor. His face sobered and he said,

"Surely Adrian, you must have realized that Gary and I are homosexuals?" I was dumbstruck to hear that - even more so, that he admitted it so matter-of-factly.

"No I didn't." I told him truthfully. I didn't add that until recently I didn't even know what a homosexual was.

"Well you don't need to worry about it," he assured me, "neither Gary, nor I, would ever think of doing anything like that with anyone." Then he promptly changed the subject and invited me to eat with him and Gary at The Cumberland Hotel.

"It's a celebration again," he told me, "Gary has just made his first million." Gary was in the antique business and owned a very nice shop in Pimlico, no armor or weapons though, but lots of furniture and rare works of art.

On the evening that we celebrated with a meal in the Cumberland Hotel, we were joined by a friend of Bill and Gary, named Michael. He was home on leave from his job as a waiter on a luxury liner. We were all seated, enjoying our meal, when a lady sitting at a nearby table, dropped her serviette on the floor. Upon noticing it, Michael exclaimed, "Oh, I must learn to relax and remember I'm not at work on board ship. I almost ran over to pick up that ladies serviette." "I hope no one rings a bell," I replied, adhering to his theme, "or I may forget where I am and grab someone in a head-lock."

"Oh, please God, let it be me!" Michael gushed. Then seeing the startled look on my face, he added, "I'd love to sample a head-lock, if it was applied by you!"

"Careful what you wish for," I told him, more than a little embarrassed by his outburst, "it could prove fatal."

"Oh, what a way to die - in your arms!" He crooned. I had no ready answer for that one, which was probably just as well. As both Bill and Gary were laughing at my discomfort too hard to have heard me anyway.

'Oh well,' I thought, 'the food is very nice.'

"You should have given him a bloody good hiding!" John Graham told me, after I had related the Lon incident to him. But the only reason he gave me that advice was due to the fact that he hated Lon with a passion. He must have also guessed the reason I had chosen to tell him about it, as he quickly added, "I'm queer Adrian, but you'll never have to worry - you're not my type!" Well I was relieved to hear that. But a little annoyed that he, like Bill Jones and Bobby Selsden, thought it was so amusing.

"I can see why Lon thinks you're cute," he continued, "but I like big men, not little boys." I didn't like being referred to as a little boy, but it was certainly preferable to a repeat performance of what had occurred with Lon.

The next time I trained with Big Sony Colindos, I asked him, why I had never seen any photos of him in any of the British Bodybuilding magazines.

"I don't think I'm good enough," he replied, "I've got size, but no definition."

"Nonsense," I told him, "why don't you go and see John Graham, I'll bet he'll think you're good enough, I'll give you his phone number, wouldn't you like to see your photo in 'Man's World'?"

"You horrible little bastard!" Roared Big Sony, next time I saw him.

"What's wrong?" I asked him innocently, while trying in vain to suppress a grin that threatened to split my head in half. Thank goodness, that the 6-foot 4 inch, 270 pound Sony, was the patron saint of gentle giants, or, I would have been in serious trouble. After calming him down, I got the whole gory story. Apparently, I had been correct. John Graham did think that Sony was good enough to pose for the muscle mags. All had gone well until the photo session had been completed and Big Sony had gone down to the washbasin at the end of a dimly light hallway in order to wash the oil off his body. As he was scrubbing away at his naked body, who should come down the hallway. Also completely naked and standing to full attention, was John Graham. Sony's description of their confrontation, made the 'loony Lon' saga pale into insignificance. I roared with laughter. Isn't it strange, how such an embarrassing experience is so much funnier when it happens to someone else. Did I feel guilty? – Not a bit. After all, what are friends for?!

****

I was still wrestling about once, or twice a week. Most of the promoters by now had, at last got my name right. But my description that underlined my name on the wrestling posters varied from night to night. Sometimes it would simply state that I was the 'Welsh Welterweight Champion'. Or, that I was the youngest professional wrestler in the World. Or, that I was 'fast and furious'. I asked 'Gentleman' Geoff Moran and Johnny Childs. How come I was recognized as the Welsh Welterweight Champion when I had never had a championship match, to enable me to win it in the first place.

"Well there ain't no more Welsh welterweight wrestlers abaht, so you must be the champion," Stated Johnny, trying to make it sound logical and legitimate, "if we get any more Welsh welterweights, then they can challenge yer for it."

"Well how come I don't have a championship belt?" I persisted.

"'Cos we ain't got one to give yer." Answered Johnny.

As peeved as I was over that situation. I was soon handsomely consoled, when the weightlifting competition came around in the Forester's club and I won the lightweight title with pounds to spare. Although I was still poor on the curl lift, I excelled so well in the bench-press and squat that I almost dethroned the middleweight champion Tommy May. In fact if it hadn't been for my poor effort in the curl, I would have won the middleweight title as well. I had my doubts concerning my claim to the 'Welsh Welterweight Wrestling title,' but I was without a doubt 'The Forester's Lightweight Champion.' Oh boy, just wait till I tell Jack Dale!

When I thought that things couldn't get much better, I received a letter from Brynmawr. It was written by my best friend Peter. It seemed that my prayers had been answered with flying colors and Peter had recovered completely, with no bad side effects from polio whatsoever. I couldn't have been happier. It was quite a long letter and Peter explained what had occurred. Including the reason he had suddenly decided to come to London prematurely, to his original plan. Peter's original plan was that before his arrival in London, he wanted to be in possession of as much cash as possible. I had already told him, that getting work in London was no easy matter. Everything was going to plan. Then one evening at one of the local dancehalls, Peter got into a squabble with some guy. And true to Welsh tradition, decided to settle the dispute in a nearby back alley. Within a few minutes, Peter had spread his adversary all over the alley and was in the process of adding a few finishing touches. When he was attacked from behind, by what he imagined was a member of his opponent's gang. Caught from behind in a headlock Peter threw himself backwards and crushed his attacker against a brick wall. Taking full advantage, Peter began to deliver a savage kicking before the bushwhacker had a chance to recover. It wasn't until after, he had inflicted a considerable amount of damage that he realized that his attacker was wearing a policeman's uniform. Horrified, Peter beat a hasty retreat. A few days later, Peter heard the rumor that the police were making inquiries as to the identity of the person who had beaten the crap out of one of their own. Fearing that the guy he had fought with might point a finger in his direction, he decided that the better part of valor would be to make himself scarce. And obviously London was the best place to get lost in. I was very surprised by Peter's uncharacteristic behavior. Although he, like me, was born and brought up in an environment that bred that kind of behavior. I never remembered in all the years I had known him, for Peter to get into a fight with anyone. Not that he lacked the courage, or the ability. He had proven that to me on the wrestling mat many times over. Peter then immediately wrote to me, telling me he would be arriving in London in a couple more weeks time. The time must have passed more slowly for Peter than it had for me. He was under the constant fear that at any time he would feel a heavy hand on his shoulder and a voice growling - "You're nicked!" On his very last day in work, with tension mounting to fever pitch, Peter said he began to feel terrible. But put it down to the fact that he had spent the last 2 weeks totally stressed out, wondering if he would be leaving for London. Or, would he get piped at the post, by falling foul of the law. When he got home from work that afternoon he found his Mother about to put his dinner on the table. He told her he didn't feel very well and would go and lay down in bed for an hour or two. When after a couple of hours, his Mother went upstairs to call him down to eat, he found that he couldn't move. The Doctor was called and Peter was rushed to hospital, where the Doctor's suspicion was confirmed, he had polio.

'But not to worry now,' Peter assured me, 'he felt great'. In the meantime the 'battered policeman' incident seemed to have blown over. So Peter had decided to get his job back until he could save as much money as possible. When he felt he had enough, he would come to join me in London as planned.

After winning the Lightweight weightlifting title of the Forester's club, I was invited by Les Clark to train with him and Phil Woods. I accepted his invitation, which turned out to be an excellent decision. Tommy May trained with his own exclusive little clique and we were only as friendly as two bitter rivals could be.

"Okay Ade, it's your turn, give me 5 good reps." Ordered Big Les Clark.

"How much weight have you put on the bar Les?" I asked him.

"I don't know - who cares? Just give me the 5 reps I asked you for!" He demanded irritably. Both Les and Phil had no respect at all for heavy poundage. Who cares what it weighs? It was just a big inanimate object, with no right at all in depriving them of the satisfaction of ramming it to arms length for as many repetitions as they thought fit. Very soon my strength on the bench and squat increased by leaps and bounds. There was no holding me back, although my curl was always destined to lag. The first inter-club competition I took part in, was held in the Forester's against 4 lifters from a rival club. Accompanied by their trainers, a couple of judges and a few score of their club's members and supporters. Each competitor was allowed 3 attempts at each of the 3 lifts, and the rules were that weight could be added but not reduced throughout the competition. That would mean, that if you over-estimated your strength on the first lift and couldn't perform the lift cleanly to the judge's satisfaction, you could not take any weight off. You could only try again with the same weight, or increase the weight. With those rules in mind it was always a good idea to make certain of your first lift. Even if it was much lighter than you were capable of doing. Because the best of each lift would be totaled up. If you didn't manage to make at least one successful lift out of each of the exercises, it would really devastate your final total. When everyone was ready the competition started. One of the selected judges asked all the competitors if anyone wanted to begin the first of their 3 attempts on the curl with any less than 100 pounds. I was mortified to find that I was the only one who raised their hands, and I sheepishly asked for 90 pounds to start. The faces of our opposing team who up until now, had been looking at my 3 team-mates with solemn apprehension, were suddenly loosing the condemned prisoner look and brightening up considerably. I managed to curl 90 pounds quite easily and breathed a sigh of relief, knowing that I had at least 90 pounds so far on my score. Relief was short lived, when the judge asked if anyone wanted to try 100 pounds, I found that once again, I was the only one to raise a hand. Again I was successful - but only just.

"Who wants 110 pounds?!" Called the judge, no one put up their hands, but everyone looked at me. I shook my head and refused it, just to piss the opposition off, as they seemed to be enjoying my discomfort a little bit too much. It immediately backfired on me, when I attempted to curl 120 pounds and got disqualified for too much backbend. The opposing club's Lightweight, choose to start his curl with the 120 pounds, I had just failed with for my final lift and he just breezed it. Encouraged by the loud cheering of his team-mates and all his club's supporters. He went on to curl 130, but failed 140. Tommy May and the opposing club's middleweight began with that weight and both managed it. Reading the opposing team's demeanor when they had first arrived in our club, I got the impression that they came not expecting to win. But hoped to at least make a good showing. Les Clark, Phil Woods and Tommy May, were minor legends and would be extremely hard to beat. I was horrified to realize that as no one from any other club knew me, I was the unknown quantity. And all my showing had accomplished so far, was to give them hope. I was their only chance to score a win against the Forester's. I couldn't stand them watching me with a mixture of smirks and hope. So I just sat on a bench and put my face down on my knees and didn't budge for all the rest of the curling competition. When the curling was over, I was relieved to learn that the Forester's had a very slight lead in spite of my less than mediocre performance. I just peeked up long enough to see that they were placing the bar on the stands, prior to the commencement of the bench-press. Then I put my face back on my knees and waited.

"Does anyone want to start with less than 150 pounds for their first attempt on the bench?!" Called out the judge. I didn't know at the time, as I was still sitting with my face on my knees, but Les told me everything that happened during the competition after it had ended.

"Every time the judge called out a weight everyone in the place looked at you expectantly," Les chuckled, "they must have thought you'd gone to sleep."

No one answered the judge until he asked if anyone wanted to start with 170 and the opposing club's Lightweight got up and nailed it for his first attempt.

"Does anyone want 180 next, no – Okay 190?" Asked the judge, again everyone looked at me, Les told me later, but I didn't move. The opposition Lightweight attempted the 170 and nailed it. For his third and final lift he attempted 200 and was again successful. Then the opposing club's middleweight did the same weight for his first lift and he nailed it too.

"Does anyone want 210?!" Asked the judge, the opposing middleweight attempted it for his second try and was successful and then Tommy May for our team went for 230 and banged it up easily for his first try.

"Does anyone want ---?!" the judge began,

"I'll try that!" I interrupted. It was the same weight that Tommy May had just successfully bench-pressed for his first attempt. I was gratified that he had lifted it first. I nailed it easily. As I rose from the bench, I caught Les's eye and he was chuckling away for all he was worth. I didn't at the time really appreciate what was amusing him. But seeing him laughing, combined with the relief I felt, for at least redeeming myself a little from my poor efforts on the curl, made me want to laugh too. But afraid of sending the wrong message to the opposition, I sat down and once again put my face on my knees. I heard Les giggling behind me. Next the opposition middleweight attempted, and was successful with 240 pounds. He was followed by their light-heavyweight who was disqualified for arching his back. Tommy went for 250 and got it. I tried it next and couldn't believe it felt so light. Tommy had already beaten the opposition middleweight, but now he had me to contend with. He threw caution to the wind and opted for 275 and almost managed it, but not quite. - I nailed it and beat Tommy on the bench for the first time, even though he outweighed me by over 20 pounds. The squat was the last lift and also my favorite. Once again, it became more of a competition between Tommy May and me, rather than us against another club. I beat him on our third and final lift and managed to put my lousy curling to the back of my mind. Les and Phil were nothing less than magnificent and with me as part of their team for the first time, we walked away with an easy win. I was happy. But not as happy as I was, after I was told that I was now officially the Middleweight champion as well as the Lightweight champion of the Forester's club. After losing the Middleweight club title to me Tommy May dropped out of competitive lifting and from that time on, it was always just Les Clark, Phil Woods and me in our team. I was now the only white man in the team and I remained the 11 stone and 12 stone champion for the next two years. Lifting a few more pounds, or performing a few more reps, on the bench or the squat seemed to be a weekly occurrence. But I thought back to the time when I just couldn't quite manage one single rep with 200 pounds. Now I was using it as a light warm-up. I wondered if I would experience the same impassible barrier when I got up to 300 pounds. On my very first attempt with 300, I was training with Les and Phil and I failed to get one rep with it. Although I felt that I was very close.

"Let me have another go with that!" I demanded of Les and Phil, after they came to my aid by helping me replace the bar on the stands.

"No, you can't do it," replied Les, "take the rest of the night off and you can try again in a couple of day's time."

"I can do it!" I insisted, determined not to relinquish the bench until I had tried.

"No you can't!" insisted Les, "You've finished lifting weights for tonight!"

"Well so have you and Phil then," I warned him, "because I'm not getting off the bench until you give me that barbell!" I lay back and positioned myself under the bar. With a huge exasperated sigh, Les took one end of the barbell and Phil took the other and aided in me getting the 300 pound barbell off the stands.

"You won't do it!" Les predicted. Which was just what I really needed him to say. I took a deep breath, lowered it to my chest and exploded it back to arms length as though there were balloons instead of heavy steel plates on the bar. Both Les and Phil were almost as delighted with my performance as I was. We three were becoming a very formidable team indeed, when we were in interclub competition, we all had our individual styles. Phil was really explosive. He acted as though he had a personal grudge against every heavy weight he came in contact with. Les appeared lazy and unconcerned and very rarely succeeded in nailing his third and final lift, in each of the three exercises. On his first lift he would make sure he used a heavy, but for him a manageable weight. On his second lift he would really go for it. And on the third he would attempt something totally ridiculous. I would do what I did in my first competition. Give the opposition hope with my mediocre curl. Then sit with my head on my lap playing dead and pretending not to hear the weights being called by the judge. Then enjoy Les's play by play, as he watched disillusionment slowly setting in our opposition, as soon as I began bench-pressing.

I credited my very dramatic increase of strength, down to the amount of meat I consumed, now that I could afford to buy it. Especially after such a long enforced abstinence, due to no work and no money. I imagined that both Phil and Les, must be massive meat eaters, to be possessors of such superhuman power. But after questioning them on the subject, I found much to my surprise, that that was not the case. Phil told me that he never ate meat, with the very occasional exception, of half a can of corned beef. He preferred fish. Les admitted that he quite enjoyed meat, but attributed his strength and stamina, down to a West Indian dish, his Wife prepared for him a few times a week, Banana porridge. Which, Les explained was made by simply boiling green bananas in their skins, then removing the skins and eating what was left. I couldn't wait to give it a try and must have eaten tons of the stuff. I can't say that I liked it very much, but it was much more palatable than the 'Froment' and 'Complan' I had been devouring. Froment was wheat germ granules and Complan was a chalky powder that was supposed to contain a lot of protein. I would mix them both together in water, or milk and literally force myself to drink it down as quickly as possible. It was really yucky, but I can be very masochistic gastronomically, if I believe that what I'm consuming is going to enlarge my muscle mass, or make me stronger.

****

Jean was able to take her summer holiday to coincide with mine, and I decided to take her to Wales with me and spend a couple of weeks in Brynmawr. I hadn't got any further with her, due in part to the fact that most of our courting was conducted, either in the doorway of where she lived or in the cinema. The only time I had ever got her on her own in a compromising situation was, when I was still posing for Lon. I had persuaded him to let me borrow his flat for the evening. After taking Jean to meet him, Lon made a phone call and found that he had to go out for a few hours. As I had prearranged with him, leaving Jean and I alone. I managed to get both of us down to our underwear and into bed. But we couldn't relax long enough to really get things moving, as Lon kept phoning every few minutes, to ask if I had finished yet and could he come back home. He really pissed me off. It wasn't long before Jean realized that it was a setup. And although I denied it until I was blue in the face, she didn't believe me and that was that. After two weeks together in Wales, I didn't fare much better. In desperation after returning to London, I smuggled her up into my bed-sit in Scrubs Lane. Even though I knew I wasn't allowed to. That turned out to be a total disaster. We had both been sitting on the bed fully dressed, with our backs against the headboard, when the bed-sit door seemed to implode under the combined weight of the Landlady and her husband. They burst into the room obviously hoping to catch us in the act.

"What do you think this place is - a brothel?!" Screamed the Landlady. Both she and her husband were furious - Or at least they thought they were furious, until they saw me lose my temper. I was in both their faces, as though I had been fired out of a cannon, knocking Jean off the bed in the process. They seemed to bounce off each other like balls in a pinball machine, not knowing which way to go, to escape my fury. They both collided with the open door, causing the hinges to screech under the strain. I hit the landlady's husband in the front of his shoulder, with the heel of my left hand and brought my right fist back ready to strike. The force of the blow to his shoulder had driven him back into his wife, who was now pinned between him and the ominously creaking door. She stuck her head out from under his arm and said in a much more subdued voice,

"I'll call the police."

"Yeah, and then what?" I growled, "I haven't broken the law, at least not yet!"

"You were told you were not allowed to bring guests up here, when you first moved in." She whined,

"That's your rules not the law!" I barked in her face, "And how dare you ask if I think this fucking dump is a brothel. This girl is a virgin, not a fucking prostitute!" The husband hadn't said a single word. He gazed mesmerized at my fist, which was still hovering above his face and poised to strike. "Get out of this room – NOW!" I roared. I didn't have to tell them twice. I noticed with disgust that the husband fled first. 'What a bloody gentleman!' I thought, as I slammed the door behind them. I began looking for a new bed-sit the same day. I found one much closer to the Forester's and Jean's home, where I was allowed guests, as long as they left by 11 pm. The bed-sit was in Mostyn Gardens, in Kensal Rise. A short walk from where both Uncle Fred and Bobby Selsden lived. I still had to share the bathroom, but my own room was much larger, had a sink with hot and cold running water. A full sized cooker and best of all a double sized bed.

****

The wrestling was going well and had the potential for doing great. I had found a new promoter, Tony DeMarto, who was running anywhere from 1 to 4 shows a week, mostly in the London area. But there was good news and bad news. The good news was, after calling him, he told me that he had heard of me and was willing to give me a half dozen or more matches a month. The bad news was, that he wouldn't pay me more than I was still getting from Childs and Moran and that was 2 pounds 10 shillings a match. All the other promoters I wrestled for, were paying me 4 or 5 pounds. I decided I would accept his offer and after he had met me and watched my performance, I would talk to him about increasing my wages. My debut for DeMarto Promotions was held at the Stone-Cross Hall, in Harlow New Town. The date was August the 10th 1959, a date I wouldn't forget in a hurry. I remember, after arriving outside the venue, looking at the Wrestling Posters and was excited to see, that I was at last wrestling against a champion. Although I must admit, it was a champion I had never before heard of. His name was Ricardo Conlon and he was billed as the Lightweight Champion of Spain. 'Things are definitely looking up,' I thought, 'I should soon, easily be able to negotiate an increase in wages with Tony DeMarto, if my first match was against the Champion of Spain.' I checked out the rest of the card and with mixed feelings, saw that at last, at the age of 18, I had been usurped as the 'World's youngest professional Wrestler,' by a 16 year old named 'Young Sullivan' from South Africa, who was wrestling that night against Pat Kloak from Ireland. I wondered if my opponent would be able to speak English, but soon found that he spoke it very well, But with a distinct Lewisham accent. Everyone that I introduced myself to in the dressing room seemed quite friendly, until I introduced myself to 'Irish' Pat Kloak. He pointedly ignored my proffered hand and glared at me balefully, with the eyes of a dead Cod.

"Who'dga say yer wuz?!" He asked. He had a fat, pale face, dull sandy colored hair and wire rimmed spectacles. He didn't look remotely like my idea of what a wrestler ought to look like, but had the cheek to ask me,

"Are you a wrestler?!"

"Of course I am." I replied.

"Show me your wrestling license!" He demanded.

"What wrestling license?!" I demanded.

"Do yer have a wrestling license or not?!" He roared, I had never heard of wrestling licenses and I told him so.

"No I don't have a license for anything and I don't know, what the fuck you are talking about!" I replied.

"TONY!!!" He screamed to the promoter, "Come here at once," Tony DeMarto came running, "did you know this man hasn't got a wrestling license?!"

"Er – a – no I didn't, 'e tol' me on the phone 'e 'ad one." Lied DeMarto.

"If you use unlicensed wrestlers on your cards, as secretary of the British independent wrestling alliance, I will see to it, that you are blackballed by every one of our members. And you'll never run another show." Stated 'Irish' Pat Kloak.

"I'm sorry Pat, I did'n' know." Groveled DeMarto.

"Well I won't mess up your card tonight. He can wrestle this time, but then that's it. From now on - any more unlicensed wrestlers and you're finished." He threatened.

"Fanks, Pat." Mumbled a subdued DeMarto.

"And you!" Barked Irish Pat, turning his fat, pale, be-speckled face in my direction, "If yer wanna be a wrestler, get a license!"

'Well this is a great start,' I thought, "Where do I get one from?" I asked, straining to keep my temper. He took a brief case out of his wrestling bag, opened it and produced a pen and pad, on which he wrote an address.

"We have a members meeting - a LICENSED member's meeting, in St George's Tavern, at the Elephant and Castle every Sunday morning," he told me, "you can go there any Sunday morning and apply." He added.

'Oh well, that sounds easy enough.' I thought, I also liked the idea of having a license, that I could flash at anyone who doubted, that I was a professional wrestler.

My opponent Ricardo Conlon, stood 5"10" tall and weighed about 170 pounds. He's no more a lightweight, than he is Spanish, I thought. Our match was to be fought over 4 x 10 minute rounds, which would be the first time, I had wrestled anything other than 5 minute rounds. The match started and everything was going well, with plenty of reaction from a packed house. Just towards the end of the first round, Ricardo linked the fingers of both his hands into mine and dropped backwards, to attempt, what I thought would be a stomach throw, or his own version of a 'monkey flip'. Instead, he brought his feet back, curling himself almost into a ball, then he jerked me towards him and straightened out his legs, with all the force in his body. Both his feet exploded into my face and almost kicked my head off, I felt red hot sparks, shooting from my neck right down between my shoulder blades. My lips were split against my teeth and my nose began to bleed. I was too hurt to fall down. But the way the whole ring seemed to tilt, I really thought I might manage it after all. I had an instant migraine headache from Hell. In spite of it, I was ready to rip this bogus Spanish twat, from arsehole to breakfast time. Luckily for both of us, the bell rang to end the round, before I could catch him and ring his bell. I said lucky for both of us. It was lucky for him, because I hadn't decided what I was going to do to retaliate. But whatever it had turned out to be, it would have ended the match. Lucky for me, as the time between rounds gave me a chance to realize that if I crippled their Spanish Lightweight Champion. It would probably be appreciated about as much as it had been appreciated, when I had my first match against 'Gentleman' Geoff Moran. I didn't want to blow my chances first time out with a new promoter, who had offered me so many matches. Especially as that overly officious jerk; the secretary of the British independent Wrestling Alliance was most probably watching the match. I never really determined, whether that kick in the face was blatant vindictiveness, on the part of my opponent. I had noticed that he had been in deep conversation, with Pat Kloak, prior to my match, and wondered if he had put Ricardo up to it. Just to teach the unlicensed wrestler a lesson. That made me see red, and I wanted to see more of it. Preferably squirting out of my opponent. But, it also crossed my mind that I was possibly being purposely provoked and that my reaction could determine whether or not I received my wrestling license. I managed to temper the beast inside me. And instead of going after Ricardo's blood, I concentrated on avoiding any position where he could inflict any kind of painful injury. But I did add a little more weight and a little more pressure and leverage to anything I dished out. Without making it overly obvious to any experienced observer like secretary Pat Kloak. In Ricardo Conlon's defense concerning this incident. Over the next 14 years, I must have wrestled with him at least a couple of hundred times. And I have to say, that I have seldom shared a ring with a more clumsy, awkward, uncoordinated idiot. So giving him the benefit of the doubt, it may have been his stupidity and clumsiness rather than spite. The match was the best of 3 falls. Ricardo scored the first pin-fall in the second round. I equalized in the fourth with a submission, a one legged 'Boston Crab'. I 'accidentally' stomped on his head as hard as I could, driving his face into the mat as I stepped over him, whilst applying my finish. With one fall each the match ended in a draw, but I couldn't help wondering, who had won the first prize for the worst headache.

****

I was enjoying my new bed-sit. Especially as I could now cook myself a proper meal there. Every day on my way home from work I would pop into a Butcher's shop where I was able to buy a couple of pounds of cheap Argentinean steak, for just a few shillings a pound. Unlike my early days in Scrubs Lane, my grub cupboard was overflowing with all kinds of salad stuff, fruit, bread, cheese, eggs, milk and honey. Pinned up behind every cupboard or wardrobe door, out of sight was the very best of my 'naked lady' photo collection. Betty Page and a girl named Rosalina, who had a pair of tits that would have done credit to a Jersey Cow, were the undisputed stars. On show around the room, were photos of my favorite American wrestlers and in deep piles all along the top of the sideboard, was my enormous and ever growing collection of Bodybuilding and 'Boxing and Wrestling' magazines. I had also gained weight. Not a lot, but I had slowly crept up from 144 pounds and was now hovering around 150 pounds, which was still comfortably within the Lightweight limit which was less than a 154. Packing an extra 6 or 7 pounds of muscle didn't only add to my strength, but it also increased my upper arm measurements enough to entitle me at last, to eat one of Bill Jones's famous one pound steaks.

    I was also happy to trade cinemas and doorways for the privacy of my own room, complete with a double bed. But Jean, even though she was happy to jump naked into it, she still said no to what I really wanted. As far as my relationship with Jean was concerned, I felt it was a match made in Wonderland. Probably 'The Mad Hatter's Tea Party'. Ever since she witnessed my evil temper when dealing with my former Landlady and her husband, instead of being put off, she seemed obsessed with provoking it. First I'd get the silent treatment.

    "What's wrong?" I'd ask her, "You're very quiet tonight."

    "Oh, nuffink." She'd sigh, then more silence, this could last for hours. Then after relentless coaxing, eventually she'd 'reluctantly' tell me what was bothering her. Some guy who had been riding a bike past her house, had stopped and said hello and flashed his dick at her. I was shocked. Then another time. The middle aged grocer who owned a shop on the opposite side of the road from where Jean lived, grabbed hold of her and tried to kiss her when she went in there to buy something - I was horrified. Then on another occasion her older brother Dave, had hit her - I was furious.

    I spent two days absent from work waiting for the flasher. On the first day, after hanging about outside Jean's house for hours, I finally saw him peddling down Kensal Road. I ran out into the middle of the road and signaled to him to stop. Instead, he began peddling like hell and managed to swerve past me. I chased after him up the road, but even with my hot temper as fuel, I was no match for a scared man on a bike. The next day I waited again, but hid in a doorway with just one eye peering up the Road. Hours passed, but eventually I spied him hurtling down the road towards me. This time I took no chances. I waited until the last second, before rushing out of my hiding place in order to intercept him before he could ride past. But as I dashed out I almost ran headlong into a car, coming in the opposite direction.

The car swerved and the driver blasted his horn. I refused to be distracted from my goal, and I launched myself feet first at the cyclist and dropkicked him. The cyclist flew off his bike and cart wheeled headfirst over the front of the car onto the sidewalk. I scrambled off the road and dived right after him. I delivered and scored a savage kick at his arse, as he struggled to find his feet. But he managed to maintain his balance and using the impetus of my kick, he broke into a run for an entrance to a high rise. I caught up to him and grabbed his hair and the arse of his trousers. I redirected his charge so that he smashed headfirst into the heavy iron railings, which surrounded the building. then I was on him, punching and kicking, while he was screaming and blubbering. It was only then, that I became aware of the driver of the car and his lady passenger yelling abuse at me. Also every balcony on the high-rise was lined with people, leaning over the walls and screaming curses down on my head. I tried to explain to dozens of hostiles, the reason for my savage assault. They were not interested, they just continued to hurl abuse. Jean got into a slagging match with some of her neighbors and was screeching obscenities at them, that even made me wince with embarrassment. It turned out that the flashing cyclist, wasn't right in the head. People who knew him, would either turn a blind eye, or an admiring one. At his 'harmless habit' of unbuttoning his trousers every time he was suffering with one of his very frequent erections. Instead of being regarded as a public nuisance, this beloved eccentric was treated with extreme sympathy. I came very close to being lynched by the whole street. The next morning after Jean had told me about the grocer, I marched straight into his shop. I managed to control my temper long enough, to explain to him, why he was about to receive the beating of his life. His wife, who must have heard my loud threatening voice, came hurrying into the shop from the living quarters at the back of the building. She ordered me out of their store. So, I decided to make her husband's punishment embarrassing, as well as humiliating and painful. By taking the time to explain to her, the reason why her husband was about to receive the beating of his life. After I'd enlightened her, I sighed and said,

"Okay, the commercial is over, now it's play time!" As I

advanced, they both tried to hold the counter extension flap down to prevent me passing from my side of the counter to theirs. Their panic didn't come close to equaling my anger and I smashed it out of their grasp. They both screamed and the man fled leaving his wife alone, behind the shop counter. I ran after him down a passageway into their kitchen and arrived in time to prevent him opening a back door, from where he had hoped to escape. I grabbed the hair on the back of his head and flung him back into the middle of the room where he collided with the table, knocking it over against the wall. I quickly leapt after him and hit him underneath his nose with the heel of my hand, while almost simultaneously driving my knee into his fat stomach. His wife burst into the kitchen and took a vicious swipe at me with a large shovel. It missed and I grabbed it out of her hands and swiped her husband across his back with it, knocking him face first into a corner. The poor bugger was groveling and squealing like a pig, with his hands on his head. In spite of my resolve, to inflict maximum damage; I couldn't bring myself to hit him again. I derive no pleasure out of beating something that won't fight back. Although, I did make some further use of the shovel. It came very handy to knock most of the shops produce off the counter and the shelves, as I made my way back to the front exit. An hour or so later, as I was standing outside Jean's house and was giving her a blow by blow of what had just occurred. We looked over at the shop and saw that it had the 'closed' sign on the door – and that's where it stayed, the shop never reopened. I'm sure Jean must have regretted telling me about her older brother's bullying. I was livid,

"I'll break his fucking neck!" I told her, beside myself with fury.

"Oh no you won't," she argued, much to my surprise, "you leave him alone!"

"What do you mean, leave him alone," I demanded, "do you think I'm going to allow anyone to hit you and get away with it? I'll break every fucking bone in his body!"

"You leave him alone!" She screamed, "I don't want my brother beaten up by some -----!" Her words died in her mouth, as she saw my expression darken.

"Go on, finish what you were going to say," I challenged, "by some what?!"

"Nuffink, you just leave him alone that's all." She said quietly, realizing she'd gone too far.

"By some what!?" I insisted.

Just then as if on cue, who should come strolling down the road, on his way home from work, but Jean's bullying Brother, Dave.

"Now you leave him alone." Pleaded Jean and she grabbed my arms with her own, in an attempt to pin them to my sides. As her brother approached, he obviously sensed that something was amiss, but still gave me his usual contemptuous glare. I stepped towards him aggressively, in spite of the fact that Jean was clinging to me like a leach.

"If you ever hit Jean again, you hatchet faced twat," I snarled at him, "I'll rip your fucking throat out and make you eat it!"

"I'm not afraid of you!" He told me, trying to temper his startled expression.

"Oh yes you are," I corrected, "you may be stupid, but you're not that stupid!"

He opened the door, entered the house and slammed the door closed in our faces.

"By some what?!" I demanded of Jean again, I had been really hurt by that remark and I never really forgave her for it, I made my mind up there and then that she wouldn't get away with it.

Jean had four brothers and one Sister, her brother Dave was the oldest. Then Jean, then Brian, then her Sister Shirley. Next was John and finally Tony who was just a little Baby at that time. Her brother Dave as you may have gathered. I wouldn't have spit on even if he'd been dying of thirst. Her brother Brian, I liked immensely and my fondness for him grew more, the longer I knew him. Shirley was a sweetie. Her brother John was just a small kid, but I like most kids and as I said Tony was just a Baby. And Babies are okay, as long as they're not shitting or squawking. I found Jean's parents unfriendly, Especially her Father, who was a total creep. But as they both seemed to disapprove of my relationship with Jean. It only tended to prolong its longevity, if you take my nature into account. Jean and I were light years apart in many ways. She was painfully shy and one of the most insecure people I had ever met. I, on the other hand was brash, cocky, arrogant and extremely confident. But what we did have in common, was extreme possessiveness, jealousy and gross immaturity. I don't know for certain. But would be willing to place an odds on bet. That Jean was receiving boy – girl relationship advice, from her married workmates, at the sewing sweatshop where she worked. She was dumb enough to heed their advice and I was unlucky enough to have to endure the brunt of it. For some reason, I always felt guilty about leaving her for her friend Maureen, when I had been going out with her previously. Even though I considered, she'd asked for it at the time. But I seemed to be willing to put up with a lot of shit, in order to make amends. And, if you think that Jean didn't take full advantage of that fact, you'd be as daft as I was for putting up with it. She was always quizzing me about 'other girls',

"How many girlfriends have you had?!"

"I don't know," I told her, "quite a lot."

"How many of them have you slept with?!" She'd demand.

"None of them." I'd reply truthfully. Jean was one of the very few people to whom I would admit my virginal status. But she didn't seem to believe me and would demand constant confirmation of my unwanted celibacy. She could also wind herself into a frenzy over a pretty girl walking along on the other side of the street. Even though I soon learned it was best to look anywhere but at her.

"What are you looking at her for?!" She'd snap at me.

"Looking at whom?" I'd reply, trying to appear innocent. Then there was,

"How many women work with you in Paddington?"

"I don't know," I'd reply, "next time I'm in work I'll count them."

"Is there any of them you fancy?" She'd persist.

"No there isn't." I soon got sick of telling her.

"Yeah, I'll bet." She'd conclude, giving the impression that she wasn't convinced. And then sulk for an hour or more, in order to confirm it. She also never seemed to tire of pushing the damned envelope ever further, to see just how much she could get away with. Out of the dozens of examples, there were two incidents that really pissed me off. The first was when we were on holiday in Wales. We came back to my Parent's house late one night and found that everyone had gone to bed. I was ravenously hungry, but before I went into the kitchen to find something to eat I asked Jean what she wanted,

"Nuffink," she replied, "I'm not hungry." So off I went to prepare something for myself. I was surprised to find the cupboard and the refrigerator bare, as normally there would have been plenty. All I managed to scrounge was one slice of stale bread and about an ounce of sweaty looking cheese. After toasting the bread, I sliced up the cheese laid it on the toast and returned the toast under the grill to make a very simple Welsh rarebit. A dish I have always been very partial to. One slice was not as much as I would have liked. But at least it would be something to put into my stomach before I went to bed, as I don't sleep well if I'm hungry. I was just about to take the first bite as Jean came into the kitchen. And I made the mistake of explaining, how I had managed to create one of my favorite little delicacies, even though there was not another crumb in the house.

"Well what am I going to eat?" She demanded.

"I thought you said you weren't hungry." I replied.

"Well I'm going to want somefink before I go to bed." She said.

"This is all that's in the house," I told her again, indicating my solitary slice of cheese on toast. "If you want something to eat you can have that." I told her gallantly. Hoping that she'd at least offer to share it. With the huge exaggerated sigh of a martyr and a look of total distaste on her face, she picked up the plate baring my precious meal and carried it into the sitting room. I followed, still hoping I might at least get a bite. I watched as she took a small bite, chewed it around her mouth a few times, then instead of swallowing it, spat it out onto the side of the plate and took another bite. She continued to bite, chew and spit until the whole of my Welsh rarebit, was a half masticated mess on her plate. Then she returned to the kitchen, in order to scrape it off the plate, into the trash can.

"Why did you do that?" I asked her.

"I wasn't hungry." She replied. I do remember not sleeping well that night, and hunger only being a small part of the reason why.

Then there was the time I was late for a date with her, due to working overtime. Having said that, I must admit, that there were many times I would be late for a date with her, due to working overtime. I knew she didn't like it, but I have never been afraid of work. And, if I have the chance to earn some extra money, then I am going to go for it. I've always been that way and I will never change until the day I think I have more money than I want. On this occasion, as many times before, I had arrived home a couple of hours later than I was supposed to meet Jean at her house. I knew that by now she would have figured that I'd been working overtime, so I saw no reason to go rushing down to see her without first having something to eat. Plus, on my arrival at my bed-sit that evening, I found that the package containing my long awaited back issues of 'Boxing and Wrestling' magazines had arrived from the States. I couldn't wait to have a quick browse through them while I cooked and ate my meal. There were 6 magazines in all and in the first one, I found there was an article on Steve Stanley. The Stanly brothers were obviously bodybuilders and both possessed very strong muscular physiques. In most of the photos in this particular magazine, Steve was wearing a one strap leopard skin leotard, reminiscent to those I had seen worn by Circus strong men, and he looked fantastic in it. I placed the magazine on the edge of the table, without reading one word. I was sure that I wouldn't find anything in any of the other magazines that would interest me as much as that one would and I wanted to keep the best one for last. I was sitting at the table eating the meal I had prepared for myself and browsing through the second of my magazines, when an angry Jean burst into the room.

"Hey Street," she accused, "I fought you were supposed to meet me about 3 fuckin' hours ago!"

"I was working overtime." I replied, while I continued to eat and browse.

"Yeah right, chattin' up the birds more like it!" She accused again. A brief sigh and a roll of my eyes, is all I rewarded her with for that remark. We had been down that road so many times before, I refused to pursue it any further.

"I got my 'Boxing and Wrestling' magazines from America today," I told her in order to change the subject, "They're really excellent."

"Huh, you're always working overtime and then you waste your money on that fuckin' rubbish!" she answered; I stuffed another mouthful of steak into my face and went back to my magazine. Jean began to undress, as she probably realized that that would present the attention I was squandering on my magazines, with some serious competition. I succeeded with difficulty, in depriving her of that satisfaction. Completely naked, she walked towards me and snatched the magazine I had discarded earlier, off the table. She got into bed, opened the magazine and began looking through it.

"What a load of fuckin' rubbish!" she declared. Still refusing to take the bait, I took my plate over to the washbasin, then I undressed and got into bed beside Jean. Who, instead of welcoming me, slammed the magazine down on the bed and turned her back on me. I got back out of bed, gathered up my magazines off the table and placed them on the bedside table, where I could reach them. I chose one of them and recommenced reading. This was an exact re-enactment of a scene, that had occurred dozens of times before. I knew from experience, the harder I tried in order to pacify Jean, the harder she would make it. So, as I had done many times before, I wouldn't waste my time trying. On one occasion in the past, we had gotten to this very same stage. And I paused while reading, to slide my hand down between her legs and fiddled long enough to get a response. Then, instead of pursuing the obvious possibilities, I used my wetted finger to turn the pages of the book I was reading. At first, shocked by my audacity, Jean soon recovered and saw the funny side of my action. She screamed with laughter, I laughed too - ice melted, we got back to a normal footing. This time however Jean had picked the wrong time to play the stubborn, injured Angel. I was too interested in my newly acquired magazines, and I decided to let her stew in her own juice while I read about the American Wrestling scene. Eventually as time went by, she must have realized that I had forgone the tedious coaxing and was more than happy reading. So with a sigh, she turned back over and picked the magazine up she had thrown down on the bed.

"Rubbish." She repeated as she re-opened it. I knew, that she knew, that belittling my magazines would piss me off, but I still refused to respond to her spiteful mood. In retrospect I wished that I had responded. As with a sigh, she held the magazine out in front of me and slowly began to tear it in half. I was absolutely furious, I couldn't believe that she would do something so mean. But although I was seething inside, I still refused to give her the satisfaction of a response. Then she tore the magazine into quarters. The magazine I had been saving for last, with the article of one of my favorite wrestlers Steve Stanley. It was completely ruined, and before I had even had a chance to read it. I gritted my teeth and my head began to pound. But I was still stubbornly determined, not to show Jean the slightest bit of emotion. She screwed what was left of my magazine into a tight wad. Then she leaned forward, and I thought that she was getting out of bed. It was fortunate for me, that I was still gritting my teeth, as she suddenly smashed the jagged remains of my ruined magazine right into my face with all the force she could muster. Blood spurted all over the bed, as I received a severe gash under my nose and my lips were cut to ribbons by the rough but sharp paper. Afterwards, even if I'd been made to swear an oath on a Bible, as to what I actually did, I wouldn't be able to answer. As all I remember is the sight of Jean's bare arse in the air, as she turned a summersault over the settee, that was placed a couple of yards from the bottom of the bed. And her landing with a thump, a couple of feet shy of the window. One yard further and she would have found herself in the small garden one floor below. Well she was always trying to see how far she could go - this time it was almost through the window.

****

The very next Sunday morning, after my first match for Tony DeMarto, I emerged from the underground tube station in The Elephant and Castle. I asked the first person I met for directions to St. George's Tavern. Upon entering its crowded and smoky confines, I looked around to see if there were any faces I recognized. There were a few, but none that acknowledged my presence. I was, after all, 'unlicensed'. I asked one of them if this was where the wrestler's meeting was held and he explained that it was the correct building, but the meeting was always held upstairs. There was a private hall, that was rented every Sunday morning for that purpose. The wrestler I had spoken to, turned his attention back to his pint as I made my way over to the stairs that led to the next floor. There were a few wrestlers ascending the stairs in front of me, and amongst them was Tony Scarlo. It turned out that Tony, like me was also here on a quest to obtain his wrestling license. We both marched into the hall as though we owned it, and were promptly ordered out, after stating our business.

"If you haven't already got a license," we were told, "wait outside the door and we'll let you know after our meeting is over, if you have been voted in by a majority of our 'licensed' members." We walked back out of the hall with our tails between our legs, and waited for what seemed days, for the wrestler/promoter meeting to conclude. 'The last time I remember waiting like this,' I thought, 'was back in school, standing outside the headmaster's office before being admitted and caned.' When at last the meeting ended, both Tony and I were allowed back into the hall, to be told that they had not had time to discuss and vote, whether we would be licensed or not. They had more important issues to discuss. - Maybe we would like to come back next week and try again. Disappointed, we both left. This went on week after week, and we both began to despair that we would ever be admitted into the hallowed halls of 'licensed pro wrestlers'. It occurred to me, and later confirmed, that even on the odd week when we were discussed, and a vote did take place. We would be extremely lucky, to be voted into their number. Other wrestlers would worry that as licensed members, we would be in a position to take wrestling jobs away from them. The less wrestlers there were, the more work there was to go around. On about our third attempt, I recognized Ron Harrison and after introducing myself to him, I told him that he had been the first professional wrestler, I had ever seen enter the ring. He seemed to be quite flattered that I remembered so much about his match. While we were chatting, he asked me where in London I lived. I told him Kensal Rise and he told me that he lived less than a mile from me in Queen's Park. He gave me a lift home in his car, and before he dropped me off, he invited me to accompany him back and forth to St. George's Tavern each week. We soon became very good friends. It was Ron who confirmed my theory, of wrestlers being wary about voting in new wrestlers who might take a match or two, that they could have had for themselves.

In the meantime, I managed to do something characteristically stupid, that would have made it very difficult to wrestle, even if I'd had a license. I had just clocked out after finishing a day's work and was walking along one of the platforms. I came across a number of my workmates standing around a trolley loaded with large solid steel rollers. In turn, they had been trying to lift the two back wheels of the heavily laden trolley off the ground, by gripping a couple of curved bars that enabled one trolley to be attached to another. I watched their efforts with interest, and it soon became evident, that none of them could come even close to succeeding. Always the showoff, I ordered them to give me room. I squatted behind the trolley gripped the bars, keeping my arms as straight as possible. Then straightening my legs I lifted the trolley wheels easily, a foot or more off the ground. As I laid it back down I got a mighty cheer from everyone around me. The commotion brought more people around to see what all the fuss was about. When told, they wanted to see for themselves. So once again I lifted the trolley to a roar of approval. Soon there was a large crowd, of both workmates and passengers who were happy for a distraction, to relieve the boredom of waiting for their respective trains. So I repeated my performance a couple more times. Inspired by such an appreciative audience, a few of the guys who had been trying to lift the trolley earlier, wanted to try again. Reluctantly I let them all have a turn. With renewed vigor, they tried to emulate my performance and to my delight they all failed miserably. Once more, I stepped forward to show them all how it was done. With a mighty heave, I wrenched the trolley up as high as my thighs, and waited until the cheers subsided, before with added flair, I hurled the trolley forcefully back to the platform. But as the wheels struck the concrete surface, with a loud resounding crash, one of the steel rollers rolled off the trolley and landed on my right foot, flattening it like a pancake. There was a great murmur of, 'Oow! – Ouch! – Shit! which I thought most appropriate, accompanied by a few guffaws and a 'serves him right!' I managed to roll the roller off my foot. And feeling every bit as foolish as I appeared, I hobbled away, ignoring inquiries concerning my welfare. My foot was in agony, or at least I thought it was. It had also been numbed, but as I sat on the bus on my way home, the blood and the feeling began to return to my foot in full force. I truly didn't know what the hell to do with myself. I remember the bus conductor standing next to my seat with a puzzled look on his face, and his hand outstretched, waiting expectantly for my fare, while I writhed in pain. And in too much agony to even be able to tell him to fuck off. Fortunately the next day at work, we were not very busy. Tom decided to take advantage of that fact, by going off to take care of some private business. While he left me to take a break at the depot, after I had loaded only about a dozen parcels that we would deliver later. I had just hobbled to the coffee stall and ordered a coffee and a couple of cheese rolls, when I heard a voice behind me say,

"Are your feet still bothering you?" I turned around to find my old driver Bill sitting on a wooden bench, drinking a cup of tea. I saw Bill most mornings at the depot, but we were usually both too busy to exchange more than a nod, or a hello. Bill seemed to think that my feet were still damaged from the time I had injured them wrestling in Birmingham, when I was still working with him.

"No Bill." I answered, and went on to explain that my feet had been fine, until I had decided to show everyone how strong I was, only the day before. As I expected, I got no sympathy from Bill, who thought that what had happened was very funny. And he was only sorry that he had missed seeing the incident himself. In order to change the subject, I asked him how he was doing, and I also asked after Ted Flock.

"Oh Ted's okay," he replied, "but he misses you a lot." Bill's face broke into a big grin as he answered me. And correctly interpreting the look I gave him as a result, went on to explain, "You know Ted fancied you, - right?"

"What the fuck are you talking about, Bill?!" I inquired.

"Ted is queer." he replied. He could see that I was anything but convinced, so he continued, "Why do you think his nephew Albert, is his sole heir," –

"Cheap servitude." I interrupted,

"He's not married and he's got no kids of his own, because he doesn't like Women." Bill insisted.

"That doesn't make him a queer," I argued. Ted was usually quite jovial, but evidence of his violent temperament seemed to lurk very close to the surface. Especially when Albert's performance didn't come up to par. "Now I'll tell you whose queer!" I told Bill, and went on to relate the 'Lon of London saga'. It's strange how that subject seems to attract attention. By now, all of the snack bar vendor's customers, who I'd been aware had been eavesdropping, ever since the word 'queer' had been used. Were now blatantly gathered around, hanging on every word. I, with my chronic aversion to receiving attention, was soon mimicking Lon's mincing gait, while I shrieked,

"Oh Christopher is such a clever cat. I've even taught you to play the piano, haven't I Christopher?!" and "Oh Adrian, you've got such lovely long eyelashes and your skin is simply gorgeous!" Everyone, even the cynical Bill, was in stitches, while I performed a reenactment of Lon's outrageous antics. Just then, Tom drew up in his van and called me back to work. As I left the snack bar, I did so in character. Blowing kisses to my audience and mincing very Lon like up to the van, while I acknowledged Tom as my Prince Charming. While I was his Cinderella, about to be transported to the Ball.

Prince Charming never even cracked a smile. But as I sat beside him in the van, he dropped a bombshell, by simply saying,

"Yer feet got better fast, didn't they?" Now that really gave me food for thought. The very mention of my foot and it began to throb again. But while I'd been showing off to an audience, I had all but forgotten about it. That reminded me of the time I had hurt my feet wrestling. I'd walked a couple of miles in agony, while I looked for a taxi. It only took a few minutes of chatting to Becky Big Tits and her mates, for me to put the pain to the back of my mind. 'There has to be a practical use to the ability, to be able to do that.' I thought. Unfortunately, I soon had the chance to put that theory to the test.

I began to experience a pain in my left ear, which soon evolved into the earache from hell. I couldn't swallow food and could hardly swallow liquid, it hurt that much. The only thing that gave me a small amount of relief, was if I held hot coffee in my mouth and turned my head onto one side, to heat the area inside my ear. As I was unable to eat, my weight soon dropped back down to 144 pounds. Trying to sidetrack the pain just didn't seem to work this time, as it even hurt to talk. But just when I thought the pain would drive me completely out of my skull, it gradually seemed to ease off and get much better. I had barely got to the stage where I could swallow a little well chewed food, when I began to experience a similar pain in my right ear; in fact the only way it differed, was that it was even worse than the pain I had felt in my left ear. After miserably suffering the agony for about a week, I went to the Hospital in Praed Street. Upon being examined, I was told that I had an abscess in each of my ears, caused by four wisdom teeth that needed to be removed. Surgery would be required and they gave me an appointment for that very same weekend. I was told to bring certain items to the Hospital with me, including a pair of pajamas, a garment which I hadn't owned, or worn since I was a child of seven. On my way home from the Hospital, I bought myself my very first pair of adult pajamas.

Jean was with me at my bed-sit the night before I was going to the Hospital. As I had to be there early the next morning, I got all the things together that I needed to take with me. Then as usual, I walked Jean home. She was very silent all the way, and hardly spoke a word. When we reached her house, I told her that it would be best if I went straight back home, in order to get a good night's sleep. Rather than hang about for an hour or more saying good night as we usually did. But she began to cry as though her heart would break. As usual, it took half the night to find out exactly what was bothering her. then she told me that she didn't want me to go to the Hospital,

"Why not?" I asked her, "I've been in bloody agony for weeks and I don't think I can stand much more of it." She came straight to the point.

"There'll be Nurses there, trying to get off with you." She sobbed.

"Don't be daft," I told her, "I'm going to Hospital for surgery not sex."

"What if you're unconscious?" She bleated, "Then you won't

know what they'll get up to."

"If I'm unconscious," I replied, "I wouldn't know anything about it, even if they did get up to anything, so what difference would it make?" She would not be pacified. She had convinced herself that every Nurse that worked in Praed Street Hospital, was just waiting for me to admit myself. Then indulge in a weekend of debauchery, that would make Sir Francis Dashwood's Hellfire Club look like a Sunday school picnic. In the end, in a display of selfless stupidity, I promised that I would suffer the pain I was in. Just so that she would not have to worry, over the remote possibility. That I would have to endure a nocturnal seduction, at the hands - or anything else that they might bring to the party. Of a bunch of imaginary, sex crazed Nurses. So I gritted my wisdom teeth and didn't go to the Hospital. Eventually, they did bother me so badly that I had to have surgery after all - but that was not until almost 24 years later. 'Jean and I must suit each other,' I thought, 'I've finally found someone even more selfish than I am.'

****

Eventually - our weekly pilgrimage to St George's Tavern, paid off for Tony Scarlo and I. We were finally invited into the 'Licensed' member's presence and informed that we had been voted in as licensed members. There were a few new promoters at the meeting, I approached for work. And I got the promise of wrestling bouts from Frankie Price, Len Briton as well as matches from promoters I had wrestled for in the past such as 'Black Butcher' Johnson, 'Dropkick' Johnny Peters and Milo Popocopolis. I couldn't wait to show Tony DeMarto my brand new wrestling license. He was so pleased, that he gave me a half a dozen matches immediately. DeMarto, was promoting wrestling shows regularly in The Caledonian Baths, Leyton Baths, The Stone Cross Hall, Poplar Baths, Hadley Cinema and Dagenham Roundhouse. I am positive that the reason Tony Scarlo and I, had at last been allowed to join the hallowed ranks of licensed profession wrestlers, was due to the fact that wrestling's popularity seemed to have suddenly exploded. For months before I received my license, I had noticed dozens of wrestling matches advertised in many of the local news papers. Wrestling posters were being plastered all over London. Many of the former Dale Martin's wrestlers now seemed to be wrestling for the independents. Including World Lightweight Champion, George Kidd, Big Shirley Crabtree, with brothers Max and Brian. The Great Bolo, 'Judo' Al Hayes, Eddie Capelli, Linde Caulder. Plus many new Stars that I had never heard of before. Such as 'The Monster', Big Bruno Elrington, Hans Streiger, Collage Boy, Lord Bertie Topham and the macabre masked man Dr. Death. The first time I ever watched Dr. Death in action was at the Caledonian Baths, and he was definitely something else. I had seen any number of Masked Wrestlers by now, since the first one, The Emerald Phantom in Newport. But none of them had prepared me for Dr. Death. To me all the others were merely wrestlers wearing masks; Dr. Death was the real thing. Facial expressions, are almost as important to a professional wrestler as having two arms and two legs. Pride, anger, distain, frustration, determination, pain and viciousness, are all displayed via their face. To cover it with a mask in my opinion was to rob it's owner of the most vital of elements. In order to compensate for this, Most of the Masked Wrestlers that I had seen so far adopted huge, exaggerated almost Shakespearian like gestures, to express their mood. Dr. Death's approach was completely opposite. Instead of vastly overstating, he subtly understated. Instead of performing an act from 'Julius Caesar', he would merely adopt a pose while standing in his corner of the ring, waiting to be announced that would relay an uneasy feeling of impending doom. Like the Grim Reaper incarnate. He could revert the heckling that his introduction would evoke, to the sound made by a scalded puppy, with a slight turn of his head towards the perpetrator. Introductions complete, he would remove his ankle length 18th Century style Highwayman's overcoat. And wearing his Purple Executioner Mask, black tights and boots, he would walk very slowly towards his opponent in order to receive the referee's instructions. Most Masked Wrestlers were villains of the ring. They would usually make a big deal, out of refusing to shake the hand of their opponent, in an effort to display their unsportsmanlike demeanor. After a brief hesitation, Dr. Death would slowly extend his hand to the proffered hand of his opponent. And very gently - barely touch the man's fingers in a cold fish handshake that invariably caused his opponent to recoil in horror. A chill would spread through the audience like a new Ice-age. Even after I had witnessed his entrance and introduction many times, that handshake would always send a shiver up my spine. When the action started, he would begin the slow methodical decimation of his foe. While exuding an aura of a creature, which combined the devious intelligence of a mad, sadistic genius, with the coldness of a Reptile. He was a Master of 'maximum reaction for minimum effort'. Which was only surpassed by his appreciation of 'anticipation being greater than the realization.'

I began wrestling about 2 or 3 times a week, sometimes more, sometimes less. Amongst my regular opponents was Tony Scarlo, 'The Irish Whip' Peter Kelly, Young Sullivan and a young Hungarian refugee, the shaven headed Zoltan Boscik. Due more to my extremely aggressive style, rather than intentionally breaking the rules I was often regarded as 'The Bad Guy', or the 'Villain' by the wrestling fans. My aggression soon made my opponent appear to be the underdog, and they seemed to love to cheer the underdog on. I was on the same card as the 3 Crabtree brothers at the Caledonian Baths on the night that 2 of them retired as wrestlers. The 3 brothers were matched separately against 3 Hungarians. Brian wrestled with a welterweight, Max with a light heavyweight and Big Shirley with a heavyweight. I wrestled Young Sullivan that night, in the only match that didn't include either a Crabtree or a Hungarian. Brian's match was on first and as inexperienced as I was at that time, I recognized the fact that as a wrestler, Brian Crabtree was totally useless. It came as no surprise when in one of the early rounds he was badly injured and had to be carried back to the dressing room, by big brother Shirley. Later that evening it was announced that Brian had declared that he would never wrestle again. That prompted the biggest cheer that Brian had ever had in his short, uneventful wrestling career. He did however, go on to become in my opinion one of Britain's best referees. Max was on next, and a complete contrast to Brian. I had seen him wrestle before and found him very exciting to watch. He had a great match with a very skillful opponent and I enjoyed every minute of it. I had also seen Big

Shirley Crabtree wrestle before and he was Boooooooring!!! As he waddled ungainly and ponderously around the ring, I thought, 'if his opponent was to just push him on his arse, he would probably rock himself to sleep trying to get back up.' I went back to the dressing room before his match ended, for fear that I would fall asleep myself just watching it. Shirley also announced that he, like Brian was retiring and hanging up his boots. Much to the relief of everyone present, including myself.

I don't know if my match with Young Sullivan that night was the best I had ever had as a professional so far. Or, if the response we got from the fans, was due to sheer relief, after the end of the boring travesty they had just witnessed between Shirley and the Hungarian. But they cheered, screamed and booed until they were hoarse. After the match was over and I was in the process of getting my hand raised in victory, Young Sullivan, challenged me to a rematch. The roar of approval from the crowd almost blew the roof off.

****

A few years later, Max told me the reason for Big Shirley's retirement. As well as being a wrestler Max often promoted matches too. Mostly in Scotland and also the hometown of the 3 Crabtree brothers, Halifax in Yorkshire. Thanks to their wrestling fame, the 3 Crabtrees were regarded as celebrities and heroes in Halifax. Max and Shirley often drew large crowds of fans to the matches, especially if they were wrestling against some particularly dastardly villain. Being local heroes, it was necessary for them to be pitted against the most daunting opposition available. You can't have a brave knight in shining armor, unless you have Dragons, Giants, Ogres, or Monsters to vanquish. On one fateful evening, Max promoted a show that had Shirley in a much publicized Main Event contest against 'The Mighty Chang'. The evil Butcher of the Orient and Master of The brutal 'Sumatran Death Lock.' So murderous and dangerous was 'The Sumatran Death Lock' reputed to be, that an attempt was made to outlaw its use in professional wrestling. Of course the attempt failed. But had the much desired effect of drawing maximum attention to the danger that Halifax's local hero was up against.

For weeks before the epic confrontation was to take place, the whole of Halifax and every other town in its vicinity was abuzz with anticipation. Max who is a very astute matchmaker, made sure that on the night, the matches prior to 'Local Hero' Big Shirley versus 'The Mighty Chang', was as basic and mundane as possible. The slow handclaps and jeers, accompanied by chants of "We want Shirley!" must have been soul destroying for the participants of the earlier matches. But by the time the Main event was due to commence, there was enough electricity in the air to light up Las Vegas for a month. A deafening fanfare sounded, as Big Shirley was the first to make his appearance and strode majestically to the ring. The cheers of the Yorkshire fans drowned the fanfare, as Shirley hauled his huge bulk up onto the apron and into the ring.

"Get 'im fer us Shirley!" They roared. "Watch out fer 'The Sumatran Death Lock!" They screamed. The applause went on and on. But gradually the deafening adulation began to subside, as the strains of Oriental cymbals, flutes and bells slowly asserted themselves. The sweetness and subtlety of a beautiful Japanese melody at first seemed at odds with the anticipated apparition. But as a hush fell over the hall, the plaintive tune developed a quality so sinister it made the flesh crawl. A small, slightly built, bespectacled Japanese businessman, accompanied by a white-faced doll-like Japanese Female. Bedecked in the full Geisha regalia shuffled along beside him towards the ring. It was the manager and personal assistant of the Mighty Chang. Then bringing up the rear was the man himself - the audience gasped. The Mighty Chang was huge. Covered in writhing, twisting, elaborately embroidered metallic gold and silver Dragons, his padded multicolor Kimono made his already yard wide shoulders look colossal. His enormous shaven head gleamed orange under the harsh spotlight that followed the progress of the exotic trio to the ring. Upon entering, the dainty Geisha-Girl held open the ropes, for first The Mighty Chang, and then his manager to enter, before taking off around the ring to scatter salt into the corners of the ring. And, a liberal pinch or two for Big Shirley. Dispersing any evil spirits that might be misguided enough to try to bring any misfortune to her macabre master. Once the ring was well seasoned with salt, the diminutive Japanese doll returned to

Chang's corner in order to help him disrobe. His manager introduced him in Japanese, before standing aside in order to give the Mighty Chang plenty of room to perform his pre-fight ritual. It consisted of bloodcurdling screams, grunts, savage kicks and stomps, with his feet still encased in a pair of eight inch high wooden Japanese clogs. Then furious Karate chops that would have slaughtered any Evil Spirits that had built up an immunity to salt, and may have been dumb enough to still be lingering on the Mighty Chang's battleground. The Master of Ceremonies introduced both contestants in English, accompanied by the vast Yorkshire crowd booing and cheering themselves hoarse in the appropriate places. Then the bell rang to start the life and death clash of the Hero of Halifax against the Ogre of the Orient. And clash it was. Chang strode to the centre of the ring and was in the process of bowing to his opponent. Big fat Shirley, came hurtling out of his corner with all the grace of a de-railed express train. His enormous belly struck The Mighty Chang between the eyes and the Giant Oriental flew backwards like a pea bouncing off a tank. He disappeared from sight as he rolled under the bottom rope and crashed to the floor outside of the ring. The fans roared with delight. But gradually fell silent as the ogre failed to re-appear. Eventually the shiny orange, shaven head, slowly rose above the ring apron and The Mighty Chang stood there looking up at his opponent with a look of total disbelief on his face. Shaking his head in despair, he leaned on the ring apron and addressed Shirley very theatrically, and in perfect English,

"I say, Shirley old boy, if you're going to carry on like that, someone is going to get hurt – and it certainly isn't going to be me. So I'll bid you farewell!" with a nod of his huge head and a wave of his huge hand, he turned on his heel and strode off back to the dressing-room. The crowd was outraged, and poor Shirley was so embarrassed that he shot out of the ring and got back to the dressing-room before The Mighty Chang.

"Kid," Max told me, "we were so embarrassed, we never showed our faces outside our doors for a month!" Big Shirley declared that as soon as he had honored his commitments to the other promotions, who already had him booked on their shows, he would hang up his wrestling boots for good. Unfortunately for wrestling, he changed his mind and more than a decade later was persuaded to make a comeback.

The story Max told me may have contributed to Shirley's retirement a tad. But, the real reason, was due to the fact that Big fat Shirley had been declared the British Champion, after Bert Assirati had retired. It must have really burnt Bert's arse, to have such a sorry specimen as Shirley succeed him as British Champion. He began turning up at venues where Shirley was wrestling, challenging him and harassing him. Shirley would cringe in his corner, threaten to run if Bert took one more step towards him. He literally shit himself with fright. Now that was the real reason he retired and he refused to make a comeback, until well after Bert Assirati was too old to be a threat.

I first met The Mighty Chang whilst sunbathing in the Serpentine, in London's Hyde Park. I found that the real Chang was just as strange and eccentric as his wrestling persona. As all wrestlers seemed to do in those days, the Mighty Chang only wrestled part time. His full time profession was as an actor, who's stage name was Milton Reid. I had seen Milton in a number of movies including 'Camp on Blood Island' where he played a particularly brutal Japanese POW prison guard. The huge shaven headed bare-chested Malaysian Pirate in 'Swiss Family Robinson'. In the following years he was to appear in a few of the James Bond films. First as a bodyguard to the notorious 'Dr. No' and he also played a Boxer Rebel in '55 Days in Peking'. Milton had an aversion to body hair and would shave his entire body including his eyebrows. He always wore heavy stage makeup and penciled in eyebrows and a very thin moustache. He also covered his body in a mixture of Olive Oil and Iodine, in order to give him a gleaming golden tanned look. His extensive elocution lessons gave him a very cultured upper crust English accent. That, coupled with his exaggerated Shakespearian like theatrical gestures, seemed to be at odds, with the brutal and murderous types he always played on screen, or the wrestling ring. He had a passion he told me, to play the romantic lead in an epic like 'Gone with the wind'.

"Can't you just picture me, taking the beautiful Heroine in my arms and kissing and caressing her passionately?" he asked me earnestly.

"Not really," I answered truthfully, "I can imagine the part where you take her in your arms, but then you don't kiss her, - you rip her head off."

****

It was about that time, I first met Steve Peacock and thought immediately that Steve Peacock would have made a great name for a wrestler. But 'she' preferred to be called Tony Curtis - that's right, I said she. Although anyone could be excused for thinking otherwise. Stephanie Peacock, was one of half a dozen Lesbians who all began working at Paddington Station at the same time. They were all friends and shared two apartments in Ladbroke Grove. Steve lived with two sisters, a huge buxom blond named Dorothy and a very pretty brunette named Betty. Dot really looked as though she had seen better days. Her blond hair was thin, frizzy and totally fried. A result she told me of having dyed it every color in the spectrum. In spite of having very short hair, her sister Betty put me in mind of Cassie. Especially physique wise and could have filled Cassie's oversized bra just as snuggly. Steve Peacock reminded me of myself in my Teddy-Boy days. She wore her hair in a Tony Curtis style D.A. Wore a velvet trimmed drape jacket, drainpipe trousers, thick crepe soled blue suede shoes and neon colored socks. Usually lime green or hot pink. We all became great friends and always drew a great amount of attention whenever we strolled around London together. Big Dot towered over all of us on five inch stiletto heels. What was left of her frizzy hair would be a different color every other week, but would always match one of her large collection of feathered boas. Betty always wore the tightest fitting sweaters, that really accentuated a bosom that seemed to arrive at her destination a full five seconds before she did. Steve in full Edwardian regalia who walked more like a man than I did. And I would either be wearing nothing but a pair of boots, skin tight black leather jeans, worn with a wide black metal studded belt. Which was meant to show off my bare 27 inch waist and 48 inch chest - if weather permitted, or with my fringed leather jacket if it didn't.

My driver Tom McBride, had become very much involved with the Workers Union and began to spend his spare time in their Paddington offices. With the result, that instead of remaining around the Minories for a few hours when we'd finished our deliveries in that area. We would return to Paddington, and I would be allowed to amuse myself there instead of at the Tower of London. In order to pass the time, I would often buy a whole chicken and a few pounds of mixed fresh fruit and eat the lot, while watching cartoons and newsreels in a News Theatre. Amongst the special features, they sometimes ran old Boxing and Wrestling matches from America. I had chance to see some of my heroes in action, including Gene Stanley, Antinino Rocca and Don Leo Jonathan. If I was lucky enough to meet up with Steve, Betty or Dorothy during our break, they would usually accompany me to the News Theatre. The first time I took any of them with me, it was just Steve and myself. As the movie began and the lights began to dim, I slid my arm around her shoulders as I would any girl I was very friendly with. I knew immediately that I had made a mistake, as I felt Steve go as stiff as a board. Without moving another muscle, or looking in my direction she growled through her tightly gritted teeth,

"Get your fuckin' arm off my shoulders, or I'll rip it out of its fuckin' socket and stuff it up yer fuckin' arse!" I quickly did as she bid. She turned in her seat and even in the darkness of the cinema, I could feel her eyes boring into me.

"Listen, I'm only going to tell you this once Tarzan." she snarled, "for a guy your alright, I like you. But you're after, what I'm after – PUSSY! - so keep your fuckin' hands to yourself."

****

All day I had felt like a cat on a hot tin roof. I was simply sizzling with impatience, as tonight - not only would I be wrestling Young Sullivan, in our much anticipated return 'Grudge Match' at the Caledonian Baths. But 'The Lightweight Champion of the World' the Great George Kidd was wrestling in the Main event. To add to my excitement, a few of my favorite people, including Jean and her Brother Brian were coming to watch me in action. The day lasted a week, but eventually after finishing work, meeting up with my entourage and traveling by bus across London. We arrived at our destination and I got them all comfortably seated before I hurried upstairs to the dressing-rooms to prepare myself for battle. Young Sullivan and I were wrestling each other in the semi-main event match which was the second bout of the evening. I found that my opponent was just as excited as I was, to be sharing the card with 'The World's Lightweight Wrestling Champion'.

A million volts of electricity seemed to surge through my body as I made my way to the ring. I was extremely gratified to hear the huge volume of boos and jeers my appearance evoked, from the packed Hall. It was the first time some of my friends would see me wrestle. I wanted to give them the best and most exciting wrestling match that had ever been fought. By the time I leapt into the ring and had been introduced to the noisy fans, their screams sounded like an express train hurting through my head, at the same speed that pure adrenaline surged through my veins. I was so pumped up that I felt as though I could have picked up the ring we were about to wrestle in and thrown it through the roof of the building. The bell rang to herald the mayhem and I went after Young Sullivan like a Wolverine goes after its next meal. How he got there I couldn't tell you. But as my opponent writhed in agony on the canvas in his own corner, the referee, Tony Mansi dove in-between us just in time to redirect a huge stomp of my right boot before it exploded into Sullivan's upturned face. I brushed the ref away as though he was a bothersome insect and crashed the whole weight of my body down onto my hapless, hopeless and helpless victim. Tony Mansi was determined to keep order and he grabbed me around the waist lifted me off my prey and threw me backwards across the ring, as though I was a rag-doll. I bounced off the mat and ran straight back towards Young Sullivan. My path was immediately blocked by Tony Mansi's huge bulk. He raised his palm towards me to as a signal to halt, but I would not be denied. Without missing a stride, I leapfrogged right over his head and delivered the stomp, squarely to the centre of my still prone opponent's chest. The breath wheezed out of him with the sound of a Blacksmith's bellows. All the referee's interference had achieved was delaying the mighty stomp for less than a split second and he was livid. Once again he grabbed me off Young Sullivan and hurled me backwards. Tony Mansi was an ex-wrestler and although past his prime, he was still a very formidable fighter who must have outweighed me by at least 80 pounds. He was determined to show everyone who was in charge. But I was even more determined that things were going to go my way, and I charged right through the referee. I was Blitzkrieg, Young Sullivan was Poland. I grabbed my opponent and had dragged him halfway across the ring by his hair, before an avalanche named Tony Mansi enveloped me once more and began to crush me in a reverse Bear-hug. Tony may have had the power of an old Bear, but he had never tried to squash a Weasel before. I wriggled out of his grasp like a greased eel. And, with single-minded and determined ferocity, I again began to beat on Young Sullivan as though he was an old War drum. The bell sounded to end round one. But I didn't, I wouldn't, I couldn't stop pounding on Young Sullivan. This time I saw the referee charge and I drove my shoulder right under his ample gut with all the force I could muster sending him crashing down onto his arse. He was furious, but how could he control me when I couldn't control myself?

"You're disqualified!" He roared, in a voice that would have deafened Thor. And that was that, the match was over; once again I had fucked up.

On my way back to the dressing room, I shot a glance over to Jean and company. Her Brother Brian, stared back at me with total shock registered on his white face; I don't remember gentle Brian ever attending another one of my matches. It seemed that he found my brand of violence extremely unpalatable. Back in the dressing room, I soon recovered from my disappointment with my own performance. And Young Sullivan soon recovered from the beating I had administered. We were still enormously excited at sharing the card with 'World Champion' George Kidd. The dressing room comprised of a wide corridor running along a row of separate bathrooms. We found that each of our baths had been filled with hot water for us. Our bath would have to wait we both decided. Neither of us wanted to miss one single second of the great George Kidd in action. Still wearing our trunks and boots we both forgot about our own battle, and hurried down stairs to watch the Main Event contestants making their entrance.

The World Champion's performance was as great as mine

had been awful. His unique style of wrestling all but defied description. The match ended and George Kidd's hand was once again raised in victory. Young Sullivan and I rushed back upstairs to our respective bathrooms. Both of us filled to the brim with inspiration, derived from watching a true Master of our sport plying his trade. I was delighted to learn that Young Sullivan had never seen George Kidd wrestle before that night. I had watched a few of his bouts in Cardiff. So of course - to my mind that made me an authority concerning The World's Lightweight Champion, and his extraordinary wrestling technique. Young Sullivan's bathroom was next door to mine and I found him a very eager listener, as we wallowed in our respective baths. I recited everything I could recall about the matches I had witnessed. I also explained that in spite of being, in my opinion the best technical wrestler on the Planet. George Kidd was not every wrestling fan's cup of tea. I told Young Sullivan of the night in Cardiff, when a gang of very rowdy fans heckled and booed George unmercifully. They were obviously too ignorant to appreciate the fantastic skill of a true wrestling genius at work.

"When is the wrestling gonna start?!" they chanted.

"We want to see some action!" They roared.

"We want blood". They screamed. For about 10 minutes George Kidd completely ignored their rude, unappreciative and unjustified behavior. But the hecklers were relentless. They hoped that their insults could induce George to adopt a more aggressive style. Instead he suddenly raised one hand halting the action. He walked over to his opponent and raised his opponent's arm in victory before stepping out of the ring, and walking back to the dressing room. Leaving everyone in the arena with their mouths hanging open with shock. The World's Lightweight Wrestling Champion, George Kidd was a very proud man. And when it came to displaying his skill and ring prowess, it was his way or no way. Well I talked and talked, while Young Sullivan listened and listened. No one would have thought, that less than an hour earlier, we were both facing each other in the ring ready to tear out each other's throats. It was only due to the fact that our bathwater was beginning to cool, that induced me to shut up and get out of the bath. Once dressed, I wondered if I still had time to catch the end of the last match. As I opened my bathroom door and stepped out, I almost collided with the great man himself, George Kidd.

"Oh, hello Mr. Kidd," I said, holding my hand out, "my name is Kid Jonathan." He ignored my hand and thrust his face forward towards me. I instinctively drew back to refocus on his face. It was so contorted with horror and loathing, that he looked as though he was gazing at his own rotting corpse. His pale grey-blue eyes bored into me and I began to wonder if he was about to have a fit, or go into some kind of seizure. We both seemed to be frozen in time. Suddenly he turned on his heel and walked away from me as fast as his legs would carry him, without looking back. I just stood there with my hand still extended, wondering what the Hell that was all about. I never wrestled on the same card as George Kidd again, for the whole time I wrestled for the independent Promotions. I also noticed that I didn't seem to get as many matches for them either, whenever the World's Lightweight Champion was in Town. I tackled Tony DeMarto on the subject, but he refused to elaborate, other than saying,

"George Kidd don't like yer!" It was a total mystery to me. As I had never met, or spoken to George Kidd before in my life. It was not until many years later that the mystery was finally revealed. I have to admit that seeing dozens of upcoming wrestling events advertised in the newspapers and hundreds of Wrestling posters plastered all over London, completely lost their appeal to me when World Lightweight Champion George Kidd appeared on them. As no promoter would dream of hiring Kid Tarzan Jonathan, when The Great King George was south of the Scottish border. The incident concerning George Kidd was just the first of a series of very aggravating occurrences.

****

At the Forester's later that week I was training with Les and Phil. We had finished with the bench-press and I was also finished with the squat. The poundage that Les and Phil had progressed to was far beyond my capabilities. Soon after they began using ultra heavy weights for half squats. Then, even Phil joined me and other members of the Forester's club on the sidelines, as audience to the powerful Les. He had loaded the bar with close to 700 pounds. With the aid of Bill Smith and myself as spotters, Les got under the barbell and heaved the huge weight off the stands across his broad shoulders. He took a couple of steps forward to begin his set. This was the heaviest weight I had ever seen anyone exercise with at that time and I found it extremely exciting to watch. There was a fair amount of spring in the bar and Les had got into a rhythm and was taking full advantage of the springy movement to make each rep a little easier. When all of a sudden, the bar began to bend around Les's neck like a stick of licorice. Everyone gasped in horror as the change in the balance, twisted the Herculean Les around and down onto one knee. Both Bill Smith and I dove forward in an attempt to aid Big Les who seemed to be kneeling helplessly under 700 hundred pounds of twisted metal. As Smithy and I made a grab for the barbell the collar securing the weights on Bill's side broke, and all the steel plates on his end cascaded off the bar and clattered around Smithy's feet. With no weight on one side of the barbell to counter balance it, the bar swung around and only great luck and a bit of fancy footwork on my part, saved me from the heavy side of the barbell crashing into my knees or shins. Smithy wasn't so lucky however, as the weight swung down on my end the other end swung up and smashed into the side of Smithy's head. The mighty uppercut lifted him off the ground like a rag doll and deposited him flat on his back a few yards away. All of a sudden poor Smithy was the new kid on the block, as far as our sympathy and attention was concerned. Blood poured out of his face and spread out into a puddle around his head. In the meantime Les was still adopting the attitude of The Mighty Atlas, with the weight of the World on his shoulders. I had just turned my attention back to Les in time to see him power the remnants of the enormous weight off his shoulders over his head and drop it with a resounding crash in front of him.

"Are you ok Les?" I enquired anxiously, as he got up unaided. He just stood there patting his ample tummy and replied,

"I'm fine Ade, but if it wasn't for this big belly of mine I'd be dead." He turned and looked down at his still unconscious and very bloody spotter and said sarcastically,

"Hey, thanks for the help Smithy!"

I was still wrestling, but just not as often, and on this occasion I had wrestled my way to Victory over the excellent little Wrestler from Hungary, Zoltan Boscik. A very satisfying evening indeed - until I stepped outside The Roundhouse, Dagenham and walked into a blanket of fog. I shuffled across the road, hoping that I wouldn't get run over in the process. And hoped also that I could find the bus stop, as I could hardly see more than a yard in front of my face. On my journey to the bus stop I came upon an Off License, and thought I'd buy myself something nice to drink with my supper. As I opened the door and stepped inside, I met Peter Rann who had also wrestled at The Roundhouse that night. We discussed the weather and he asked me where I had to drive to. I told him where I lived, but explained that I didn't have a car and was hoping to catch a bus. Peter offered me a lift part way, and I gladly accepted his offer. He told me he was parked right outside the Off License. In order not to keep him waiting, I ordered the first thing I saw, which was, a very large bottle of Bulmer's Cider. I hadn't drunk hard Cider since before I had left Wales, and I thought that a few glasses of that with my supper, would just fit the bill. Although our journey took about 3 times longer than normal, due to the fog, it past quite quickly for me as Peter had a great sense of humor. And, was full of great wrestling stories. I was amazed to find it was gone 1.30am by the time he dropped me off near Knightsbridge. By the time I was crossing Notting Hill Gate the fog had lifted a little. I decided to walk up Portobello Road, instead of the wider and better lit Ladbrook Grove, which ran parallel to it. The real reason I took that route, I don't think I would even have admitted to myself at the time. But it was the possible off chance meeting with Margaret, who I hadn't seen for ages. I was morbidly curious to know how she would greet me if we met by 'chance'. In my left hand I was carrying a small suitcase that contained my wrestling gear, and in my right I was carrying my big bottle of Bulmer's by its neck. I walked as briskly as I was able, considering the visual impairment caused by the dense fog. The only sound in the still night was the clip-clopping of my Cowboy boots on the pavement. When all at once, an explosion of movement to my left, as two dark figures leapt out of a shop doorway, and a large fist ricochet off my forehead. Instinctively, my arm swung back and around in a wide arc and I brought the heavy bottle of Cider right down onto my attacker's head. He went down face first into the sidewalk. But the bottle of Cider, instead of shattering on his skull as one would expect. Sent a terrific shock up my arm and bounced out of my hand over my head and landed somewhere behind me without making a sound. I leapt over the prone body in front of me, in order to attack the tall, skinny Black Man, who was still hovering on the other side of his fallen comrade. He made a noise that startled me in the otherwise silent night, that sounded like someone stomping on a cat's tail. He ducked by me and ran up the road in the direction I had been coming from. I looked after him as he disappeared into the fog, then down at the crumpled figure of a very heavily built Black Man, who hadn't moved a muscle since I'd put him there. I stepped back over my would be assailant, in search of my Cider, and found it in pristine condition, nestling on top of a box of garbage next to the curb. I must have gazed down longingly at it for a full minute, before turning on my heel and continuing on my journey. I left my precious bottle of Bulmer's, where it lay. I have a thing about garbage and I couldn't even touch a brand new unused, virgin of a garbage-can without scrubbing my hands afterwards. As bad as I felt about losing my Cider, I felt even worse about what had just occurred. I didn't know whether it had been an attempted mugging, as I would have preferred to believe. Or if the attack was racially motivated as the London Race war was still going strong. Especially in the area where I was that night. I have never been a Racist; I'm willing to respect anyone who is willing to respect me. I had always been happy that there were so many different and interesting types of Human Beings in the World, just as I was happy that there are so many species of Animals.

    A couple of similar occurrences took place a few years later. The first was in a Cinema in Brixton. During the interval between the two movies showing, I went to get an ice-cream each for Jean and myself. I was standing in a queue waiting for my turn when a Blackman pushed into the queue in front of me. I had to tell him a couple of times to get to the back of the queue. At first he ignored me, then he turned his head and said,

    "Hey Mon, fuck off!"

    He was just about to be served when I grabbed the neck off

his shirt and threw him backwards out of the queue. He pulled out a knife, began waving it about in front of me and said something like,

"I cut you up, you fooken' blad clad." Not having a ready answer, I kicked him hard in the stomach. He fell down, but jumped straight up and ran over to a group of Black men, who were standing inside the main entrance. He began jabbering away and pointing at me. I was in the process of formatting a plan of defense, when the obvious leader of the group, who my assailant was directing his complaints to, waved his hand at me. He smiled and said to the knifeman in a voice loud enough for me to hear across the foyer,

"Better you leave 'im alone Mon, or he break you in 'arf, dat's Adrian Street, de wrastler Mon, I seed 'im on de tele!"

Then on the other occasion, I had been grocery shopping in Streatham on a bright sunny afternoon and was walking along the High Road on my way home. I was carrying 3 large paper carrier bags. One in each arm, the other wedged between them. They were so stuffed with goodies, that I could barely see over the top of them. As I approached the corner near Streatham Station, I saw two Black men wearing bus conductor's, or bus driver's uniforms. The reason they caught my eye was, the fact that they were walking fast and furiously towards me, in an extremely agitated state. Waving their arms about to emphasize whatever it was they were discussing. I moved over to my left in order to give them more room to get by when they were still about 20 or 30 yards in front of me. But as I did, they both spotted me for the first time, and purposely began to move at the same hectic pace in my direction. I moved further to my left, but they still marched straight towards me. By the time they were close I was as far to my left as I could go, almost wedged up against a shop window. I stopped for them to pass, but the one on my right barged straight into the package I was carrying in my right arm, while the other one hurled himself at the centre package. I felt the shop's plate glass window creak as I was forced against it, and then the crash of glass, as 3 of the 4 bottles of Guinness I'd bought, cascaded out of one of the bags and smashed on the pavement between our feet. The Black man on my left, quickly ducked down and came up with one of the broken bottles in his fist and thrust it viciously towards my face. With both of my arms hugging the bags of groceries to my chest, I had no alternative but to sacrifice all my goodies by hurling them in the way of the broken bottle like a battering ram, in order to protect my face from the sharp, jagged glass. As the bags fell to the ground, I threw myself between my attackers and made a mad dash for the corner. No, I wasn't running away. I was never blessed with the common sense or motivation to take that route. There was a Lady on the corner selling flowers, and I had noticed that lying on the table where her blooms were displayed, a tool that was used to open wooden crates. It had a hammer head on one side and on the other, two parallel pointed metal prongs. It had the appearance of a twin bladed ice-pick. I grabbed it, turned and hurtled back towards the pair of Public Transport thugs, with extremely vicious intent. In spite of the heavy overcoats they both wore, I wasn't able to overtake them. They fled for their lives up the High Street. But I wasn't concerned and I would not be denied revenge. I didn't know of another human being with more stamina than I possessed and I was perfectly willing to chase them for the rest of the day and all night, if that was necessary. Unfortunately, a big red double Decker bus slowed down across the other side of the street. And both of my would be victims risked life and limb by dashing across a busy highway to reach it. As soon as they leapt aboard it picked up speed, leaving me in its wake and saving them both from some very serious injuries. I walked back to my groceries, which were spread all over the pavement. And before attempting to see what I could salvage, I returned the hammer to the Flower Lady on the corner and thanked her for its use.

"Yer shoulda stuck it in he's fuckin' froat." She told me sweetly.

Returning to my story, the final aggravation happened during one of our much extended lunch breaks. Steve Peacock, Big Dot, Busty Betty and I were walking up Edgware Road on our way back to the Station to clock out for the day. We were taking our time as we still had plenty of it to kill. We happened upon a book shop, and I decided to go in to see if they had any Wrestling or Bodybuilding magazines. It would have seemed strange, I suppose to anyone who may have observed us. That while I was browsing through magazines depicting muscle-men, Steve was gloating over naked Ladies in glamour mags. I didn't know what Dot or Betty were looking at, until Betty called to me and said,

"Hey Tarzan, here's some more Bodybuilding books over here."

I walked over to where she was browsing through one of them. But when I looked at the display up close, I could see that they were not, what I would term as bodybuilding mags. They had titles like 'Body beautiful' 'Adonis' and such and contained photos of 'Pretty Boys' rather than Bodybuilders.

"That's not bodybuilding," I told her, picking one out to show her what I meant. "they're all pouf's books." I flipped through the magazine, looking for a good example, I was suddenly stopped dead in my tracks,

"We've got to go!" I shouted, snatching Betty's magazine out of her hand, and throwing it back on the shelf, "Come on, hurry up!" I ordered, as I herded them all out of the shop and into the street.

"What's up with you Tarzan?" complained Steve, "We've got loads of time yet?"

"Oh, it's just later than I thought it was." I replied feebly, as I couldn't think of anything else to say. I felt my face burning like a furnace. The reason for my hasty exit was due to the fact that while I was looking in the 'Pouf's' book, for a 'good example' I came across about 4 or 5 photos of myself wearing nothing but the dreaded posing pouch. And in the photos of my back, I may as well have been completely naked, and there was no way I wanted any of my friends to see them. In spite of my suspicious behavior, and bright scarlet countenance. I thought I'd got away with it, until Betty leaned up against me, cupped her hand against my ear, and said in a loud stage whisper,

"You've got a nice arse Tarzan!"

Just then we turned left into Praed Street, and on the opposite corner the walls were plastered with new wrestling posters. As flustered as I was, by what Betty had just said, I was happy that I now had the perfect excuse to completely change the subject - UNTIL, I saw whose name dominated every one of them - Yes, you've got it in one, The Great George Kidd was back in town.

****

1959 was coming to a close, on the 5th of December I celebrated my 19th Birthday and the only aggravation I suffered for the rest of that year, I guess you could have said was more or less, self inflicted. I was very disappointed that the Birthday present that I would have liked to receive from Jean, was still a no go. I decided that if she wasn't willing to help me with my problem, I would have to resort to attempting to resolve it myself. I planned to spend the few days I had off from work for Christmas, in Brynmawr by myself. As taking Jean with me would do a lot more than cramping my style. There had always been a good number of very willing participants, in and around Brynmawr. I figured that if I took the trip alone, I would have a fair chance of a close encounter of the carnal kind. Which was more than I'd get if I invited Jean to join me. Needless to say she was furious. She shouted and screamed, sulked and cried, every night. Leading up to my departure was shear agony. But I was determined that anything she said or did, or threatened to do, was not going to change my mind.

The night before The Forester's Club closed for the Christmas holidays, the Club held a presentation. Members of the training staff gave speeches of appreciation etc. I was mildly interested in the procedure, but remembered wishing that they would hurry up and get on with it, so that I could begin my last workout before Christmas. Even though presentations were taking place, recognition given and awards presented, to various Club members for their accomplishments. I was taken completely by surprise when I was called up to stand beside Les Clark and Phil Woods. We then listened to Bill Smith telling us, and all club members, how much The Forester's Club appreciated our efforts, and success in representing their weight-lifting team in inter-club competition. Each of us was presented with an award. For representing The Club, as both the 11 and 12 stone Champion I was awarded a black v-neck Weider T-shirt. To replace the poor, worn and threadbare Weider T-shirt that I'd been wearing for years. Then everyone in attendance was amazed by my reaction when I received it. Not least of all myself. The granite hard, tougher than nails little Welshman sobbed like a Baby. It wasn't that the T-shirt was such a valuable item. I could have bought one myself for less than a couple of pounds. But I couldn't ever remember being appreciated for accomplishing something that really meant so much to me before in my life. I proudly donned my new T-shirt and promptly soaked it with tears, that just wouldn't stop streaming down my face.

I had to work half day on Christmas Eve. But I went to work prepared to catch the first train I could from Paddington Station to Brynmawr as soon as I had finished working for the day. I was utterly exhausted when I arrived in Brynmawr that evening. I was still reeling from the savage encounter I had had the night before with Jean. She was still attempting to change my mind about taking her to Wales with me. It had taken till the early hours of the morning, to finally convince her that I was going alone. We parted on bad terms. Walking to my parent's home that evening, I passed by the Tabernacle. I cringed as I recognized Dad's loud voice dominating a Christmas Carol they were singing. After greeting Mam, I told her that I'd just discovered yet another flaw in The Tabernacle's view on Religion.

"What flaw is that?" Mam inquired, with a look of resignation on her face.

"They've got Christmas mixed up with Easter." I informed her, "I just walked by The Tabernacle and heard them Crucifying 'Silent Night.'

"Don't tell Dad that," Mam replied, "or there'll be no peace on Earth this Christmas." - "Not to mention the good will." I added.

After a chat and a bite to eat, I walked down to where Ter, his Wife June and their 6 month old, Daughter Sandra lived.

"Oh, you've just arrived in time," Ter informed me, as he opened his front door, in answer to my knocking, "we're all going to a Christmas Eve party, at June's Brother's house." Although I was shattered from the lack of sleep the night before and the long journey from London to Brynmawr, I was beginning to get my second wind. After a few drinks at the Christmas Eve party, I started to feel at least half human. I began talking to a pretty girl with jet black hair, who told me her name was Maureen. We had been chatting for a couple of hours when Terence sidled up to me and whispered loudly,

"You can bring her back to my house if you want to; we've got a big sofa you can sleep on!" I looked at Maureen, who smiled timidly. Then he spoke directly to her,

"Do you want to spend the night with Adrian at my house, or not?! He demanded.

"Oh, I don't know." Replied Maureen shyly.

"Well make your fucking mind up," ordered Ter, "cos Adrian can get a lot better than you, you know!" - 'The last of the smooth talkers,' I thought. I was amazed when I heard Maureen say,

"Okay, I'll come if he wants me to." And naturally I did. We arrived back at Ter's house past midnight. After showing us the sofa in his lounge, both he, June and Baby Sandra went upstairs to bed and left us to it. As Maureen and I began to undress she surprised me again by asking me,

"Have you ever done 'it' before?" Then I surprised myself by answering,

"No I haven't."

"I haven't either." Stated Maureen, 'Yeah right.' I thought.

We both stood there naked, neither one of us believing that the other had never done 'it' before. I was convinced that there was only one of us telling the truth. Well we dove onto the sofa and got right down to 'it' and I took to 'it' like a baby Duck takes to water. Why it had taken me so many years to accomplish 'it' was now beyond me, as I found 'it' was as easy as falling off a log - only much nicer. Even though I had been totally inexperienced up until that time. I could tell that Maureen was anything but - but she gave me a back-handed compliment when she gasped,

"Now I know you were telling lies!" The fatigue of the last couple of days just melted away. Replaced by a well of energy I didn't know I possessed. I attempted to make up for all those wasted years in one night. It was 9 am in the morning, before we finally called a halt to the festivities. That wasn't because either of us wanted to stop. It was on account of not wanting to be caught in too compromising a position, when my Brother and Sister-in-law arose. Even more to the point, I remembered Dad's yearly Christmas pilgrimage. He would visit every local family member each Christmas morning. Exchange the season's greetings and drink their health. It would only be a matter of time before he'd be knocking on the front door. And there was no way

I wanted to be caught here with Maureen by Dad, after not going back to my parents house the night before. So I quickly got dressed, said, "thank you," and, "Goodbye." To Maureen and went out to visit each of our local family members in Dad's wake. Exchanging greetings and taking a drink with all of them. As fortune would have it, I missed meeting up with Papa on my pilgrimage and arrived back at my parent's home before Dad did. Mam was dishing out the dinner and I was sitting at the dining table with my knife and fork in hand, when Dad staggered in. By the time everyone was seated and had begun to eat, I was really beginning to feel the effects of too many nights without sleep and too many drinks, too early in the day on an empty stomach. I was gnawing on my first bite of Turkey leg when Dad said,

"There was some strange Girl in Terence's house when I went there today. - She looked as though she hadn't slept for a week." He looked straight at me with eyebrows raised and gross speculation written all over his face. That was all I remembered, before I keeled over and fell face first into my Christmas dinner. - 'But never mind,' I thought, 'Even if I had have drowned in the gravy - at least I wouldn't have died a Virgin.'

1960's.

Before returning to London, I visited Mamo who was Hospitalized and suffering with Cancer. Mamo had always been a very large and powerfully built Woman. Very stern and humorless, with a violent temper and seemed totally devoid of affection. But when I appeared at her bedside, she opened her arms and hugged me for the first time in our lives. And in a way that would have broken my back if she had still enjoyed her former strength.

"Oh, Adrian, thank you for coming to see me." She sobbed, in a voice so weak I wouldn't have recognized it. Her bulk had also disappeared and her strong and muscular body had been replaced, by what now felt like a bag of bones. I disengaged and tried to smile down at her. But she began to cry and I almost disintegrated. Within a few months I returned to Wales from London to attend her funeral.

****

Every Saturday night Paul Lincoln ran wrestling in The Metropolitan Theatre, in The Edgware Road. And every Saturday night The Metropolitan Theatre was packed to capacity. The fans would begin lining up outside the Theatre, hours before the doors opened, to ensure admission. That would give them ample time to admire dozens of almost life-sized, grainy, black and white photos of the wrestling Stars, that were framed in glass cases along the side of the building. Stars, who would be appearing on that night's or future shows. As well as very many great British Stars, there would be a steady procession of American and Continental wrestlers working for 'Paul Lincoln.' If I wasn't wrestling anywhere myself on a Saturday, I would be one of the fans waiting impatiently in line to buy my ticket. The first time I had gone to The Metropolitan, I had marched into the building via the stage door. Explained that I was a wrestler, and demanded to speak to Paul Lincoln, as I wanted to offer the services of Kid Tarzan Jonathan to his Promotion. In no time flat I got a response - 'Get out – and if you want to see the matches, go to the front entrance and buy a ticket!' It turned out to be as difficult to get a start with 'Paul Lincoln Promotions' as it was to get a start with Dale Martin's; I wondered if George Kidd's regular appearances on Paul Lincoln's shows could have anything to do with my difficulties?

"JESUS CHRIST – I can't believe the weight you just lifted!" exclaimed the new boy at The Forester's Club as I rose from the bench after completing my set. So naturally I took an instant liking to the newcomer. His name was Tony Woods. He seemed to be so impressed with the amount of weight I was using on all of my exercises that I took him under my wing and began to teach him what I knew about pumping iron. Tony was also interested in Wrestling. So it wasn't long before I introduced him to the mat and we began knocking lumps off each other with a passion. To show his gratitude Tony introduced me to Anne, a girlfriend of his girlfriend Marcia. And immediately Anne and I began knocking lumps off each other - but with a different kind of passion. Tony's girlfriend Marcia, was a scream. Almost everything she said was hilarious, but the way she treated poor Pussy whipped Tony was criminal. And to add insult to injury he wasn't getting any Pussy in the process. Marcia would order

Tony about, and he would just about fall over himself trying to comply with her slightest whim. I could have hated her for the way she treated my new friend, but she was so funny with it, that it was impossible for me to take offence. Even though, the treatment often included pinching, kicking and slapping. Then poor, pathetic Tony would apologize for making her do it. In spite of all the other abuse he suffered. Tony's pet peeve with Marcia was a photo that she kept in her purse that seemed to be her most treasured possession. It was of a 'very well built' and very naked Negro, standing at the table with his huge prick lain from one end of a dinner plate to the other. It had a caption written underneath which exclaimed, 'All that meat and no veggies!' Marcia was always flashing the photo and roaring with laughter at people's reaction to it, while Tony would cringe and plead,

"Hey Marcy, why don't you get rid of that disgusting fuckin' photo?" He even tried to coax me, to ask Marcia if I could borrow the photo and then destroy it, instead of giving it back to her. But I often derived as much sadistic amusement out of Tony's discomfiture as Marcia did. So I pre-warned Marcia not to give me the photo if I asked her if I could borrow it in Tony's presence. But hey, what are friends for?!

****

When it came to parting with money, Promoter Tony DeMarto was tighter than Bert Assirati's Bear-hug. I was still only getting 2 pounds-10 shillings, a match from him even though all the other promoters were paying me 4 or 5 pounds. With the exception of Johnny Childs and Geoff Moran, who were also only paying that amount. When I tackled Johnny and Geoff on the subject, they explained with a certain amount of justification, that they only ran shows in small venues. And that I owed them, as they had given me my start in the business. 'If I can get more from DeMarto,' I thought, 'I could use that as a leaver to pries at least a couple more pounds a match out of Childs and Moran.' I knew that Young Sullivan was in the same boat. So I approached him on the subject, and he agreed. The next time we were wrestling on the same card for DeMarto, our combined demand for an increase in wages, would carry a lot more weight than if we attempted it individually. An ideal opportunity presented itself when we found that we were both wrestling at Poplar Baths Hall, and then wrestling each other, the following night at The Caledonian Baths Hall. Young Sullivan and I had both debuted for DeMarto 6 months earlier, at The Stone Cross Hall.

"We've been wrestling for him since last August," I explained to Young Sullivan, "he'll have to give us something extra."

"How much shall we ask him for?" asked Young Sullivan.

"Well we both get 4 or 5 pounds off everyone else, so we should get at least as much off DeMarto - we'll ask him for 5, but if we have to, we'll settle for 4."

"What will we do if he won't pay us more?" queried Young Sullivan.

"Then we'll go on strike and tell him we won't Wrestle for him the next night at The Caledonian Baths." I replied.

"You're on first wiv' Joe Murphy," Tony DeMarto told Young Sullivan, "an' you're on last wiv' Peter Kelly." He told me as he walked into the Dressing room in Poplar Baths Hall. Young Sullivan and I had been waiting impatiently for our impending confrontation.

"Young Sullivan and I would like a word with you Tony." I told him.

"Waddya want Jonafun?" He asked, eying us both suspiciously.

"Young Sullivan and I have both been wrestling for you for over 6 months now," I explained, "and we both think it's about time we got a raise in wages."

"No Chance," He replied without a seconds hesitation, "I'm overpayin' as it is."

"We want 5 pounds a match from tomorrow night on." I demanded, ignoring his initial response.

"Nah, yer ain't worf it." He told us.

"Ok, how much do you think we're worth?" I asked, willing to parley if I had to.

"Abaht firty bob fer the pair of ya!" He informed me.

"We'll settle for 4 pounds a match starting tomorrow night!" I demanded, allowing his insult to slide over my head.

"Nah, yer ain't getting' it," he stated, "beta getcha boots on," He told Young Sullivan," while ignoring me, "yer on first."

"TONY!" I shouted, "If you don't pay us at least 4 pounds a match, we won't be wrestling for you in The Caledonian Baths tomorrow night."

"Izat right?" He retorted, directing his glare at Young Sullivan, as if daring him to condone my statement. Young Sullivan nodded his head, to indicate that we were united.

"Okay, please yourselves," he told us, then turned around and called to one of the wrestlers who was in the process of changing into his ring gear. "Hey Eddie, we're gonna be a coupla wrestlers short tamarra night, will yer wrestle twice wiv Joe? I know he'll do a double fer a couple of extra quid."

"Yes, no problem." Answered Eddie Capelli. I couldn't believe that one wrestler would blatantly do that to another one. It wasn't a very large dressing room and everyone present was aware of the gist of our disagreement. In order to ingratiate himself with the promoter and earn a couple more pounds in the Process, Eddie Capelli had cheerfully kicked the legs out from under both Young Sullivan and me.

"Okay, we will wrestle tomorrow night!" Young Sullivan yelled at DeMarto.

"What abaht you Jonafun?!" DeMarto demanded, I folded like a deck-chair.

"Yes, I'll wrestle tomorrow night Tony," I agreed, but added optimistically, hoping to save a little face, "what about 3 pounds a match?"

"Forget it," he growled, "you gonna be there or not?!"

"I'll be there." I conceded, trying my best to ignore the disappointment on Eddie Capelli's face. And the satisfied smirks on the faces of the other wrestlers present.

That incident was the only time in my life that I allowed anyone to play my bluff and to this day the memory is still a burr in my side. I promised myself that from that day on, I would never concede another ultimatum whatever the consequences.

I was still wrestling a couple of times a week on average. And still posing for physique magazines a few times a month, for various photographers. One day after a posing session for John

Graham, he showed me some publicity photos that he'd taken of an American Wrestler 'Texas' Buddy Cody. They reminded me of the large grainy photos of wrestlers, displayed in glass cases outside The Metropolitan Theatre. And I thought it was about time I had some publicity photos taken of myself. I asked John how much he would charge me to take similar shots of me.

"Maybe we can trade." He suggested and then giggled like a girl at the resulting expressions that must have crossed my face.

"Don't flatter yourself," he told me after he'd recovered, "I told you you're not my type - I was thinking you could do some of my Darkroom work, I hate doing it myself, but you may find it interesting."

"What kind of Darkroom work?" I inquired apprehensively.

"Oh, the usual stuff, developing film and printing photos." He replied.

"I don't know the first thing about developing film or printing photos." I told him.

"No problem - I'll teach you how to do it." He said.

So that was how I learned to develop film and print photographs and to say I may have found it interesting was an understatement. I loved it. While I worked in the Darkroom, which was situated behind the curtain that was used as a backdrop. John would relax in his studio, on the other side of the curtain drinking coffee and listening to his very extensive collection of classical music. I began to love the music he listened to, as much as watching the blank sheets of paper magically transformed into pieces of black, white and grey works of art.

****

There was no one except Tony to practice Professional wrestling with at The Forester's during this period. And the fact that Marcia would only 'allow' Tony to train on a Monday, Wednesday and Friday meant that we would have to share the mats with the amateur wrestlers on those nights. On Tuesday and Thursday nights, when we would use the mats exclusively for practicing pro wrestling, I now had no one to practice with. So on those 2 nights all I did was lift weights. One Tuesday night I had just began my workout when Bill Smith walked in chatting to two very pretty girls. It turned out they wanted to join the club and learn how to exercise with weights.

"Oh good, Adrian is here tonight, he'll teach you all you want to know." He said to them and winked at me, as he made the introduction. He then handed them over to my tender loving care. June and Wanda were both about my age and both blond. Wanda's hair looked natural, June's was almost white. I was unaware of it at that time but it turned out that Wanda had recently become engaged and June was already married.

I don't know how it slipped out. But after we had been exercising for about 2 minutes, I just happened to mention that I was The Club weightlifting Champion and also a Pro Wrestling Champion. And normally on Tuesday and Thursday nights, they would have been able to come over to the Wrestling building and watch me in action.

"Oh, we'd love that," cried June enthusiastically, "why don't you show us now?!"

"There's no one here to wrestle with," I told her - "I think I've probably frightened them all away." I added modestly.

"You can wrestle with us instead." Invited June, so without further ado I collected the key to the wrestling room. By the time I had rolled out one of the wrestling mats, both June and Wanda had stripped down to their Bras and Panties. So as not to mess up their brand new workout gear, they told me. All I wore when bodybuilding was a pair of leopard skin briefs and flip-flops. So although I was outnumbered two to one to begin with, we were all similarly dressed. But as both June and Wanda, turned out to be extremely dirty wrestlers, in a very short period of time we were all similarly and completely undressed.

"This is what I call All-in-wrestling." I told June, as I pinned the naked Wanda to the mat.

"Oh really," answered June, "but why bother to wrestle - when it's all in?!"

Jean had a new obsession, not that she had forsaken the old obsession of quizzing me continually about 'other girls.' She did that so often and automatically, that I began to wonder if she was still conscious of what she was actually saying. My automatic negative reply, was now tinged with a little guilt and a lot of what

I thought of at the time, as justification. Considering that I had been accused of something I had been innocent of for such a long time. Her new obsession was marriage, 'Yeah right,' I thought, 'Give me at least another 20 years and maybe I'll think about it - or maybe not.' I supposed that one day I would get married. After I had become not only a full time professional wrestler, but a very successful full time professional wrestler. With a mortgage free house of my own, a car and a very, very healthy bank account. I also imagined that one day I would possibly marry Jean, at least she seemed to be the prime candidate at that time. But as far as I was concerned, only time would tell, and I intended plenty of that going by before I ever got the urge to listen to the sound of wedding bells ringing in my honor.

BUT! Not only was determined Jean willing to compromise, she was also in command of a very powerful weapon. Namely 'The dreaded carnal carrot' which was waved in front of my Donkey-like nose, along with the promise that I could munch on it to my heart's content - AFTER, we became engaged. So I agreed that we would become engaged on her 17th Birthday, which was a few months away. Hoping that I could at least have a sample nibble in the meantime. Alas, it wasn't to be, what I got instead was,

"Are you sure you're telling me the truth?! – Because I would never get engaged to someone who had been with other girls before me." And I would reply with a sigh,

"No I have never been with other girls." And think to myself, 'how ironic. - It's so important to her, that she will be the first girl I make it with, when, if she'd played her cards right she could have been.' However, I did get a very nice consolation prize. As I now had the ability and the facility to develop and print my own photos, Jean agreed to pose for some naked pin-up photos. There was a small price to pay, if I had nude photos of her she wanted nude photos of me. I agreed to pose for one photo and the deal was sealed. It turned out to be a bad deal, as Jean's Father, for whatever reason, decided to search through Jean's purse and found the photo in question. He was suitably outraged and disgusted, and told Jean that she would probably end up with a Nigger. When Jean told me, I was outraged and disgusted. I would have made him pay dearly for his conduct and his comment, if Jean hadn't managed to persuade me to let it go.

****

The matches I had for DeMarto seemed to dwindle a tad, probably a punishment resulting from my unadulterated audacity of asking for more money. As long as George Kidd was not in town, I was getting about the same as usual from the other promoters, which wasn't a lot. I was wrestling for Milo Popocopolis in Hastings and traveled there in a car, once again with Gunga Singh and Mike Dimitri. Gunga and I chatted all the way, but to Mike Dimitri I was the invisible man. I remember telling Gunga that I was missing out on a very enjoyable training session. It was a Thursday and Both Tuesday and Thursday was June and Wanda night at The Forester's Club. I impressed him mightily, with a very detailed blow by blow description, of a typical workout. After arriving quite early in the afternoon, we had a coffee and a sandwich in a café owned by Milo, which was just opposite the arena we were wrestling in. We were served by a pretty Greek waitress and it was lust at first sight. Somehow she managed to force me to tell her, that I was Kid Tarzan Jonathan, Welter-weight Wrestling Champion of Wales, and I just happened to be wrestling in the arena across the road on the pier that very same night.

"Yes," she said, "I'd love to come and watch you wrestling tonight; I'll pop over as soon as I finish work." Gunga and I was once again sharing a corner of the dressing room and once again he reminded me,

"You certainly know how to piss Mike Dimitri off," he told me laughingly, "He said you were nothing but a walking, talking erection."

"Well he seems to know me a lot better than I know him." I agreed. I was just in the process of lacing up my boots, when my opponent walked into the dressing room and informed me there was a Lady outside asking for me. I went out and began chatting to the waitress, but was continually bombarded by autograph hunters. So in order to enjoy a little privacy, we went out of the back door onto the pier.

"I can't stay out long," I told her, "as I'm wrestling in the first match."

"Let's not waste time then." She suggested.

"Hey, hurry up Kid," shouted Peter Kelly, as I re-entered the dressing room, half an hour later, "we've got about 5 minutes to get in the ring, where have you been?"

I had noticed Mike Dimitri was there getting changed, so for his benefit, I told Peter exactly where I'd been and what I'd been doing.

We had an excellent match. With poor Peter Kelly suffering about twice as much pain and punishment as usual, in order to satisfy my ego, knowing I had at least one special spectator cheering me on. Match over and hand raised in victory. I hardly gave myself time to relish the boos and jeers, for the cruel treatment I had so sadistically administered to a very game and valiant underdog. I leapt out of the ring and made a B line for the young Grecian Beauty and whisked her back out onto the pier to begin round 2. By the time I went back to the dressing room, the second match had just finished and both the contestants, 'Iron Jaw' Joe Murphy and Peter Rann entered it the same time that I did.

"Hey, you dirty sod," Peter Kelly, called to me from across the room, "I saw where you went after the match, you went back on the pier with that Greek Bird." I saw Mike Dimitri look at me and scowl, so for his benefit, I replied in a loud voice,

"Well I've got to preserve my reputation Peter, didn't you know I'm a walking, talking erection?" seeing that my little quip wasn't lost on Mike Dimitri, I added, again for his benefit, "My motto is, if it moves I'll fuck it – and if it doesn't move I'll kick it until it does!" Everyone laughed, except Dimitri and that was the way it ought to be.

As we were getting changed, I was chatting with Peter Rann who had driven down to Hastings on his own and he offered me a ride back to London. I gladly accepted, as Peter would usually drop me off in the Knightsbridge area, which was a lot closer to home. As we drove out of Hastings Peter asked me,

"What's up with you and Mike Dimitri?"

"Search me," I replied, "I've been on the same card as him at least a dozen times and he has never spoken one word to me, so I just ignore him."

Peter Rann really had a sinister sense of humor. He asked me if I knew whether nitroglycerine was heavier or lighter than water and if it was lighter, whether it would float on water, or dissolve into it. I told him I didn't have a clue, and the only explosives I knew anything about, was the ones I'd got from dismantling fireworks. And had cleverly and successfully succeeded in blowing my eyebrows off with. Being curious, I asked Peter why he was interested in nitroglycerine. He explained, he had a bad favor to return. And in order to do so, he intended to visit the guy's house with a jar of nitro and an eye drop dispenser, which he would use to spread the nitro onto the surface of the water in his ex-friend's toilet.

"Can you imagine what will happen when he takes a crap?" he laughed and that laugh had to be more sinister than Peter's sense of humor. His eyes would close into evil slits; his mouth would spread and emit a noise that sounded like a Snake about to strike. Or the hiss of an angry Alligator. On our way to Knightsbridge, we were passing a nightclub that Peter frequented and he invited me to join him there for a drink. On our way into the Club, we were met by The Doorman who Peter obviously knew.

"Hey Peter," he called, "have you been wrestling tonight?"

"Yes Fred," Peter answered, "Hastings - have you met Kid Jonathan?"

"No," Fred replied.

I held my hand out towards him intending to give him a good firm handshake, but his hand shot out and back to his side in a flash, barely touching the tips of my fingers.

"Peter's in there." Fred told Peter.

"Okay, thanks for warning me," Peter replied, "I'll see you later Fred." – "Don't look over there." Peter warned me, as we entered the club and approached the bar. So obviously, I looked, in order to see what I was supposed, not to be looking at. The first thing that caught my eye, was the very shapely legs of a Lady with a very short skirt leaning over a table talking to a man. The man was sitting between a woman and a Blond Girl, who looked too young to be in a Club that sold alcohol. I couldn't see the man properly, as the Lady with the legs was partially blocking my view of him. As she had her back to me, I didn't recognize her either. Until she turned around and made her way towards us, accompanied by the woman who had been sitting with the man and young girl. It was Cassie, Margaret's Sister, she brushed right passed us and didn't seem to recognize me. Maybe I've changed I thought. But she hadn't, same big tits, same angry scowl. I redirected my attention to the man sitting with the very young blond girl. He looked like a cross between a Frog and an overweight Martian, complete with a silvery white suit and wearing just a little less jewelry, than that worn by Mr. T. In his Frog like mouth, he sucked on a cigar the size of a cucumber.

"I've seen that guy before somewhere." I told Peter.

"So have I," Peter replied, "He's my Boss."

'Polish' Peter Rachman did not resemble the picture I had of him in my imagination. His head was completely bald and looked like a huge round cannonball. If his body had been in proportion with his great big head he would have been a giant. But he had a fat stumpy little body with short arms and legs and dainty little feet and hands, reminiscent of the little blond girl, who was sharing his table. In spite of his diminutive size, he seemed to carry his own spotlight. His very presence, seemed to make his corner of the club glow. I immediately began scanning the club for wrestlers, who I thought may have been present to guard his body.

"You met one of them outside," Peter Rann informed me, when I told him what I was looking for. "No one is going to bother Peter Rachman, while 'Mad Fred the Ear-biter' is on guard." So that was 'Fred the Ear-biter'. Again, I was surprised by the way reality contrasted with my imagination.

"What's he doing outside if he's supposed to be guarding Rachman? I inquired.

"Serge Paplinski got him a job as a bouncer for Stefan de Faye, the club's owner." Peter Rann explained. And then told me that Rachman and his head honcho, Serge Paplinski, had helped secure a job as doorman at the club in an effort to distance themselves from Mad Fred, after the ear-biting incident, which had generated very much unwanted attention. "Serge is a very good friend of mine," Peter told me, "but he's really mad at me at the moment. His home is full of enormous aquariums, which house his collection of very expensive and exotic Fish. He couldn't understand why I found them so amusing. Until he realized that I had been bombing them with Alka-Seltzer tablets." Again, that hissing laugh. As I may have mentioned, once or twice before, if you have friends and family you don't need enemies. But that was nothing compared to the 'favor' rendered to Stefan de Faye when he employed Mad Fred the Ear-biter at Polish Peter's bequest. To begin with Fred proved to be an exemplary employee. No undesirables would ever, in their wildest dreams imagine that they could get past him, if they were not welcome in the Club. But he was a very strange bird indeed. And if Fred took a dislike to anyone, whether they were high rollers, big spenders, prized customers or even personal friends of Stefan, they would not be allowed entrance while he was on the door. Stefan complained bitterly and warned Fred again and again that if he didn't severely adjust his attitude, he would have no alternative but to fire him. Stefan's ultimatum did nothing to temper Fred's behavior, if anything his resentment at being threatened only made him worse. In a final fit of exasperation, Stefan fired Fred and ordered him never again to set foot on his premises. But instead – being fed up with Stefan's continued complaints, Fred threw Stefan out of his own Club and warned him not to come back. Business at 'Esmeralda's Barn' seemed to continue as normal, but with Fred still commanding the door and Stefan no longer at the helm, things were not destined to improve. Stefan obviously appealed to Serge Paplinski to sort the situation out. But Serge was a very intelligent man. Intelligent enough to appreciate that in spite of his own incredible martial-arts prowess, he was no match for 'Mad' Fred. As Stefan was unable to successfully terminate Fred's employ, a Thug was contracted to do the job for him. It was a very costly enterprise for Stefan, as he ended up paying out good money for nothing. It was an even more costly enterprise for the Thug, as he had to suffer a total loss of dignity. Not to mention a substantial loss of blood and nasal tissue. He was chased down the road, by a very Mad Fred the Ear-biter. Who seemed to have modified his diet a tad and bitten off the end of the Thug's nose, in their very brief but very violent confrontation. Not to be deterred, Stefan decided to bring in the big guns. On this occasion, Fred was inside the club when two Thugs walked in and met Fred face to face, as he was making his way towards the exit.

"I'm sorry Fred," said one of the Thugs, "this isn't personal." as he leveled a revolver at Fred's chest. It was too long a speech, Fred's hand shot out in a blur and snatched the gun right out of his would be assassins fist. The Thug repeated himself in a shriek, as he and his henchman fled for their lives,

"I'M SORRY FRED - IT WASN'T PERSONAL!!!" They barely managed to put the club door between Fred and themselves before Fred emptied the revolver into it.

Peter Rann told me that the conflict was eventually resolved and Stefan got possession of his Club back, but only after Peter helped negotiate a very lucrative severance plan for 'Mad' Fred the Ear-biter.

Being the eternal optimist, when our Summer Holidays came around, I invited Jean to spend them in Wales with me. But as far as any serious action was concerned, Jean was still determined to wait until she had an engagement ring on the third finger of her left hand. While we were in Wales we visited my cousin Marina, who was in Hospital waiting to give birth to her first child. Her Husband Billy Reynolds, meantime was given the chance to work overtime. Contemplating the extra cost of a new addition to his family, he accepted it. In the tradition of our family, Billy was a coalminer and while his Wife Marina was giving birth to their Daughter Debbie, both Billy and Billy's twin Brother were killed in a cave in – As I remember my Father saying, 'working in the pit was hard work, dirty, unhealthy, poorly paid and dangerous.'

****

Tony's and Marcia's relationship was off and on, like a horny Buck Rabbit in a Warren full of very pretty Does - and at the moment it was very much off. As much as I liked Marcia, I tried to convince Tony that he was better off without her, as she really did treat him like crap. But Tony could not be convinced. Marcia worked in a hole in the wall Kiosk in Craven Park Road, in Harlesden that sold candy and tobacco. It was just a small box of a shop, that barely gave Marcia room to turn around in. She sat between shelves on either side of her, stacked with confectionary and cigarettes and a window that opened into the street. It enabled her to peddle the produce directly to customers as they passed by on the sidewalk. There was a Café directly across the Street, that became Tony's new favorite watering hole. He was always asking me to accompany him there and although they only served 'fried' steak, it wasn't too bad, so I often did.

Marcia and Tony weren't even speaking to each other. Whenever Tony entered or exited the café, he would make a huge deal of not, looking in her direction, but would ask,

"Is she looking over here, has she seen me?" I soon learned to tell him,

"Yes Tony, she looked over here and saw you." Whether she did or didn't, because if I told him she didn't see him, he'd find some excuse to go back into the café and try again. Whenever Marcia did spot us she would wave at me and I would wave back to her. Eventually, Tony suggested that I should go over and talk to her and tell him what she said about him. So I began crossing the street whenever we'd finished our meal. Tony would stand about outside the café, pretending to be waiting impatiently for me to finish gossiping with Marcia. He would wear sunglasses whether the weather was sunny or dull. That way he could pretend to be looking down the road, while he was really gazing at Marcia through the corner of his eye. This must have gone on for best part of a month, when Tony had an idea he thought might peak Marcia's interest.

"Tell her that I've started wrestling pro." He told me. So over the street I went.

"How's the love life Marcia?" I asked as way of a greeting, but before I could tell her about Tony, she beat me to the punch.

"Good Adrian," she replied, "I've been going out with a Boxer, - HEE – HEE!"

"What's so funny about that?" I inquired.

"He's a bleed'n sex maniac!" she answered, "HEE – HEE – HEE!"

"Oh, that's nice." I said.

"Yes," she agreed, "the first night I went out with him, we were having a cuddle in the lane behind my house, when he suddenly said, 'Oh, I'm sorry Marcia.' And he stood back and dropped his trousers in front of me - BLEED'N HELL! He had a dick as big as that black geezer in the photo - HEE – HEE – HEE!"

'Tony will be pleased.' I thought and to change the subject, I told her, "Tony is wrestling pro now." I don't think she even heard what I said, as she ploughed straight on describing one lurid detail after another of her exciting new relationship. While I listened patiently, I glanced over the road at poor Tony, still trying to look nonchalantly heroic. Marcia's tirade wound down, as she became aware that I was looking over at Tony.

"What's that silly bleeder been up to?" she asked.

"Oh, Tony?" I replied, "He's wrestling professionally now."

"Is he any good at it?" she inquired.

"Of course," I told her modestly, "look who taught him." As if on cue, Tony looked over, squared his shoulders and started to walk across the street assuming a gait that he thought appropriate, for a young, powerful professional wrestler. He had John Wayne, King Kong, Robert Mitchum and Tarzan of the Apes All rolled into one.

"Oh, why is he walking like that? Marcia wanted to know, "did he hurt himself wrestling?" I roared with laughter and the fact that Marcia had sounded so genuinely concerned made it even funnier. I had hardly recovered, when Tony stepped beside me blew himself up like a Puffer fish and drawled in a gruff voice,

"How's the love life Marcy?"

'Oh my God,' I thought, 'I hope she doesn't tell him.' While I laughed until I went cross-eyed.

As it happened, Marcia didn't tell him, but later I did. - Hey, what are friends for?

"I'll kill the bastard!" he growled.

"Why would you want to do that?" I asked him, "it's not his fault that Marcy isn't going out with you - he probably doesn't even know you exist."

"I'll wait for him to walk down the alley when leaves Marcy tonight." He told me.

"And then what?" I wanted to know.

"I'll beat the shit out of him and tell him that if he ever bothers Marcia again, I'll cripple him!" he stated.

"I don't think Marcia was bothered," I reminded him, "in fact

I think there's something about him, she really seems to fancy."

"She won't after I've finished with him!" he promised.

"Well you do have an advantage over him." I told him.

"What advantage is that?" he asked,

"Well you know that he can Box, but he doesn't know that you can wrestle," I explained. He thought about that for a while and then suggested,

"We could both wait for him tonight; he wouldn't stand a chance against the two of us."

"Forget it." I said. Poor Tony was devastated. But I knew how I could cheer him up, while turning occurrences to my advantage. As he wasn't going out with Marcia anymore, there was now nothing stopping him from training on Tuesdays and Thursdays, as well as the other weeknights. Today was Thursday,

"Come to the Forester's tonight," I invited, "I've got just the thing to take your mind off Marcia." That night at The Forester's, I introduced Tony to June and Wanda.

****

One month after our return to London from Wales, and on Jean's 17th Birthday we became engaged. Much to my surprise and delight, there was no big double cross and true to her word, the very next day was spent in bed doing what came naturally, at long last. Did it cure me off chasing 'other girls'? Yes, most definitely, if Jean was close by and available. But put enough space between us and enough temptation in my way and all bets were off. At the time, I probably wouldn't have been able to put a finger on the main ingredient that was the cause of my chronic promiscuity. Jean was a very attractive Girl, so I definitely had no excuse on that account. What I've come to appreciate is, that being brought up in a sexually stifled atmosphere. Where a 10 year old kid, would get almost beaten to death by his own Mother, for sticking girlie photos in a scrapbook, didn't help. Neither did Dad and the other bloody sexually repressed denizens of the dreaded Tabernacle. I have always been very much attracted to pretty girls, from as far back as my memory allows, as were my friends. And being as gullible as we were, we really believed each other's boasts of our fantasy sexual conquests.

Whether they felt as inadequate as I did, as a result I don't know. I did know I wanted to be a man who was strong and completely fearless. I would fight anyone, or anything, I would never back off from any challenge. I would even go as far as climbing any cliff or mountain, the more daunting the better. Even though it terrified me to do so, only to turn to jelly and go running away sniveling with terror, when confronted with a pretty girl, who was offering to make my idle boasting, a reality. The realization that I wasn't man enough to step up to the plate, resulted in a vast inferiority complex, that was totally incompatible with the image I was willing to perceive of myself.

My Christmas Eve triumph, with Maureen completely shattered my inhabitations. Once that formidable dam was breached, I was ill equipped to control the resulting deluge. One come-on smile from a pretty face was a gauntlet hurled at my feet and I could not refuse the challenge. It seemed that every failure from my past needed a hundred victories to erase them. To walk away, would once again cast self doubts I couldn't live with. – Hey, that's my excuse and I'm sticking to it.

I was still 11 stone and 12 stone weightlifting Champion of the Forester's Club. And doing my bit in making sure that we met and defeated any and every challenge we were confronted with from other clubs. I would also wrestle as much as possible, preferably pro style. If I was fortunate enough to have an opponent to practice with, if not then Monday, Wednesday and Friday were amateur nights and I would be happy to wrestle that style as a last resort. William Stockford had been wrestling as an amateur for more than 15 years, and had never had the faintest ambition to ever turn professional. But one evening, he told me that he had been receiving overtures from Dale Martins and had decided to give their offer some serious consideration. A week or so later, he informed me that he had received a list of venues he would be appearing at. And a few weeks after that, he showed me a handful of Dale Martin's wrestling programs, bearing his name in preliminary bouts. William Stockford was a bit on the long side to print on their posters, so they shortened his professional name to Billy Stock. Billy, had never possessed the desire to become a professional wrestler. And now, here he was showing me a handful of Dale Martin's programs with him in them. I thought it was bloody unfair, after all the effort I had put into my quest to wrestle for them. I told Billy that I was as jealous as Hell. The Maori Giant John DaSilva from New Zealand and the classy Welshman Tony Charles, who both wrestled as amateurs in the 1960 Empire Games were also approached by Jack Dale and accepted an offer to turn pro. Dale Martins seemed to be recruiting new wrestlers like never before.

The volume of venues promoted by Dale Martins, had been steadily increasing, since a 25% post war entertainment tax had been abolished by Chancellor Peter Thorneycroft in the 1957 budget. As a result, venues previously deemed to be unviable, were now capable of generating a healthy profit. Add to that, the recent television début, that overnight had elevated one of the World's oldest sports into the undisputed 'new kid on the block' and onto the threshold of a popularity explosion without precedence.

'Timing is perfect.' I thought and off to Brixton I raced as fast as public transport would convey me and for the thousandth time, ushered myself into the august presence of Jack Dale,

"Hello Mr. Dale," I said, "I'm ready to begin wrestling for Dale Martins."

"Yeah, right," he yawned, "come back when you're older - bigger and a bloody good amateur."

Tom McBride had retired from driving and was now involved on a full time basis in the Railway Workers Union; I had been re-paired with a new driver named Angelo. Angelo was Italian, but spoke fairly good English and we got on very well together. Although I did miss Tom, who I now regarded as one of my best friends. As with both Bill Waller and Tom McBride, Angelo and I would endeavor to put our day's pick-ups and deliveries behind us, in order to enjoy as much free time as possible. Angelo was a keen swimmer and we would spend the remainder of each working day after we had completed our deliveries, visiting various swimming pools in, or close by our area. Although he was married Angelo, was also a keen Womanizer, who changed Girlfriends more often than Imelda Marcos changed her shoes. He then burdened me with the dubious chore, of having to pacify a number of his many disgruntled ex-conquests. It was dirty work, but someone had to do it. 'Oh dear,' I thought, 'no peace for the wicked.'

****

"Be careful of the bottom step." I whispered, as we crept stealthily down the stairs, reminding Jean of the loud creak it emitted, which seemed to amplify dramatically after the clock struck 11pm. A bright light flashed on before our eyes, freezing both Jean and I in mid step. We stood transfixed, as there before us in all his Heavenly Glory - in spite of the stern look on his face, appeared the Angel Gabriel. The Angel Gabriel wasn't as tall as I imagined he would be, and I was also surprised to see that as well as the stern face, he was also wearing an ankle length, grey and black plaid dressing-gown. 'Obviously to hide his wings' I mused. He spoketh – and although his voice did have that Heavenly booming quality, it also contained a nerve rending whining undertone.

"Mr. Street," it thundered, "how many times have I told you, that guests have to leave by 11 o'clock?!"

The Angel Gabriel evaporated, to be replaced by my ever disgruntled Landlord. He still seemed to be wearing his heavenly Hallo, which turned out to be an effect caused by the bright hallway light reflecting off his bald head.

"What time do you call this?!" he demanded.

"About 10 past 11." I replied hopefully, whilst attempting to reassemble my grimacing features into a disarming smile.

"It's gone one o'clock in the morning!" he informed me. This scenario had become an all too common occurrence. Almost every night, after completing a round or two of bedtime Ballet, Jean and I would both tumble helplessly into the cozy arms of Hypnos. Then strenuously snore in unison, before awakening, hopefully, by or before 11 pm. The chances of that actually happening however, proved to be an all too elusive occurrence. Anytime between midnight and 3 am, or even 4 am, was not at all unusual.

Losing consciousness every night after a carnal encounter or two, may not have seemed very complimentary to my partner. Especially if you take into account that I was such a newly recruited sex addict. But let me describe a typical day to you, before you pass judgment. I would awaken at 6 am, wash, shave, get dressed and leave my flat, walk a mile and a half to a bus stop on Harrow Road. Ride the bus to Paddington where I would alight and walk almost a mile to the depot to clock in. I would then make my way to the loading bay and begin loading packages, parcels, crates, boxes etc, into the back of the van. After that we would drive to a nearby refreshment stall and breakfast on crusty rolls and coffee. Then our deliveries would start. I would carry the various contents of the van, into shops, stores, warehouses, downstairs into basements, upstairs to offices or high-rises. Make deliveries to other depots, where we would pick up more packages, to be delivered to various locations. Or, taken back to Paddington Station and unloaded at the end of our working day. In our free time, of which we usually had plenty, I would be alternately plunging into a swimming pool, or into one or more of Angelo's ex-conquests. When work was over for the day, I would clock out, walk a mile to the bus stop. Ride to Kilburn Lane. Walk a mile and a half home, grab a bite to eat, then walk a mile and a half to The Forester's Club. Lift weights for an hour and a half, make my way to the wrestling room, roll out the mats. Wrestle for an hour and a half, roll up the mats and take a shower. Then on my way back to my flat, I would call for Jean. We would walk the mile and a half, grab another bite on arrival, begin our Ballet lessons. Fall asleep, wake up, creep downstairs and try to avoid the creaky step. Walk Jean a mile and a half home. Stand in her doorway saying goodnight for an hour. Then walk the mile and a half back home and grab another bite, before falling back into bed for a short nap, before getting up and begin doing it all over again.

****

I thought that the night I had introduced Tony, to June and Wanda had been a great success. After locking ourselves in the wrestling room and rolling out the mats, there had been lots of grunting, groaning, groping, gripping, gurgling, gargling and giggling and lots of fun was had by all. A very memorable night indeed, unfortunately it was made even more memorable by the fact that I never, ever saw June or Wanda again. Why I'll never know, but it did remind me of the fact, that no good deed ever goes unpunished.

Talking of deeds going unpunished. 'Polish' Peter Rachman, had never paid a penny in tax, in spite of the fact, that by now he owned literally hundreds of properties in London. Although the rent act passed by the Tory Government in 1957, hogtied most 'legal' or 'honest' Landlords, it was a windfall for 'Polish' Peter. Who was able to take advantage of it, through any unscrupulous method he could devise. He converted cellars into nightclubs, Drug-dens, or Cribs for Prostitutes. Instead of making a huge dent in his empire, the 1959 Street Offences Act, that drove the 'Night-Ladies' off the pavements of London, was also a Bonanza for Rachman. The Girls would pay 10 pounds each a day, for a room to ply their trade. Even in a small house with only 7 or 8 rooms, 'Polish' Peter could make well in excess of 20,000 pounds a year, from a property that would have cost him only about 4,000 to 5,000 pounds to buy.

By 1959 the slum Lord was wealthy enough to invest in better class flats, hotels and even office buildings. He lived in a Mock-Georgian Mansion in Hampstead Heath, which had enough garage space to house each of his 6 cars. He wore white Sharkskin suits, elevated Crocodile skin shoes, gold chains and diamond rings. He was rarely seen without dark glasses, large cigars in his mouth and a young Girl on his arm. He ran gangs of vicious enforcers, rent collectors and West Indians, whose job it was to drive out stubborn sitting tenants. Then he could replace them with prostitutes, or other higher paying tenants. He was married to a pretty Lancashire Lass named Audrey O'Donnell, but that did nothing to curb his relentless pursuit of young girls and money. His favorite pastimes, were being seen, gambling and watching naked girls wrestling. In spite of his dubious dealings, 'Polish' Peter Rachman was never once found guilty of an illegal act.

Even though his notoriety eventually earned him his own spot in the Compact Oxford English Dictionary - 'Rachmanism' Noun Brit – The exploitation and intimidation of tenants by unscrupulous Landlords - origin named after notorious London Landlord Peter Rachman 1919 – 62. His name wasn't generally known until 'The Profumo scandal' in 1963, by which time he was either dead, or doing an excellent job of pretending to be.

At the Club's year ending ceremony, I was once again awarded a Black V-neck Weider T-shirt for remaining 11 and 12 stone Champion. In spite of my resolve not to embarrass myself, I once again bawled my eyes out at the presentation. Jean and I spent Christmas in Wales, where our new revised relationship made for our most enjoyable visit yet.

****

1961 turned out to be the biggest roller-coaster ride of my life so far. With more ups and downs, than the zigzag war paint I had worn on my face, when I made my grand entrance to St Mary's Junior School, dressed like a Red Indian.

My disgruntled Landlord, grew ever more disgruntled. I lost count of the ultra ultimatums I had received, concerning the time my guests left each night. Plus, the continual squeaking of my bed at all hours, couldn't have done much to calm his ragged nerves either. Well, I can't say I wasn't warned; in fact I had been warned - warned and warned again. Now I was told to leave, so once more I began looking for a new flat. That was bad. After much searching I found a very nice one on the ground floor in Liddell Gardens about a half a mile away from Mostyn Gardens. That was good – or at least I thought it was at the time. There were a few drawbacks, but nothing I couldn't live with. Both the bed and the room itself, was smaller than the one I had just vacated. It was a half a mile further away from the bus stop, the gym and Jean. But there were no restrictions as to what time my guests left at night, or even if they left at all. So that more than made up for the minor inconveniences. So, that was also good. My new Landlady was Polish and a couple of months after moving into my new flat, the Landlady's Brother Michal came to stay with her. It turned out that as a result of losing his job, he also lost his Wife and a place to live. So now, until he could straighten his life out, he would be staying with his sister. He seemed like a very nice and friendly guy. A bit too friendly I thought, one day after inviting him into my flat for a coffee. As we chatted he strolled around scrutinizing everything in the room. He even opened my wardrobe and a couple of cupboards and only desisted and sat down, after I asked him if he was looking for anything in particular. He explained that as the house was not very large and I was now living in the only spare room, the only place left for him was a tiny converted, windowless utility room, less than half the size of my small room.

"Oh, this is very nice - very nice." He'd tell me, every time he entered my space.

At the Forester's I was still helping our team win, that was good. I was still Occasionally wrestling that was so-so, as I wanted to wrestle more often, for more money. Working for the Railway with Angelo was good, very good. But then they put me to work with another driver, bad, in fact it was very bad, as I was told that I would now be working nights. Working nights pole axed me, as it meant that I couldn't wrestle pro. I couldn't even wrestle in the Forester's, or represent our club in competition. In fact I couldn't train with weights at all and I very rarely had time to see Jean. When she was working, I would be trying to sleep. I couldn't eat properly either. At night and until the early hours of the morning, the only places I could get food was at various coffee stalls, frequented by truck or taxi drivers. They sold little else but hot-dogs, which I hate. Just the revolting smell of fried onions was enough to make me gag. The modest amount of weight I had managed to gain, as a result of getting a job, after my long abstinence from both work and food fell off my bones. Bad – bad – bad! I complained bitterly to the Management and was told, that if a position on day shift became available they would keep me in mind. I soon made a thorough nuisance of myself, reminding them on a very regular basis, that I was very unhappy working nights. But they displayed superhuman patience and ignored my request in a way that was reminiscent of Jack Dale, whenever I asked him to give me a start for Dale Martins. Most of our deliveries was back and forth to Covent Garden, Billingsgate Market and Smithfield Market. As much as I love Flowers, I soon began to hate Covent Garden, and all that meat and poultry at Smithfield and Fish at Billingsgate, only reminded me of all the food I was missing out on. And hard earned muscle that I was losing as a result. Bad - very bad. As I was now unable to train at The Forester's I began to perform free exercise at home, after I returned there from work. Pushups by the hundred for upper body, sit-ups by the hundred for my tummy and a thousand reps of Indian squats for legs and endurance. I usually kept my window wide open, where I would do my deep breathing in between sets of exercise. Michal would often knock on my door and join me for a coffee, before he went out looking for work and I went to bed and tried with mediocre results to get a little sleep - Not good. As sorry as I had become for myself, I felt even sorrier for poor Michal. I fully appreciated how hard it was to get work in London during that period. At least I had a job, even though I hated it very much. During my first few weeks on night shift, I had accepted a number of wrestling matches and feigned sickness as an excuse to take time off from work, in order to wrestle. But thanks to my big mouth and treacherous workmates, it had got back to management. I had been warned not to become sick again, if I wanted to keep my job – Bad. One morning dizzy with fatigue, after another boring and strenuous night, humping all kinds of produce and packages around Covent Garden, Smithfield Market, Billingsgate Market and Paddington Station. Sustained only by a diet of dried up crap, I arrived home more than ready to hit the sack. 'But, it will take more than that to stop me from exercising first.' I told myself, in an attempt to stir my lack of enthusiasm with a little inspiration. I stripped down to my briefs, courtesy of Lon and forced my body into a set of Indian squats. After completing 100 reps as a warm up and wake up, I dropped down and did 50 push-ups. I then walked to the open window, in order to breathe deeply until breathing became easier and I would then perform my next set.

The first time I stood at the window, I saw two men standing on the pavement directly across the other side of the road, staring straight at me. I just stared back and continued breathing until I was ready to continue exercising. I continued, but every time I returned to the window, the same two men, in an otherwise empty street just stood and stared. Once I had began my workout it became easier, as getting motivated enough to do my first set was always the hardest. Another 100 squats, followed by another 50 push-ups and I returned to the window gasping for oxygen. And there was the two men still staring as though mesmerized. On about my fourth or fifth set as I returned to the window, I saw both of the men walk across the road without taking their eyes off me, until they walked out of my line of vision. Seconds later, they began knocking on the front door. While I began another set of squats, I heard Michal's voice from the hallway after he had answered the door, followed by a muffled conversation. I was surprised when there was a loud knocking on my door. Swearing under my breath, at being interrupted before I finished my set, I opened my door. After flashing their badges and introducing themselves as Plain Clothes Policemen, my two visitors told me, there had been complaints concerning indecent exposure and according to them, 'while investigating the complaint they had caught me in the act'.

"What fucking act?" I wanted to know, "I'm trying to have a bloody workout."

"Get dressed!" they ordered, "You're coming with us to the Station."

I was sweating rivers, but slipped into my jeans and T-shirt, feeling hot, sticky, wet and pissed off. I then followed them outside and around the corner to their parked car. One Policeman opened the back door and motioned me in, then they both got into the front. No one had spoken a word, until the policeman driving, started the car and he growled 'loudly' under his breath,

"I hope they throw the bloody book at you, I would have been off duty now if it wasn't for you." The other Policeman, who was sitting in the front passenger seat, turned and looked at me with that resigned, 'well you can't really blame my partner grumbling' look. But still didn't say a word.

"You'll probably get 6 months." The driver told me, as he caught my eye in his rear-view mirror. His partner shifted in his seat uneasily, as though sympathizing on my behalf and gave me a sad, baleful look in order to confirm it.

"6 months for what?!" I demanded.

"Filthy little pervert." He growled more to himself, but obviously for my benefit. He carried on in that vein. In what I would normally regard as fighting talk, but under the circumstances, I refused to respond and just sat silent and stony faced. His partner on the other hand, who's profile was facing me, only took his eyes off the driver to give me an occasional, almost apologetic look. He winced visibly, when his partner's remarks were particularly barbed and poisonous. The Police

Station was in Harlesden, no more than a few hundred yards away from the first flat I had lived at in London. I was escorted in there from the car, with the obnoxious driver on my left grabbing a handful of my shirt. The passenger on my right, walking close but not touching me. I was hurled into a large room and was grateful to see it was occupied by a number of Police, including Police Women. I thought as a result, that the use of any rough house tactics would be less likely. Nevertheless, the driver flung me towards a desk with all the force he could muster and screamed at the top of his voice,

"Sit there!!!" Indicating a chair next to the desk, "Right let's get your statement!" he shouted, as he walked around the desk and pulled out a chair facing mine.

"Okay, calm down," his partner told him, "I'll take his statement, you go and get yourself a cup of tea and try to simmer down a bit." I was looking around the office, embarrassed by the first Policeman's loud outburst and was surprised to see that no one was taking the slightest bit of notice. I was also very happy to see the first Policeman's back disappear through the door by which we had entered, after taking his partner's advice. I then turned and faced the partner, who I shall refer to from now on as TGC and the one who had gone for tea as TBC.

"I'm sorry about that," apologized TGC - the good cop, "my partner has had a really rough night. He was just getting ready to piss off home, when we were told to go and investigate a complaint, all the way over in Kensal Rise. Now he's really pissed off, that it just turned out to be a complete waste of time." You can't imagine how gratified I was when I heard him say, it was a complete waste of time.

"Listen, this is the best way for us to play it," he told me lowering his voice and glancing around at the other denizens of the cop-shop, as though this was going to be our little conspiracy.

"The best thing you can do is to plead guilty. It's a first offence, so it'll just be a little slap on the wrist and a couple of quid fine."

"Why should I plead guilty?" I asked, "You were there and you know I wasn't flashing."

"Yeah, I know that," he conceded, "but if you plead not guilty, they'll lock you up until they can set a court date. That will involve bringing in witnesses ----"

"What fucking witnesses?!" I interrupted.

"Well my partner for a start," he replied, "put him on the stand in the mood he is in and he'll rip you a new arsehole - he figures, it's your fault that he's not home in bed. As it is he's going to be really pissed off, when they let you go. But if we can keep him off the stand, there's fuck all he'll be able to do about it." He was making it sound as though, in the name of justice and fair-play, he was siding with me, against his own partner, who was tired, stressed, and as a result, totally overreacting. "Take my advice," he continued, "plead guilty, pay a couple of quid fine. Then you'll be free to go home and get some sleep and let my partner do the same." I decided to take his advice and fell victim to the classical, patented 'good cop' – 'bad cop' scenario. But, I didn't appreciate it until TGC – The Good Cop took the stand and blatantly and cheerfully perjured himself, by stating that I had been completely naked, when he saw me breathing at my ground floor open window. I was ordered to spend 3 weeks on remand in Wormwood Scrubs Prison. It was to gradually dawn on me, that being on remand was the equivalent of being in Purgatory. Where observation of one's performance, while under sufferance, would determine whether you would advance to heavenly freedom, or to a spell in Hell. When my 3 weeks in Wormwood Scrubs Prison was completed I was to return to court where sentence would be passed. They would either set me free, or send me back into the fiery pit of incarceration for whatever period they saw fit. As I was being escorted to a holding cell, to await transport to 'The Scrubs' TGC came up to me and said,

"Damn, I'm sorry about that. I would have laid a bet, that you'd have been on your way home by now." I just gave him that look and thought,

'Yeah right – and I believe you!' Within the hour, I had been placed in a sitting down coffin of a compartment in the back of a black van. It had a solid door on my right and a little slit of a window on my left, from which I could press my eye and watch all the 'free people' going about their daily business as I drew closer to jail. I had often looked at the prison from Wormwood Scrubs Common, when I was running barefoot in an attempt to toughen my feet for wrestling before I wore boots. But I had never, in my wildest dreams imagined that I would ever see the inside of the place. Upon arriving at the prison about half a dozen or so prisoners, including myself were released from our coffins. Then marched into the building and deposited, one at a time into a small cell each and left alone for what seemed hours, to ponder our fate. I couldn't believe this had happened and willed myself to wake up from this awful dream. What would happen to my job, if I didn't turn up for work for 3 weeks – or more? Especially after the warnings I had received for taking an odd night off occasionally in order to wrestle. What would happen to my flat, if I wasn't there to pay the rent for 3 weeks – or more? But worst of all what would Jean think about all this? What would she do when I didn't call for her? What would she think when she came looking for me at my flat and find I wasn't there? Much to my embarrassment I had noticed Michal, peeking through the crack of his door, as I had been escorted out of the house by the two Policemen. Perhaps he might tell Jean what happened? But then what would she think? Would she believe me, or my accusers? Especially as I had been conned and had stupidly pleaded guilty. I was only too aware of Jean's fanatically suspicious and jealous nature. I could only hope and pray, that she would believe me and not the arseholes, who had placed me in this terrible predicament. This wasn't just bad – this was fucking insane. A short eternity later, my cell door opened and a guard entered. He handed me a mug of milky tea, stepped back out and with a loud resounding clang, slammed the door closed again. I held the mug as far away from me as arm length would allow. My mind was in turmoil, as I would now have to make a monumental decision. When I was about 12 or 13 years old, I had read in a bodybuilding magazine that tea was not good for you. As my Mother was a very big tea drinker, I told her what I had read.

"Okay if it's not good for you, don't drink it." She told me, as she took another gulp out of one of her best bone china cups. I took that as a challenge and replied,

"Okay I won't." and from that date, not one single drop of tea had touched my lips. But here I sat, about 8 years later in a prison cell. I hadn't eaten or drank anything since about 3 o'clock that morning, when I had devoured an elderly cheese sandwich. Its only defense against me, had been the Shirley Temple tight curl of the bread, which was washed down by an evil cup of stewed, lukewarm coffee. I was now starving and parched. My weight had dropped since I had started working nights and I realized, that my future could prove to be very precarious, to whatever bodyweight I had left. Would I still have a job? – would I still have somewhere to live? Would I still have Jean? Would I be able to afford food? I decided there and then, to eat and drink anything and everything I was offered while I was incarcerated, as I couldn't even begin to guess what the future held in store for me when I was released. Even though I realized that my decision was only common sense, I felt as though I was flunking a challenge. It was almost as though I was committing a gross act of sacrilege as I gulped the sweet, sickly brew down to the last dreg.

"Fuckin' Mary - look at the body on that fuckin' twat!" shouted a loud raucous voice and realizing that the author of that statement, was referring to me, I turned and shot a warning glare across his bows. But the glare bounced off his timbers, without inflicting a dent or even a splinter. As a scruffy, skinny looking kid of about 18 years old continued,

"Hey, ain't chew the Phantom Flasher? – Shit!" He continued, while blatantly pointing an accusing finger between my naked legs, "If I 'ad that fuckin' thing I'd be a bleed'n flasher too!" His name was Freddy. And he, like me and about 20 other new prisoners, were all standing naked waiting to be issued our prison togs, after being told to strip off our own clothes and hand them in. It was easy to remember, after I had learned his name was Freddy, as he was so much like a younger version, of the Freddy I had been fired from Wembley Stadium, for punching out it was creepy. Same look, same attitude and all the time issuing the same ear shattering audio. – If anything, the new 'Freddy Mark 2' was even more devoid of diplomacy than the original 'Freddy Mark 1' had been. And it almost got me into the trouble I was determined to avoid, as well as Freddy.

After we were all dressed as proper prisoners, and as an extra effort to cosmetically complete our shabby ensemble, we were all marched to the Prison Barber Shop. My long Tarzan like locks were shorn in a way that would have made an Australian Sheep sheerer proud and Dearest Daddy Dance with Delirious Delight. I had walked into the Barber Shop sporting the magnificent mane of a Jungle God and walked back out with a head that looked like a rusty old cannonball. My hair had never been so short in my life – including the day I was born.

"You fuckin' stupid bastard," Freddy told me, after I had explained the circumstances leading up to my present predicament, "why did you make it so fuckin' easy for them? You should never plead guilty, even if they catch you in the fuckin' act."

Freddy basically confirmed the conclusion that I had arrived at in retrospect. In order to obtain that all important conviction, it seemed that nothing - including trivial items, such as fact or truth, were worthy of consideration. In Freddy's case, he had been caught running down the street, with his arms full of Woodbines, after he had broken into a Tobacco Kiosk. Similar to the one that Tony Woods' ex-girlfriend, Marcia worked in.

"I didn't plead guilty," he told me, "even though they caught me red-handed, wiv' me arms fulla fuckin' fags - I didn't make it easy for them." He added proudly.

"You're still in here though, aren't you Freddy?" I reminded him.

"Yeah, but I didn't make it easy for them, though, did I?" he argued - " see? That's my point." - 'Oh, how devious the criminal mind.' I thought.

For the duration of our stay, in The Scrubs, we occupied a large dorm, rather than separate cells. It had a desk occupied by a supervising guard and rows of beds, lining two opposite walls. There was 4 beds that were to be avoided at all costs, I was to learn. One either side of a young West Indian kid, who was reputed to have a dose. And another 2 beds, one either side of a boy of dubious sexuality, who had a tendency to get lonely in the middle of the night. Our days consisted of polishing, scrubbing and cleaning the dorm. Other times we would be allowed to either read, or play some kind of table game. Incidentally, that is where I learned to play Chess. Also each day we would go outside for some form of exercise and fresh air. Exercise consisted of walking around and around, in a circle in a small, rectangular yard whilst suffering a bombardment of ribald and embarrassing remarks, aimed at us by a similar circle of adult prisoners. Or else, we would be taken to a much larger yard, where a guard would order us to run as fast as we could to a distant wall and then back again to where the guard was standing.

'Excellent training' I thought, 'to make it much more difficult for any criminal to be caught while fleeing from the Police'. The rules were, that the last one of us to get back to the guard, would have to drop to the ground and perform 10 pushups. I had already decided from my first day, that I would keep a low profile. I'd do everything I was ordered to do without displaying any attitude whatsoever, never mind how mundane or ludicrous, the task proved to be. BUT – as I witnessed the unbelievably sorry performance, displayed by the last to arrive runners. When, with trembling arms, they crumpled onto their noses, after completing just a few repetitions of their designated ten pushups - my ego once again betrayed me. After purposely coming in last and being ordered by the guard to drop and give him 10 pushups, I made a token show of being hesitant and even reluctant to comply.

"Drop and give me 10 pushups at once!" he repeated very loudly.

With a huge sigh of resignation, I dropped down into the pushup position and gave him 100 repetitions. All the other prisoners chanted out the score as I performed each rep. I hopped up triumphantly and faced the 'screw' - who looked totally unimpressed,

"Okay," he sneered, "seeing you've got so much energy to spare, drop down and give me another 100." I dropped down and to the screw's chagrin and the other prisoner's delight, I gave him 101 reps. When I stood up and faced him for the second time, he still looked unfazed and told me,

"Okay - so you're good at doing pushups. Let's get you all running again, and you," he added, glaring straight at me, "if you're last, just one more time, I'll have you cleaning every fucking shit house, in this fucking nick."

I found his little speech truly inspirational. So much so, that every time we raced after that, I was always guaranteed to be amongst the first runners to return.

A few days after my arrival at The Scrubs, I was told I had visitors and was escorted to a room and then placed behind a glass window, which made me feel like a bloody Goldfish in an aquarium. I didn't know for sure who it was that was visiting me, but hoped it would be Jean. Although I was bursting with apprehension, not knowing how she was going to react to me being where I was – or, more to the point, to the reason why I was where I was. It was Jean, accompanied by Tom McBride, who had volunteered to drive her to the prison, after she had phoned him and told him what had happened. I was ecstatic to find that my apprehension had been unfounded and that neither Jean, nor Tom believed for one second, that I was guilty of what I had been accused of. Especially after I explained how I had been tricked by the Police.

"BASTARDS!" Exclaimed Jean and Tom in unison. Which didn't come anywhere close to my own thoughts on the subject. Before they left I asked Jean to mail me a photo of herself and she promised she would, that very same day.

I imagined that I would be allowed, to receive a photo that was mailed to me. As Freddy had recently got a letter from his Girlfriend that was not only extremely X-rated, but was accompanied by an illustrated story, she had made up and drawn for him. Her artwork was excellent and only surpassed by her weird imagination. Where she had gotten her ideas from was beyond me - until Freddy filled in the blanks.

According to Freddy, in spite of his 16 year old Girlfriend being an insatiable Nymphomaniac. She would absolutely refuse to have any kind of sex with him at all, unless there was at least one or more, of her Girlfriends present to witness the action. Then all stops were pulled out, and then there were no depths of depravity, to which she wouldn't plunge, in order to impress and entertain her audience.

We were all sitting at desks in a classroom, when I received my letter from Jean containing her photo. Freddy in the meantime, had received a couple of letters from his Girlfriend containing similar drawings to the first one he had shown me. Today, however Freddy was disappointed and hadn't received any mail at all. The guard in charge, after collecting a couple of pages of a questionnaire from each of us, that we had been told to fill in, left the classroom with them. Telling us all to keep quiet and to remain seated until he returned. The moment the door closed behind the guard, Freddy shot out of his seat to see if I had received the much anticipated photo, that I had told him I was expecting. As I mentioned earlier, I was well aware that Freddy was no Prince of diplomacy and was guaranteed to blurt out the first thing that came into his mind. Even so, I was still shocked. As he took the photograph I'd handed him, he shouted loudly,

"SHIT! I'd like to fuck her!" Well I bounced out of my seat. My fist bounced off Freddy's face - Freddy bounced off the wall, then bounced off the desk he had bounced onto and then bounced onto his head in the corner of the classroom. Just then the door opened and I quickly bounced back into my desk. The guard reentered and Freddy crawled out of the corner, with the aid of the desk he had bounced off. Freddy only had a small gash under his left eye, but as I studied it the whole side of his face swelled up like a Halloween Pumpkin. "I fell down!" Freddy volunteered, before he was asked.

"You were told to stay in your seats," barked the screw, "sit down and stay put until I get someone to take you to the infirmary." With that he again left the classroom, giving me time to dive under a desk in order to retrieve my photo.

"I wouldn't drink that if I were you." I recognized Freddy's nerve grating voice, as I took a long draught from my mug of sweet, sickly, milky tea.

"Why not?" I inquired. Freddy looked encouraged that I had actually answered him. As the only response he had received from me since the photo incident, was to tell him to 'fuck off' - every time he had attempted to engage me in conversation.

"Well they put Bromide in it, don't they?" He answered.

"What's Bromide?" I asked.

"The stuff they put in yer tea." He told me.

"Okay, why do they put it in your tea?" I demanded impatiently.

"Well it stops you getting' a hard-on, don't it?!" He replied. I never really forgave Freddy. But I selfishly tolerated him again, for no other reason, than to share and enjoy the next sexy installment of his Girlfriend's artwork. But, the initial deluge of mail from her seemed to have completely dried up. Both Freddy and I feared that his mail had finally been opened and censored by the Screws. However, our fears proved to be completely unfounded. And I must admit that I was as excited as Freddy was, when he at last received another letter from his Girlfriend. Only to be disappointed when we found that this time it contained no artwork. It turned out to be a 'Dear Freddy' letter. Apparently, her itchy twat couldn't tolerate the eternity of another few days wait, till she and Freddy might possibly be reunited. She informed Freddy that his own best friend had gallantly offered his services. He was now bravely filling the breach, that had been left empty by Freddy's absence. And, that both she and her audience were extremely satisfied and impressed by his very enthusiastic performances. Poor Freddy was devastated. I felt almost as sorry for him as I did for myself, after I found out that his letter didn't contain any drawings - Hey, but isn't that what friends are for?

Eventually the much anticipated day arrived and I was returned to the courtroom, where my sentence was to be passed. - Would I be set free or would I be making a return trip to Hades? I truly had the feeling that they were well aware of the fact that I shouldn't have been here in the first place. Sure enough, I was to be released and I was told with no blot on my record. Nevertheless, I was still ordered to pay about 30 pounds court costs. I immediately told them that I had no money at all and would therefore be unable to pay them anything. Okay, they told me we will arrange for you to pay it in weekly installments - BUT, miss one payment they warned me and I would find myself back in that courtroom in a flash – Pun intended. As I walked out of the courtroom, I was met by TGC – The Good Cop,

"How are you doing?" he asked me, in a way that was meant to convey that he actually gave a flying fuck.

"Wonderful." I replied, in a way that I hoped would convey how much I truly appreciated the implied sincerity of his concern.

"How are you getting home," he asked me, ignoring the implication in the tone of my reply, "do you have a ride?"

"No, I don't," I told him, "but now I have a bit more room to maneuver, the walk will probably do me good."

"Don't you have any bus fare?" he continued unfazed.

"No I don't." I replied. After fishing in his pocket he produced a handful of small change and handed me 4 shillings,

"That will get you back home." He told me.

'Bloody conscience money!' I thought – it crossed my mind to mention that the traditional fee for betrayal was 30 pieces of silver not 4 and my first instincts were to tell him to stick it up his miserable arse. But for once I swallowed my pride, as I realized to my dismay that without money, I would not be able to afford to swallow anything else. And my stomach was already growling viciously, at the prospect.

"Thank you!" I told him, without much conviction and turned to walk away.

"Make sure you keep up your installments," he advised me, arresting my departure, "or you'll find yourself back here real fast."

"I'll do my best." I told him taking another step.

"Yes, you'd better keep your nose clean," He continued, "and that includes any retaliation against Mr. Gorzynski. Touch one hair on his head and they'll be down on you like a ton of bricks." I took one step back,

"Mr. who?!" I asked.

"Mr. Gorzynski," he replied, "the other bloke who lives in your house."

"You mean Michal?!" I confirmed, "What's he got to do with anything?!"

I walked all the way from Harlesden to Kensal Rise with wings on my feet. In spite of a conscious effort to slow down and think things through. The thing that I wanted the most, I also feared the most, and that was a confrontation with Michal. Had TGC's implication been an effort to shift, or share the blame? Or had he been planting a seed that would cause me to take an action that might lead to a bigger and better conviction for him to add to his score? I had liked Michal, I thought he had liked me and I didn't want to believe the thoughts that had been placed in my mind. But the acid cauldron in my guts, that had replaced my earlier hunger pangs, caused me to fear the worst. I hadn't taken the bus for a number of reasons. For one, it would be too fast. Another, I didn't want the distraction of other people around me in a confined space. And last but not least, I wanted to protect that precious 4 shillings for as long as possible. I walked up to my front door with the enthusiasm of a man walking to the gallows. The way I saw it was, that Michal's only defense, and my only consolation, was the fact that the implication, that had led me to my present state of mind, had been given birth by a motivated liar. I opened the front door and my heart leapt into my throat, as a figure inside quickly scuttled from the hallway into the owner's quarters. Slamming the door closed behind them. Disappointment mingled with relief, as I recognized the figure as belonging to the Landlady and not to Michal. Although, the very fact that she wasn't now standing in front of me, smiling with her hand wide open for the owed rent, was definitely food for thought. And then, I thought of food for the first time since after leaving the courtroom. But once again, as I stepped into my room my appetite evaporated and for the first time in my life I felt sympathy for the Three Bears when they discovered Goldilocks. As, just like the three Bears, somebody had been sleeping in MY bed! When I had left my flat with the two policemen three weeks earlier, I hadn't been to bed that day and my bed had remained perfectly tidy. Now the bedclothes were in complete disarray and I could still see the impression left by someone's body. I forced my fury to the back of my mind and told myself that food and coffee might improve my mood. I was in the act of cutting a thick slice of green mold off a small block of sweaty cheese. And scraping a layer of mold off a couple of slices of stale bread, with the idea of making some melted cheese on toast. When I caught sight of a strange garment hanging on the inside of my flat's door - then I realized it was anything but a strange garment. It was the dressing gown that was constantly worn by Michal, when he was at home. It seemed that the scheming bastard, just couldn't wait to move into my room. My watering mouth dried like ancient parchment. I left my food where it was, I couldn't get out of the house fast enough. If I had the misfortune to bump into Michal here and now, I knew for a fact that I would be looking at 20 years to life.

I am certain that you will agree, that my story so far already contains a very fair quantity of Soul bearing. But here comes a real scoop, I am about to unveil for the first time ever, something that I never admitted or discussed with anyone. Including Tony Woods, Peter Inge, Tom McBride or even Jean. In fact it was something that I couldn't even discuss with myself. It was just too contrary to my nature and my own personal code. Which goes something like this. If someone blackens my eye, not only will I blacken both of theirs, but then I will wait patiently until they heal up, so that I can blacken them both again. Harm me in anyway and there will be a reckoning. But in Michal's case, I was possibly more afraid of a confrontation with him than he would have been with me. Especially as he was probably ignorant of what I was capable of doing to him. This was something I could not discuss with anyone, as I felt it would have completely shattered my reputation not to retaliate. And, I was so very ashamed and disgusted with myself for not responding - but too afraid of the consequences if I did. To walk away, without exacting a terrible and what I considered to be, a very justifiable revenge, would be one of the most difficult things, that I had done so far in my young life. I tried to congratulate myself for being sensible under the circumstances. But being sensible under any circumstances where I feel a little violence is called for, is something for which I am not famous. After leaving the flat the first thing I decided to do was take a trip to Paddington, in order to find out if I was still employed. On my way there it played on my mind that working nights, had been the beginning and cause of my misfortunes. And unfortunately as a result I found I was unable to temper my attitude, when I walked into the office. I told them, that under no circumstances, would I ever work the nightshift again. They seemed happy to assure me that I wouldn't have to. They handed me a week and a half's worth of back pay and my employment cards. Once again I was out of work.

I could hardly wait to get back to the Forester's and temper my frustration, by hurling a few large bodies across the mat and once again experiencing that comforting feel, of a very heavy barbell in my hands. But I realized that a new roof over my head, while searching for work was my first priority. I began looking for another flat in the Kensal Rise area, the cheaper the better. Much to my amazement I found what I was looking for within the first couple of hours of my search. It was the smallest, dingiest and most depressing little hole that I was ever to live in.

It was great to be reunited with Jean again. Especially after suffering an unbearable 3 week abstinence. But in spite of our enthusiasm I was surprised by experiencing a diminished intensity, which seemed to deaden the pain and lasted a few days before returning to normal. It caused me to wonder if there was indeed any credence to Freddy's claim concerning Bromide.

I had never been more desperate for work. Even more than the prospect of losing bodyweight, I feared the consequences of not being able to pay my fine. I tried to get work from a Lumberyard in Paddington, with no luck. I took a return trip to Smithfield Market. Carrying huge half carcasses of beef was something I imagined I would excel at, but no dice. I couldn't call any of the photographers that I posed for, or any of the promoters that I wrestled for, both for the same reason. Tarzan had lost his hair, there was no way that I could wrestle or pose without my trade mark mop. My hair would grow and thank goodness, it would grow fast, but it would still take more time than I could afford, to grow it from a mere shadow into any resemblance of its former glory.

'Oh well,' I thought optimistically, 'at least I won't have to spend any money in the Barbers shop for a while.' In the meantime, I even contemplated taking a trip across London to pay Ted Flock a visit and inquire whether I could at least resume the part time job I had had with him breaking cars. Or, even as a final resort ask him to put a word in for me to get some form of employment from 'Polish' Peter Rachman.

As a result of first working the night shift and then taking an enforced 3 week vacation, it had been well over a couple of months since I had even set foot in The Forester's Club. I knew that if I did return there, there would be a lot of embarrassing questions, concerning my prolonged absence. Not to mention the speculation that my latest hair-do would provoke. Nevertheless, I decided to brave my emotional turbulence, with the thought that I had come to London to follow my dream of becoming a full time professional wrestler. And not to fret over how I was perceived, by any other living soul while I strived to accomplish my quest. I was saddened to learn, that I had missed out on a few competitions in my absence. But an event that could have only been triggered by my return to the Forester's, more than compensated for any of the negative aspects that my return might have generated. After bringing Tony Woods up to speed, he promised to inquire if there was any possibility of me obtaining work with the Company that he was employed with. True to his word, just a few days later, he told me he had arranged an interview for me. I got the job, and at the beginning of the next week. I began working for Turriff's, who were contracted to The London Water Board. After reporting for duty I was handed a couple of instruments that I was very well versed in the use of. A pick and a shovel. My new job was digging holes in the streets of London, while looking for water leaks. Although we were now both working for the same company, I only saw Tony occasionally during working hours. It turned out that there were a number of gangs of Laborers working in various districts of London, who dug the holes where a suspected leak might be, but Tony was a specialist his services were only required after the leaks had been discovered and then he would go to each of the various districts as needed in order to fix them.

There were two characters in my gang who were the most memorable, First was the foreman Giles who for some reason hated my guts and everything surrounding it and a tubby white haired Irishman named O'Bryan. I don't know why Giles disliked me so much but it seemed that throughout my life that people in authority and I, are very rarely compatible. The reason that O'Bryan stood out was his thick meaty hands and a huge, muscular pair of Popeye proportioned forearms. Which I jealously coveted, from the very first time I saw him rolling up his sleeves. O'Bryan worked all day long with a huge and very heavy pneumatic drill, which I immediately attributed to being responsible for his very disproportionate forearm development. With that thought in mind, I also jealously coveted O'Bryan's job. The day came when I had my chance. And, in order to cinch it, all I had to say to one of the other laborers, but in clear earshot of Giles was,

"Oh shit, O'Bryan is not in work today, I hope that Giles doesn't ask me to work that bloody great big drill!" A few minutes later, Giles gave each member of his gang their respective day's assignment and when it came to my turn, as I expected he yelled,

"O'Bryan's out today, so Street - you'll be working the drill." In spite of my excitement I managed to moan, "Oh shit, why me?!" but just for Giles's benefit.

Within the first few minutes, I began to realize that I had

made an awful mistake. The tremendous vibration from the heavy machine numbed my hands and arms right up to my shoulders and neck. Which would have been more comfortable, if they had also been numb instead of in agony. The vibration became so severe, that I had to clench my jaws to prevent my teeth from chattering, or even shattering, while my brains felt as though they were in a blender instead of my skull. In spite of my distress, which became more outrageous by the second. I refused to complain in an effort to deprive Giles getting a huge measure of satisfaction at my expense. After what seemed like the longest, most pain ridden day of my life. I staggered home feeling as though I had just finished a very long wrestling match with Bert Assirati. That night in the Forester's I was as strong as Samson - only without his hair. The next morning, I crawled out of bed feeling as though I had slept all night in a suit of armor that was about six sizes too small. On my way to work that day, I hoped that I could make myself sound convincing when I mentioned to one of my workmates, while in earshot of Giles, that I really hoped that I would be working with the drill again, to insure that I wouldn't be. Thank goodness I didn't have to, as O'Bryan was back and I for one could not have been happier to see him. Even so, as I worked I cringed in pain, every time I threw a shovel full of clay out of the trench I was digging. I was convinced that even Torquemada with his very best inquisitors, urged on by Dad, couldn't have devised a more efficient torture, than one full day with the pneumatic drill. As I picked and shoveled away, I kept glancing over at O'Bryan drilling furiously, while he barely had the decency to show a little sweat. He handled the dreadful, mechanical monstrosity as though it were a toy.

As the Spring turned to Summer and the days grew longer and warmer, I began to enjoy my job more. Stripped to the waist, I felt as though I was being paid to sunbathe. But unfortunately, it resulted in a very uneven tan. Working in a hole hunched over a shovel all day my back soon darkened until it resembled polished Mahogany. While my front remained shades lighter. My legs, clad in heavy working jeans and boots remained a lighter shade of winter pale. Uneven tan or not, I soon became a magnet for every Artist and photographer, who seemed to inhabit that area in extremely prolific numbers. And as a result I acquired yet another source of income. The very first time I was approached and asked to pose for photographs, was during my lunch break, while working in Lisson Grove, which was near Lord's Cricket Ground. Having just finished a half a chicken and a couple of bananas. I was still sipping from a pint bottle of milk while sitting on a bench reading a newspaper. A yellow sports car pulled up to the curb, the driver leapt out brandishing a camera. He asked my permission to take a few snaps while I continued to read and drink. He then asked me if I had ever posed for any physique photos and I told him that I had. He handed me a card with his name, address and phone number and told me that he would like to photograph me in his studio. I told him that I was a professional model and also the fee, that I would expect to be paid if I accepted his offer. He agreed, and we made arrangements to take photos at his studio that very same evening after I had finished work for the day. I had noticed that he had given me some strange looks, from the first time he had introduced himself, and I had told him my name was Adrian. I went on to explain that I used the name Kid Jonathan when my photos appeared in Physique Mags. I thought that the strange looks, were possibly a result of him recognizing me from the magazines, or that he could have been a wrestling fan. It turned out that the strange looks, were the result of me not recognizing him, as he had expected me to. Especially after he had told me his name was Desmond Carrington. Desmond Carrington was an actor, who played Dr. Chris Anderson, one of the main Stars in the popular TV Series of that time, 'Emergency Ward 10'. I had never seen it, as I hadn't watched television since before I left Wales. Nevertheless, he was quite a good photographer who also developed and printed his own color photos, which was quite an accomplishment in those days. I was approached by Richard while working on deepening a hole, just a few yards up the street from the house in which he lived,

"You can call me Dick if you like" he simpered coyly. Richard was an excellent Artist, who would work from photographs that he would take, rather than from a live stationary model. His apartment was decorated with many examples of his own artwork. Plus, photographs of male nudes, a Household Cavalryman's helmet, adorned with a white horsehair plume.

And a large statue of David, which only differed from Michael Angelo's original masterpiece by the fact that this version had a set of genitals that would have looked more at home on a Clydesdale Stallion. As I wasn't overly impressed with the photos he took of me. I showed Richard some of the ones that had been taken by 'Mark' and he agreed, that they were much better than his. He chose one of those to work from instead of his own. The result of his artwork did resemble me, but looked more like Elvis with muscles and blond hair. The hair surprising me the most, as Elvis didn't have blond hair and neither did I in those days. But fortunately, by now at least it had grown back.

Then there was Monica.

"Oh, where did you get all those muscles?!" she asked. I was once again working down a hole. And thought at first that it was Tony Woods, assuming an effeminate voice and taking the piss. He was due to arrive at any time, to fix one of the leaks that we had uncovered. Until I looked up at a pair of bare legs a mile long. She looked like a model, with shoulder length Blond hair. A very pretty face and a sensational figure.

"I wrestle and lift weights." I told her. And as I was eye level with her shapely ankles, I casually moved to a vantage point, where I could almost, but not quite check out what color knickers she was wearing.

"My Husband is a photographer," she told me, "mostly physique or glamour shots, I think that you would make a very fine subject for him."

"Oh yes, I do quite a lot of that sort of thing," I answered, adding, "I make as much money posing for physique magazines as I do from digging holes all over London." Just to let her know I expected to get paid for my services.

"Oi, have you finished work for the day?!" Shouted Giles, interrupting our conversation.

"My name is Monica," she told me, as she turned to retreat, "what's yours?"

"Adrian." I answered.

"Okay Adrian, I'd better go, I'll talk to you again." She said and with that, she glided down the road leaving me in the full glare of Giles's miserable eyes.

I saw her again later as she walked by, but she just waved,

smiled and said,

"Hello Adrian." Which earned me another glare from Giles. The next day while we were all sitting on a low wall adjacent to our trench, waiting for Tony to arrive and do his thing, Monica came by again. Most of the gang were smoking, including Giles which gave him less excuse to grumble when Monica stopped in front of me, produced a pen and pad on which she began to write. She then tore off a page and handed it to me,

"That's our address and phone number," she told me, "my Husband Michael will be home all day. So why don't you come around for a coffee, when you take your break and I can introduce you - Second turning on the right, 9 houses down." She added.

"Okay, I'll see you later." I agreed, as she glided off down the street.

"Cor Mate, I fink she fancies you!" said Charlie, one of the gang. I shot a quick glance after Monica's retreating figure, to make sure she was out of earshot, before I struck my best muscle pose and replied smugly,

"Well you can hardly blame her can you?!" Giles snorted and took a deep drag of his fag, then blew the smoke out with disgust.

Monica answered the door and invited me in. Her Husband Michael, waved through an open door of a small converted office, as he carried on a conversation he was having on the phone.

"We'll be in the kitchen." Monica told him.

"Coming Darling." He replied, as he put down the phone. Unwound his long legs and offered me his hand, after he had stood up and crossed his office in about two strides. Monica was very tall, Michael was even taller. 'Now I know what Gulliver felt like in Brobdingnag.' I thought, as they both towered over me.

"This is my Husband Michael," Monica said as she introduced us, "and this is Adrian," she told Michael, "he really does have a gorgeous body." I remembered Lon saying the self same thing. But it sounded so much better coming from Monica.

"Help yourself," Monica invited, as we entered the kitchen, indicating a tray laden with food, and then added, as she correctly read the blank expression on my face. "Smoked Salmon on

Poppy seed Bagels - and how do you like your coffee?" I had never tasted Smoked Salmon before and I immediately remembered the past gastronomic disasters I had suffered from my first taste of other unfamiliar Seafood. But I was hungry and decided to chance it. It was delicious and I suffered no unpleasant aftereffects.

"Bring your coffee with you," Michael invited, "I'll show you my studio - will you have time for a posing session now?" He asked.

"Well I've only got about an hour," I replied, "and I'm filthy dirty from work."

I had only swilled the clay off my hands and forearms in a bucket of cold water, before I had come to visit.

"Oh, that should give us time," he assured me, "and you can take a shower first."

The studio was of medium size. Comprising of a white wall which was decorated with items of a nautical nature, like fishing nets, a small anchor and buoys, etcetera. Over head rails with a variety of curtains of different shades, that could be slid across to serve as an alternate backdrop, plus lights, tripods and cameras.

"This is the shower-room," he told me, as he opened a door adjacent to his studio, "you can get changed in here - posing trunks are in this cupboard." He added, as he pulled back the shower curtain and turned on the shower for me. "Monica tells me that you have done quite a lot of posing for Magazines." He continued as I undressed, "towels are here." He added, pointing to a rail. He could not have indicated the whereabouts of the towels, at a more opportune moment. The door opened and Monica entered with an armful of towels as I was about to step into the shower completely naked.

"Here are some more towels if you need them." She said, and chuckled at my embarrassment, as I grabbed a towel off the rail and held it in front of me. That was the first time Monica entered a room and caught me in a state of complete undress, but it certainly wasn't the last. It seemed that every time I was in the process of changing from one pair of posing trunks for another, she would be right there. She reminded me of Aladdin, who would rub his wonderful lamp, to make a Genie appear out of thin air. But in order to make Monica appear the same way, all I had to do was drop my drawers.

When I returned to work that afternoon, after my first posing session for Michael I had left the posing oil on my body and was gleaming in the sunlight like a Knight in Shining armor. I chewed at another bagel I had been given for the road. As all my workmates, including Giles were looking at me as I approached, I stopped and studied my bagel for effect and mused,

"MMMM-MMMM, this Smoked Salmon is really excellent you know." As though I actually knew what I was talking about.

"Cor, she musta fancied yer!" Chimed Charley, as Giles scowled his usual scowl. And in order that his scowling wouldn't go to waste, I dipped my hand into my pocket from where I produced and brandished my 5 pound note posing fee.

"For services rendered!" I sighed, punctuated again with my favorite muscle pose.

The next morning, as we all began collecting our tools from our work camp, Giles called out,

"Hey Street, you stay here today and mind the camp." It was not unusual, for my mood to be a little fractious first thing in the morning, after the very late nights I kept. But my miserable response to Giles's order that day turned out to have an extremely favorable result.

"Yeah, and do what all fucking day?! I grumbled.

"Light the fire, tidy up and put the kettle on fer the blokes tea at one o'clock an' make sure nobody nicks any of our tools," He ordered, "you kin manage that can't yer?!" he added sarcastically. Giles had succeeded in making my day sound as mundane and as boringly useless, as he could. And my miserable early morning disposition, had caused me to rise to his bait. I also realized that his major motive, for keeping me hidden away at the camp, was to put an end to the attention I drew, while working in the streets. And the extra cash I generated as a result. To him, Monica had been the final straw. But I was to find out that the new job he had ordered me to do, was anything but, boring or mundane.

It didn't take me long to learn, that as long as I stayed in the vicinity of the camp, my day was virtually my own. As soon as everyone left, I loaded and lit the brazier. Filled the kettle with water, ready to pop onto the fire when needed. Give the camp a sweep, oil up any spare tools and line them up at the back of our portable shed. Then the remainder of the morning was my own. By the time the gang came back for their break, I would have their tea ready for them. When they went back to work, I'd look longingly after them, as though I wanted to join them – But only for Giles's benefit. Then after they'd gone, I'd wash the dirty mugs, tidy up and the afternoon was mine, until the gang came back when their day's work was complete. If they had to work overtime in order to finish a difficult job, then I would also get paid overtime for doing nothing more than sitting and waiting for them. The present location of our camp couldn't have suited me better. On the north side of the bridge, where the Harrow Road crosses over the Grand Union Canal, was a pavement that was more than wide enough to contain our camp and still leave plenty of room for passing pedestrians. It was quite easy to scale a fence, which divided our location from the canal, which had footpaths on either side of it, that was fantastic to run or walk on. It was lined with grassy banks, that were tailor made for sunbathing. Very soon, the polished Mahogany on my back spread all over my body.

Along the footpath, on the right-hand side of the canal, was a Hospital. It sported a number of Tennis Courts, between the Hospital building and a fence, which divided the Hospital grounds from the canal bank. One day, as I was taking my early morning jog beside the canal, I noticed there were two Ladies wearing very short, white dresses playing tennis. I was never particularly fond of tennis, but was particularly fond of pretty Ladies wearing very short dresses. So I decided to sacrifice my morning exercise in order to become a tennis fan. I really began to appreciate the skill and agility that both participants displayed. But not nearly as much as I appreciated what else was displayed as a result of a strong gust of wind. Or, when one of the adversaries bent over to pick up the ball - 'there's more to tennis than meets the eye,' I decided. I had only been watching for a few minutes, before the Lady with the dark brown hair became aware of my presence and greeted me with a smile. Which alerted her opponent, a Lady with light brown hair, to turn around and do likewise. I returned their smiles, waved and called out,

"I didn't think I liked tennis, but it's a great spectator sport isn't it? And much to my delight, the Lady with the dark hair kicked one leg up, like a Can-can Dancer. Which made it obvious that she knew exactly what I liked best about her chosen sport. I cheered them both for about another 20 minutes. But, only when I got a glimpse of something worth cheering for. That seemed to amuse them both almost as much as they were amusing me. With the result that their tennis match, soon seemed to degenerate very nicely into a panty flashing competition. When they finished their game and exited the tennis court, they came over to the fence,

"That was the best tennis match I've ever seen." I truthfully told them,

"Yeah, I'll bet it was." Replied Del. Del, the Lady with the light brown hair. Brenda was the Lady with the dark brown hair. They were both in their mid twenties, both worked as Nurses in the Hospital and were both now off duty after working all night. After chatting for a while, they told me that they were going to get changed and go home. We said goodbye, but as they started to leave, Brenda asked me,

"Will you still be here in about 15 minutes?"

"Definitely," I told her, "if you're coming back."

I only ever saw Del and Brenda playing tennis on one other occasion. But on most weekdays, I would meet either one of them in the morning. With the result that the skin on my back, soon became much darker than my front again.

One day I was in the process of swilling out the gang's tea mugs, after their break, when a waitress from the 'Pie and Eel Restaurant' came over and invited me to eat. I explained, that the very thought of eating Eels, whether stewed or jellied, was sufficient in itself, to cure my most aggressive hunger pangs. She suggested, that I should at least sample their famous 'Pie and Mash'.

"Why don't you come over now?" she suggested, "The first one is on the house."

As the price she quoted, was well within my budget and the waitress was very pretty, I accompanied her back across the road. It turned out that Janet, the Waitress had come over and invited me, at the bequest of Mary, who was the Daughter of the restaurant's owners. Mary lived in an attic apartment on the top floor of the building above the restaurant, with her one year old

Baby. Her husband, she told me, had left with an under aged Girl, just after the Baby was born. After eating, I was also invited up to Mary's apartment for a couple of hour's worth of desert.

It seemed that if you have enemies, you don't need friends. Thanks to Giles, I had Del or Brenda for Breakfast. Mary as an afternoon snack. Which kept me happy, until I met Jean, for the main course at night. Also the fact that Giles was so determined to keep me away from the hard work, I had been used to doing, I also had lots more energy, to spend on more pleasurable pursuits.

Even though Giles did his best to keep me hidden away, I still posed occasionally for some of the contacts that I had already made. I still posed for Desmond Carrington and had been posing for Michael about once a week. I probably would have posed for him a lot more, if I had accepted his offer to pose for full frontal nude photos. But I had refused Michael, as I had refused Bill Jones, when he had made me a similar offer. It seemed as though, most physique photographers had many clients, who they termed as 'Private Collectors.' Who would happily – or should I say gaily, pay top dollar for photos of musclemen willing to bare it all. In spite of my love of money, and my willingness to do whatever, in my quest to accumulate as much of it as I could, there were many things that I would draw the line at. And that was definitely one of them. As far as I was concerned, Physique photography was about displaying an athletic, muscular body built as a result of hard training, with heavy weights and not cheapening it, by posing as a 'Private Collector's' naughty fantasy. On the very same day that Michael had propositioned me about posing nude, he asked me,

"Do you find my Wife attractive?"

"Yes I do," I replied, "I think she's very pretty."

"Would you like to fuck her?" he asked.

"NO!" I lied. I was extremely shocked by his question and didn't know whether it was an accusation or an invitation. - When I said I 'lied' – that wasn't strictly true either, - I did find Monica very attractive and under the right circumstances -? But, I knew her Husband Michael and I liked him. So, I wouldn't have been comfortable screwing his Wife, whether he approved or not. On the other hand, if I hadn't known him - or even if I had known him and didn't like him - well what can I say? – Monica was very attractive.

There was only one more incident that I can recall, while our camp was still beside The Grand Union Canal. O'Bryan had used his pneumatic drill to take the hard surface off the road and I had been left on my own, to complete digging the hole. Meanwhile, Giles and the rest of the gang, went off to dig elsewhere. From where I was digging, I could also keep half an eye on our camp and merely pop over at the appropriate time to get the tea ready for the gang's lunch break. As I was working, I saw a man and a girl walking along the pavement towards me. The girl gave me such a radiant smile that I automatically returned her smile, which caused the man to get right into my face.

"Who d' fook are yer laughin' at?! He wanted to know.

He was a tall, dark haired, rawboned individual and if his eyes had been any closer together, he would have passed as Polyphemus's shorter twin brother.

"I wasn't laughing at you," I told him, "I wasn't even looking at you." I added reasonably, "I was smiling at the Lady."

"I'll kick yer fookin' teet' out!" he threatened. "Not if I break your bleed'n' legs first." I warned him.

"Go'n fetch Patrick!" he told the girl, and she shot off around the corner into Harrow Road. Realizing he was now on his own and within reach, The Cyclops moved back a couple of paces. Before Polyphemus and I could exchange another nicety or two, the girl came back around the corner. She was accompanied by Patrick and 5 others which included another girl. Patrick immediately reminded me of Big Sean, who I had had bother with outside the Acton Bolt Factory. But thankfully a smaller version.

"Dis fooker wuz takin' thu Piss jus' 'cos we're Irish, Patrick!" complained Polyphemus to Patrick.

"This cross-eyed idiot, is a fucking liar, Patrick," I countered, "I never even spoke to him until he got in my face and I didn't know he was Irish, until he opened his trap."

"What have you got against the Irish?!" Patrick wanted to know. I used my shovel to knock my pick flat at my feet. Out of reach of any of the Irish gang, before I began burying it with clay, at the bottom of the hole I was standing in.

"I've got nothing against the Irish, or anyone else," I told him, as I leapt out of the hole and placed my shovel over my right shoulder, "unless they have something against me. I told you this idiot is a liar," I added pointing at Polyphemus, "if I had anything detrimental to say about the Irish, I could say it right now and there's fuck all any of you could do about it. And I'll cut the first of you fuckers in half with this shovel who tries. Like I said, that cock-eyed cunt is a liar."

"No, I'm not, OUCH! Yelled Polyphemus, as Patrick gave him a smack in the ear.

"You're always causing trouble, when dere's no need of it!" Patrick told him. And then to my surprise, the girl with the radiant smile began screaming,

"HE DID PATRICK, He said all the Irish, wuz a load o' bastards!"

"You shut yer mouth too!" Patrick warned her and she retreated to the corner as Patrick took a threatening step towards her. For no apparent reason, the stupid bitch wanted to see my blood.

"Are yer gonna let 'im git away with it?!" she screeched, as she disappeared around the corner. Patrick turned and looked at me, raised his eyebrows, sighed, shook his head in exasperation. He turned and walked back around the corner, followed by the remainder of his gang and that was the end of that. 'Being the leader of a gang of Irish idiots, can't be a lot of fun.' I thought. I walked to the corner, to assure myself they were indeed leaving, before returning to my work and continuing enlarging the hole.

Early the next morning, while we were waiting for the truck to arrive, on which our camp would be transported to a new site, I popped into 'The Pie and Eel' to say goodbye to Mary. The restaurant was closed that time of the morning. Mary opened the door to my knock, wearing nothing but a dressing gown. So we bade each other farewell. After a brief encounter, symbolically on top of the table, that I had sat at on the first afternoon that I had been invited there to eat.

****

I was still working out hard at the Forester's; I usually posed about once a week for various physique photographers and wrestled for various small time promoters, about 5 or 6 times a month. Although the wrestling business, seemed to have exploded in popularity to unprecedented dimensions, it also seemed, as though it was leaving me in its wake. While people like Billy Stock, who had never possessed any pro aspirations, rarely had time any more to attend the club, as he was now wrestling for Dale Martins almost every night. At the zenith of my despair, out of the blue I received a letter bearing a logo I was very familiar with. It was a picture of a Wrestler in the throes of being caught in a flying head scissors by his opponent. It was the trademark of Paul Lincoln Promotions. I opened the envelope as carefully as I could, so as not to damage the logo that I had admired for so long. I found to my delight, that I had been offered my first professional wrestling match from a 'Big Time Wrestling Promoter'. The match was to be held in Finsbury Park, in London and I would be wrestling against Jon Cortez from Spain. He would be the biggest name I had yet faced in the ring. I had seen huge double crown sized wrestling posters, all over London bearing a photograph, that covered almost one half of the posters of Jon Cortez, with his equally famous Brother, Peter Cortez. Together they were billed, as the Tag-team Champions of Spain. When I told Bill Jones of my good fortune, he was almost as excited as I was. He decided immediately, that he would come to Finsbury Park to watch me wrestle. I remembered being very flattered, as Bill had never been to a wrestling match before in his life. I had called up Bill and a couple of other photographers, in order to earn a little extra money, that I used to invest in some new wrestling wear. I was well aware of the importance, of a first impression. And there was no way, that I was going to leave even the tiniest detail to chance, after being given the biggest opportunity of my wrestling career, so far. The arena stood right beside the Park that had given Finsbury Park it's name. I must have stood on the opposite side of the street, just gazing at the building, for 15 minutes or more. Just savoring the thought, that this was going to be the venue, that was going to launch my career and would eventually elevate me to grappling stardom.

'Yes,' I thought, 'this is going to be my new beginning.' When I entered the dressing room the response to my greetings only earned me a silent scrutiny, that ranged anywhere from blank stares, to glares of unfeigned hostility. But, as that was not an unusual reaction for most newcomers to evoke, from their more experienced peers. I just shrugged my shoulders and found a place to sit and get changed. I recognized Jon Cortez from the photos I had seen of him on the wrestling posters and introduced myself to him, as his opponent for that night. He looked totally unimpressed and seemed to regard me in a way, that was mirrored by most of the other dressing room's occupants.

'Oh well,' I thought, 'maybe they'll come around a bit after they see me wrestle.'

Jon Cortez was probably only a few years older than I. He was about my height and weight, good looking with a very lithe, muscular, athletic physique. As one would expect from a wrestler who was reputed to be, as fast, skilled and as agile as anyone in our profession. Our match was to be the opening bout of the evening. And I don't think I had ever performed in front of a larger or more enthusiastic audience before. It was fantastic. I found new strength and stamina in the very air. It seemed to buzz and vibrate from the cheering fans and rewarded me in full measure from the first sound of the bell till midway through the seventh round. When my hand was raised in a victory over one of the best Lightweight wrestlers in Europe. I was ecstatic, as the huge crowd roared their approval, this was it – I had arrived! This was what I had sweated, toiled and bled for. What I dreamed of night and day for more years than I cared to remember. I felt that every drop of sweat, blood, time and tears had been very well spent. Now this was my time - my time to shake the wild and wonderful world of wrestling to its very foundations. I was loathe to leave the ring and relinquish the adoration being poured on me by my beloved fans. But also, I couldn't wait to witness the change in attitude, that my triumph would provoke amongst the formally hostile occupants of the wrestler's dressing room. Not to mention the offer of more matches – maybe even full time employment from Paul Lincoln. To say I was taken aback when I reentered the dressing room would definitely be an understatement. The only thing that made this entrance differ from the first one, was that the expressions of hostility on the faces of the occupants seemed to have increased tenfold. No words of congratulations. Not one word of encouragement.

'Jealousy.' I thought - but that was all the time I had to think. The dressing room door imploded as a furious Jon Cortez burst though it and hurled himself right into my face,

"WHO THE FUCK TOLD YOU, YOU WERE A WRESTLER!" He demanded.

"Well I just beat you didn't I?!" I replied.

"YOU COULDN'T BEAT ME ON THE BEST DAY OF YOUR FUCKING LIFE!" He claimed.

"Okay," I responded, "let's pretend this is the best day of my life and we'll go outside and test your theory." I was aching to grab him and hurt him, but didn't think that it would enhance my chances of a future with Paul Lincoln's Promotions if I did.

"Where do you work out?!" He snarled.

"The Forester's Club," I told him, "Why do you want to know?"

"Okay," he stated, "I'll come up there one night and we'll have it out on the mat."

I had noticed that his voice had lost some of its volume. And that his face had retreated from a few inches to a few feet away from my own, as he realized that I was impervious to his attempted intimidation. But that last statement really pissed me off. I'll come up to the Forester's and we'll have it out on the mat indeed. I wondered why he hadn't challenged me to a vicious game of dominos.

"FUCK OFF," I told him, "I'M IN THE MOOD FOR YOU RIGHT NOW. THERE'S A PARK RIGHT NEXT TO THIS BUILDING, AND NO ONE'S THERE THIS TIME OF NIGHT TO INTERFER WITH WHAT I'M GOING TO DO TO YOU - PLUS, THERE WILL BE PLENTY OF FLOWERS TO COVER YOU UP WITH ONCE I'M FINISHED!"

"I'll come up to the Forester's one night soon." He promised with menace, and walked away. Needless to say that he flunked on his promise. I didn't set eyes on Jon Cortez again for a few years. But it seemed that the damage was done. And it also seemed that I had flunked my big chance. I was paid 6 pounds for wrestling that night - the most money I had received for a single match so far. But there was no offer, or even the mention of any more matches for Lincoln. After I had dressed, I went out of the dressing room to join Bill, who was still watching the wrestling.

He was amazed to see how despondent I had become after my previous exhilaration at the end of my match. But my medley of emotions was chockablock full of bad ingredients. My hopes had been flying so high only to freefall without a safety net, and land flat on my face.

"That was a great match!" Bill told me.

"Fuck wrestling," I growled at him, "I've had enough of it."

"Oh, I think that would be a mistake," argued Bill, "the audience loved you; I really think that you've got something." It was amazing, I thought, how much that would have meant to me under different circumstances.

Jon Cortez's attitude certainly hadn't helped my cause. But I realized that as one of Paul Lincoln's top Lightweights, my victory over him was very hard for him to digest. And his actions - or should I say, overreactions, I felt had provoked me to the brink of violence which had colored me as the troublemaker. But I was eventually to learn, that this little fracas was scarcely the tip of the iceberg. I may have known more about wrestling than Jon Cortez had given me credit for. But when it came to wrestling politics, I was an absolute dunce. For instance, there was a basic formula in the way that a wrestling show was presented. The main event was the all important match on the card. It was the match that was designed to bring the fans back in droves after witnessing a controversial conclusion. With the suggestion, that the controversy would be settled in the return match that would be held the on the next show. Very much in the fashion of the old Saturday morning serials that would always end with a cliffhanger. Therefore it was considered that the first match would always be a preliminary, designed to warm the fans up, but not too much. The second match would be to wet their appetites a little more. Then the all important main event would pull out all the stops, that would usually raise the roof off the building. It would have the fans leaping and screaming, and filled with whatever emotion the match was meant to evoke in order to bring them back to the next show. The fourth and final match was known in the business as 'the send 'em home happy match.' That was just enough to settle the fans down and in many cases, prevent a riot that the main event may have come very close to causing. Too late I was to learn that Paul Lincoln Wrestling

Promotions exercised the strictest adherence to that rule. Even an opening match that was considered slow and boring, would be tolerated by the promotion with more enthusiasm than a match that generated the slightest bit of excitement. Excitement was not for a preliminary wrestler to enjoy. That pleasure was strictly for the main event. Just like a four course meal in a good restaurant, the soup course was merely an appetizer. The fish course a tantalizer. The meat or poultry was the main course designed to bring the diner back. And then the desert to top the meal off, satisfy a sweet tooth, and send the diner home happy. A preliminary wrestler was not supposed to dominate a wrestling show, any more than a lowly bowl of lukewarm leek soup, was intended to dominate a four course meal. But, even though I may have been regarded as an insignificant appetizer in the wrestling world. I was nevertheless, a bowl of leek soup with Chateaubriand aspirations.

In my match with Jon Cortez, he may have attempted to keep the match flowing at a more temperate pace. But he was up against a runaway buzz saw with no off switch. His outburst in the dressing room, was probably meant to convey two messages to the promoter. First, that he was not to blame for the huge amount of excitement our match had generated, and secondly that he was not happy with the culprit gaining a victory over him. But from my own point of view, I've said it before and I'll say it again and again and again - I AM NOT A TEAM PLAYER! I didn't become a professional wrestler for the sake of any of the promoters I had wrestled for, or was destined to wrestle for. I didn't become a professional wrestler for any other wrestler, or even for the wrestling fans. I became a professional wrestler for ME! The way I saw it was, if you are happy dancing in the chorus-line, you'll never become a Prima Donna.

In retrospect Jon Cortez's reaction may not have been as out of line as I thought it was at the time. Nevertheless, I did hate him a lot and hoped that if he did come up to the Forester's Club, 'to have it out on the mat'- he would come on a Tuesday or Thursday night. 'That way,' I thought, 'I could take him over to the wrestling room and lock just the two of us in there. Where I was sure that I would have a lot more fun with Jon Cortez on his own, than I ever had with both June and Wanda together'.

****

My less exuberant demeanor as the result of 'The Finsbury Park disaster' may have contributed to Giles once again tolerating my presence, and putting me back to digging holes in the road. We had moved camp from beside the Grand Union Canal, to Bayswater Road. I didn't like it there as much as our former camp, but it did have some advantages. For instance at lunch time, I could either jog up to the Edgware Road and just have time to grab a Steak or a Chicken and baked potato, at the Rotisserie before jogging back to work. Or else, I could bring a pre-packed lunch with me, and then find myself a pleasant spot somewhere in Hyde Park to eat it. Many times when I was working, I would scrutinize the buildings on the opposite side of the road and wonder which, if any of them might belong to 'Polish' Peter Rachman. Or even have been the home of the notorious Jack Spot, when he and his wife were brutally attacked, by the two vicious henchmen of rival gang leader Billy Hill.

One afternoon, digging as usual in my hole, I became aware of being watched. I looked up and I locked eyes with a bearded man walking along the pavement towards me. He was huge, close to 6 and a half feet tall and weighing in the region of 300 pounds, he stopped, smiled and said,

"Hey Kid, you're in great shape, where do you workout?" I detected an American accent, but as he had addressed me as 'Kid' I wondered if he had recognized me as a wrestler. It turned out that he didn't know who I was, and that he had addressed me as Kid was just a coincidence.

"The Forester's Club." I replied, then asked him, "Are you a wrestler?"

"Used to be," he told me, "but I'm in movies now - I'm just taking a break between films, and doing a bit of talent scouting for the casting director."

He went on to tell me he had been dressed in a Gorilla suit, and had played a giant Gorilla in his latest movie which he said, had been filmed in Italy.

"Do you know 'Tiger' Joe Robinson?" he asked me.

"Not personally," I replied, "but I know who you mean, he

was a wrestler and he was in that movie 'A Kid for two farthings' with Primo Carnera and Diana Dors."

"Yes, that's him," he agreed, "he's in Rome now and doing great. You know you would do great out there too. They'd give you work, no problem. You're in much better shape than Joe Robinson, and he's making some excellent wages. If you're interested, I can give you a letter of recommendation. And in the meantime, I'll phone the casting director and tell him to expect you." He handed me his card, and told me he was presently living further down Bayswater Road in the direction from where he had been walking. And, that I should come there after I had finished work for the day. He would write me the letter and fill in the details. Apparently the Muscle Movies made famous by the legendary Steve Reeves when he starred in 'Hercules' a couple of years earlier, were still going strong – pun intended. Arnold Schwarzenegger's bodybuilding and muscle movie career probably did more to popularize muscular physiques, but Steve Reeves was the first. He started the ball rolling, when Arnold was just a twelve year old kid.

The big guy's name was John Smith, and he answered the door of his second floor flat wearing a dressing gown. When I entered, the first thing that caught my eye was a partially covered, otherwise naked girl laying fast asleep in a double sized bed. John just chuckled and said,

"Let's go out on the balcony - would you like a beer?" There were two seats, one either side of a small table on the balcony which overlooked Bayswater Road and Hyde Park. As I sat down, John came out with the letter that he had already written for me and a couple of bottles of beer. He apologized that the beer was not ice cold, but then added that I would probably enjoy it better that way. He had been told British men liked their beer warm. I corrected him, and told him it was only Mild Ale that was drank at room temperature, the rest we also enjoyed cold. As we sat and supped our beer, he explained the situation in Rome. Where I was to go, who I was to ask for, and what I was to say.

"You'll fly out to Rome," he explained, "give this address to a Taxi driver, and he'll take you to where you need to go."

"What about the airfare?" I asked.

"No problem," he assured me, "they'll reimburse you for all

of your expenses, as soon as they sign you up." Actually there was a problem. I had only just finished paying my court fine installments, and the rest of my money had gone into force feeding myself, in an attempt to regain my depleted bodyweight. I had no money for airfares, and for some reason, I was too embarrassed to tell him. Instead I gave him an excuse, that I would have to take care of a number of loose ends before I would be able to leave the country, which would include obtaining a passport. Another problem was Jean, who would not be happy when I told her that I was off to become a movie star in Italy. She would convince herself that I would immediately be sexually assaulted, by both Sophia Loren and Gina Lollobrigida the second I stepped off the plane.

"I wouldn't leave it too long," John advised me, "the sooner you can get out there the better." So I started saving every penny I could scrape together in order to finance my trip to muscle movie stardom. The more I thought about it, the more sense it made, and I really began warming to the idea. Even though the Gladiator-Barbarian movies that were being churned out of Italy, at that time were really corny, badly dubbed and featured actors with extremely questionable talent, I was still their biggest fan.

"What are you going to do with all your muscles when you get them?" My Mother had asked me, when I had first begun bodybuilding.

"Use them to become the best professional wrestler in the World." I had replied, But now it seemed that I might find another use for them, and it was a use that really appealed to me. I was suddenly overwhelmed by a sense of urgency. I felt that if I were to allow any more grass to grow beneath my feet in my quest to travel to Rome, I would arrive only to find that the muscle movie craze was over.

At last I was ready to leave. But I had only saved enough money for a one way ticket, and maybe a Spaghetti dinner after I arrived, providing the taxi ride wasn't too expensive. Which would mean that I would have to endure that all too familiar empty feeling once again. I braced myself and girded my loins in readiness for the conflict that I was convinced would ensue with Jean, when I broached the subject concerning my immediate travel plans. When I received another letter with an offer of work

- this time from Dale Martin's Wrestling Promotions. The date I received the letter was mid July 1961 and there was an offer of 8 matches - beginning the very next month. I was surprised that the letter was signed by Les Martin, who I had only rarely spoken to, and not Jack Dale. Now it seemed that I faced the dilemma of my life. Would I ignore the offer of 8 wrestling matches from Dale Martin, and go to Rome? Or would I cancel my plan of traveling to Rome and the movies, to wrestle for Dale Martin's?!

It truly was a dilemma, as obviously I couldn't do both. The very thought of exploring the Mighty Coliseum and viewing many of the other Ancient Roman sites. Plus the very real possibility of meeting one of my biggest heroes, Steve Reeves. And maybe even appearing in a movie with him. As other wrestlers such as Primo Carnera and Quasimodo had already done was mind boggling. On the other hand, I remembered standing and staring at the wrestlers in action in the ring in Dumfries Place Drill Hall, in Cardiff and promising myself - one day I will wrestle for Dale Martin's. And one day I will wrestle in that ring. I must admit that I did view my upcoming journey to Rome with a certain amount of apprehension, due entirely to the money situation - What if for some reason my face didn't fit, in spite of Big John Smith's assurance that it would? Then what? – No return ticket, no money, no food, and no way to get back home. Nevertheless, before I received Les Martin's letter, I had been determined to take the chance. I am a staunch disciple of the saying 'nothing ventured nothing gained.' But why had I lifted weights and wrestled all these years, and why had I left the Welsh Coalmines for the bright lights of London in the first place? To become a full time professional wrestler - Well I made my choice and that was, to try once again to become what I had set my heart on becoming originally. I have often wondered what adventures, or misadventures I may have missed or avoided by my decision to remain a wrestler and not attempt to become an Italian film star. But I am also a staunch believer in another saying that was attributed to Napoleon Bonaparte, that made my mind up once and for all -

"When you set out to take Vienna – take Vienna.'

I hope that you enjoyed BOOK 2 of my autobiography - if you did you will love the sequel BOOK 3 - **'SO MANY WAYS TO HURT YOU.'** - Big time wrestling in Britain's 'GOLDEN AGE OF PROFESSIONAL WRESTLING.'

PHOTOS

My first pro opponent, 'GentleMan' Geoff Moran, 1957.

Me as Kid Tarzan Jonathan, 1958. Photo by Mark.

Me as Kid Tarzan Jonathan, 1958. Photo by Mark.

Me with Jean in Brynmawr, 1958.

Me with Jean in Hyde Park, 1959.

Me as Kid Tarzan Jonathan, 1959. Photo by Mark.

Me as Kid Tarzan Jonathan, 1959. Photo by Mark.

Me as Kid Tarzan Jonathan, 1959. Photo by Lon.

Me as Kid Tarzan Jonathan, 1959. Photo by Lon.

Me as Kid Tarzan Jonathan, 1960. Photo by John Graham.

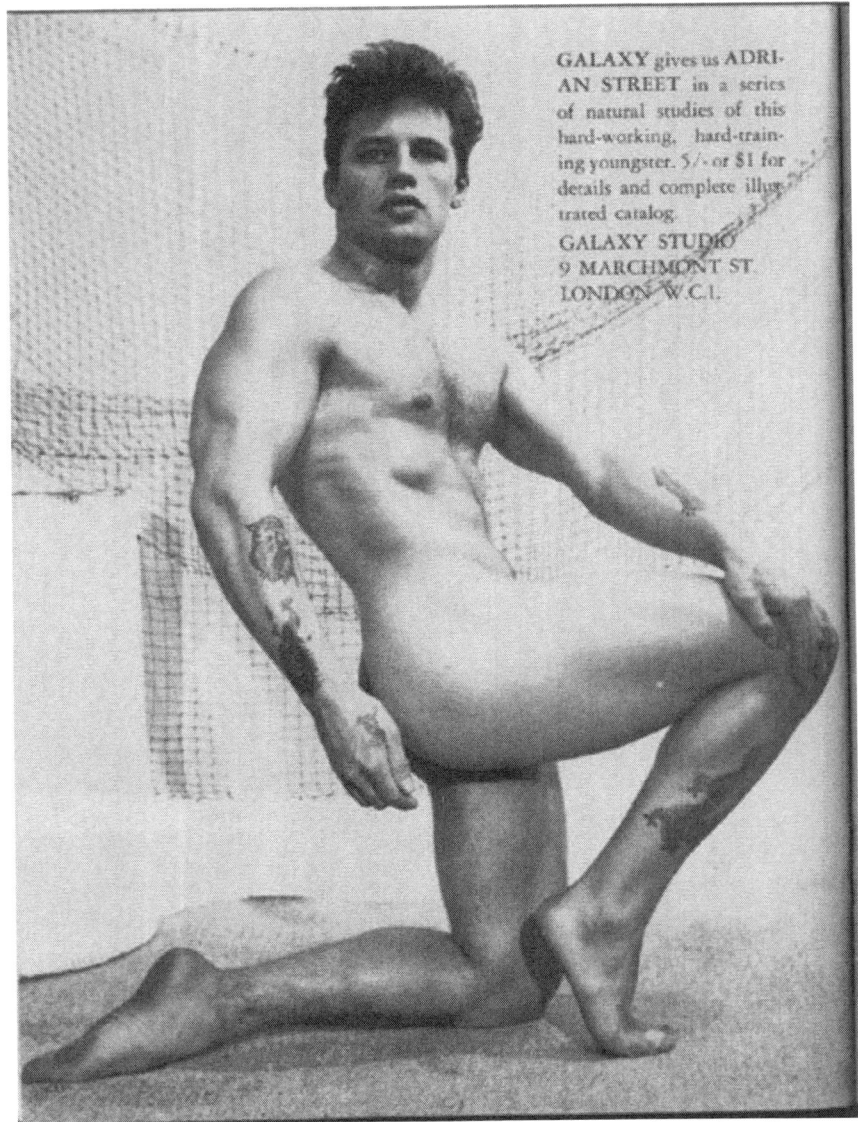
Me now as Adrian Street, 1961. Photo by Galaxy Studio.